THIS IS MY BELOVED COMPANION

JEWISH CHRISTIAN LADY EVANGELIST. Combinations of these words can cause a fuss. A little over a century ago, even more so. Back then, crowds of thousands of women and men, of all classes, in cities, towns and villages across Australia, New Zealand, North America and Britain, flocked to hear Emilia Baeyertz tell her story of romance, tragedy and hope and exhort them to follow Jesus the Messiah.

In *This Is My Beloved: The Story of Emilia Baeyertz, Jewish Christian Lady Evangelist*, Betty Baruch and Amanda Coverdale told Emilia's remarkable story as a novel. *This is My Beloved Companion* will help you delve deeper into the life and times of Mrs Baeyertz with:

- A selection of historical extracts, reports, letters, interviews, pictures and addresses

- A complete list of characters in the novel, both historical and fictional

- A detailed chronology

- A list of places where Emilia preached

- Hundreds of notes on the novel with background, sources, references, connections and curiosities.

THIS IS MY BELOVED COMPANION

FOR READERS OF
THIS IS MY BELOVED
THE STORY OF EMILIA BAEYERTZ,
JEWISH CHRISTIAN LADY EVANGELIST

Edited by Garth Coverdale

Emilia Baeyertz Society
Melbourne

Published by Emilia Baeyertz Society Inc.
5 Laughlin Avenue, Nunawading Victoria 3131, Australia
© 2017 Emilia Baeyertz Society Inc.

Editor: Garth Coverdale
Producer: CATTAC PRESS
Printer and distributor: Ingram

The image of Emilia Baeyertz on the front cover is from the September 1886 edition of *The Pioneer* published in Launceston, Tasmania.

This work is a companion to *This is my Beloved*, the 2017 novel by Betty Baruch and Amanda Coverdale published by Emilia Baeyertz Society, Inc. ISBN 9780994572400 (paperback). This companion includes addresses by Emilia Baeyertz and other historical works. For attribution, please refer to the endnotes, footnotes and bibliography.

All Bible quotes are from King James Bible unless otherwise acknowledged.
Typeset in Garamond Premier Pro.

Apart from any use permitted under the Copyright Act 1968, no part may be reproduced by any process without prior written permission from the copyright holder. Every attempt has been made to trace and obtain copyright. Should any copyright not be acknowledged or copyright not be observed, please write to the publisher.

National Library of Australia Cataloguing-in-Publication entry
Title: This is my beloved companion : for readers of
   This is my beloved, the story of Emilia Baeyertz, Jewish Christian
   lady evangelist, by Betty Baruch and Amanda Coverdale /
   Garth Coverdale (editor).
ISBN: 9780994572417 (paperback)
Notes: Includes bibliographical references.
Subjects: Baruch, Betty. This is my beloved.
   Baruch, Betty–Criticism and interpretation.
   Coverdale, Amanda. This is my beloved.
   Coverdale, Amanda–Criticism and interpretation.
   Baeyertz, Emilia, 1842-1926–Fiction.
   Guided reading.
Other Creators/Contributors: Coverdale, Garth, editor.

Foreword

This *Companion* is intended to be read with *This Is My Beloved* by your side.

So, if you haven't got your copy of *This Is My Beloved* with you, please collect the novel and companion together and then, when you are ready, go to your favourite reading spot to settle down to read the words—on paper or under glass.

If you are the reader who likes to devour a story as it is written, read *This Is My Beloved* straight through then, perhaps after some reflection, dip into this *Companion*.

If you are the reader who wants questions to be answered on the journey, and who isn't bothered by spoilers, start with this *Companion* open at the Contents page as you begin to read *This Is My Beloved*.

If you are the reader who is mostly interested in the sources, this *Companion* will make a lot more sense if you also read *This Is My Beloved*.

If you are the reader who is also looking for chapters on Emilia's context, theology, spirituality, themes, achievements, role or career, I refer you to another worthy companion to *This Is My Beloved* in its own right: *Emilia Baeyertz—Evangelist* by Rev. Robert Evans OAM. You can order a paper book, or download an ebook, through revivals.arkangles.com.

Garth Coverdale

Contents

Characters in *This Is My Beloved*	1
Historical Accounts	7
Works of Emilia Baeyertz	109
Consecration	113
The Jewish Passover	121
Holiness	135
Seven Steps to the Blessed Life in Psalm 32	147
The Young Ruler and Bartimeus	151
The Jewish Day of Atonement	155
Notes	163
Places where Emilia Baeyertz preached	205
Chronology	209
Bibliography	239
About the Editor	251

Characters in *This Is My Beloved*

Fictional people are in listed in *italics*, historical people whose real names we know are in **bold** and historical people with fictional names are in ***bold italics***.

Jessie Ackermann, a crusader
Arthur Aronson, a brother of Emilia
Charles Aronson, a brother of Emilia
Charlotte Aronson (née Myers), the second wife of George
Emily Aronson, a sister of Emilia
Frederick Aronson, a brother of Emilia
George Aronson, a brother of Emilia
John Aronson, father of Emilia
Julia Aronson, a sister of Emilia
Leah Aronson, wife of Lewis
Lewis Aronson, a brother of Emilia
Maria Aronson (née Lazarus), mother of Emilia
Nuriel (or Norman) Aronson, a brother of Emilia
Philippa Aronson (née Solomon), the first wife of George
Rachel Aronson, a sister of John Aronson
Saul (or Samuel) Aronson, a brother of Emilia
Bella (or Isabella) Baeyertz (née Johnston), wife of Charles N.
Carl Baeyertz, a son of Charles N. & Bella
Charles Nalder (or N.) Baeyertz, son of Emilia and Charlie
Charlie (or Charles, jun.) Baeyertz, husband of Emilia
Charles Baeyertz, sen., father of Charlie
Emilia Baeyertz (née Aronson), our saint

John Baeyertz, brother of Charlie
Maida Baeyertz, a daughter of Charles N. & Bella
Marion Baeyertz, daughter of Emilia and Charlie
Mary Anne Baeyertz (née Treleaven), mother of Charlie
Abraham Berens, husband of Eliza
Amy Berens, daughter of Eliza and Abraham
Eliza Berens (née Aronson), a sister of Emilia
Jonathan Bernard, a doctor
Sally Blackland, wife of Will
Tommy Blackland, son of Will
Will Blackland, cousin of Nancy Wait
Godfrey Blunden, a musician
R. C. Blunden, an organist
Lila (or E. W.) Booth, an evangelist
Sarah (or S. C.) Booth, an evangelist
Henry Brett, a publisher
Otto Brickmann, a goldsmith
Wm. Christopher (or Chris) Bunning, a pastor
Matthew Burnett, an evangelist
Robert Calvert, a pastoralist
A. J. Campbell, a minister
H. Clark, captain of a sailing ship
William Clark, a pastor
John Coley, an apprentice goldsmith
Ernest Colman, a solicitor
John Colton, a politician
Mary Colton, a suffragist
Sir Arthur Cotton, an engineer
Elizabeth Cotton, an author

CHARACTERS IN *THIS IS MY BELOVED*

Mr Cutler, a real estate agent
Mr Dimant, a manufacturer
Mr Dinsley, a coach operator
Isaac D'Israeli, father of Benjamin
Benjamin Disraeli, an author
Mary Anne Disraeli, wife of Benjamin
Mr & Mrs Edwards, citizens
Richard Gibbs, husband of Suzette
Suzette Gibbs (née Baeyertz), sister of Charlie
Mary Ann Gibson, an evangelist
William Gibson, a farmer
Mr Gregson, a missionary
Thomas (or T. C.) Hammond, an evangelist
Brian & Edna Harris, farmers
George Higinbotham, a politician
Maurice Isaacs, a doctor
Violet Jackson, a friend of Emilia
Eliza Johnston, mother of Bella
Kerr Johnston, father of Bella
Lizzie Jones, a daughter of Mrs Jones
Mrs Jones, an employee of Aronson, Rosenthal & Co.
James Kirkland, a doctor
Martin Langmore, a doctor
Mr Larcham, a bank manager
Alexander Lazarus, a brother of Maria Aronson
Dora Lazarus, wife of Alexander
Dr Ledler, a chemist
Emily Macartney, a friend of Emilia
Hussey (or H. B., jun.) Macartney, a vicar

Henry McCoy, a YMCA General Secretary
James McCulloch, a politician
John MacNeil, an evangelist
Daniel Matthews, husband of Sarah
Sarah Matthews (née Johnston), sister of Bella
William Matthews, a brother of Daniel
Mrs Melrose, a cook
Louis & Bertha Monash, passengers
D. L. Moody, an evangelist
Mr & Mrs Morris, friends of John & Maria Aronson
Susannah Moss, grandmother of Robert Newfield
Daniel & Lily Newfield, parents of Robert
Robert Newfield, fiancé of Emilia
Mrs Parkinson, a caterer
John G. Paton, a missionary
Charles & Sarah Perrin, evangelists
Olivia Phelps, fiancée of John Baeyertz
Alice Porter, a friend of Emilia
Thomas Rae, a doctor
Henry & Margaret Reed, evangelists
Boswell Reid, a surgeon
David Rosenthal, a jeweller
Thomas Sabine, a vicar
Ira Sankey, a singer & songwriter
Mrs Simpson, a friend of Emilia
John Singleton, a doctor
Joseph R. Smith, a fence
Alexander Somerville, an evangelist
Charles (or C. H.) Spurgeon, an evangelist

Thomas Spurgeon, an evangelist
Harry Stockley, a friend of Charlie
Mary Stewart (née Thomson), an evangelist
Wm. Downie Stewart, husband of Mary
T. B. Swift, a minister
Henry Varley, an evangelist
Mr & Mrs Vogel, friends of Abraham & Eliza
Lydia von Finkelstein, a performer
Nancy Wait, a friend of Emilia
David Walker, a YMCA General Secretary
Walter Walton, an employee of George Aronson
Mrs Weinbeck, a factory manager
Mr Wilks, a sailor
Mr & Mrs Williamson, pastoralists
William Wood, a vicar
Thomas Young, a goldsmith
Bob, a friend of Emilia
Billy, a groundsman & groom
Beatrice, a maid
Cook, a cook
Nurse, one of three different nurses

Historical Accounts

EVERYWHERE THAT EMILIA WENT, OVER FOUR DECADES, HER PUBLIC ministry was recorded. I have selected some extracts and illustrations from those historical accounts and present them for you in date order.

For each of these selections, I show, to the best of my knowledge, the location and date of the event or article and a title. Footnotes include my sources. There are no note numbers in the novel itself; those notes are grouped by chapter at the end of this *Companion*. So, if you have read or are reading *This Is My Beloved,* or you want to know more about the life and times of Emilia, or you simply love books with titles that start with *The Annotated ...* , please read on.

The presentation of my references in the footnotes and endnotes is based on a commonly-used style of the American Psychological Association. For example, a note with (Evans, 2007, p. 218) refers to page 218 of the book described in the Bibliography as Evans, R. (2007). *Emilia Baeyertz—Evangelist*. Hazelbrook, NSW: Research in Evangelical Revivals. That bibliography, in turn, refers to the book *Emilia Baeyertz—Evangelist* that was written by Robert Evans OAM and published under the Research in Evangelical Revivals imprint in Hazelbrook, NSW, during 2007.

References to Watson refer to Sydney Watson, Emilia's nineteenth-century biographer. Where there are two dates, the first is of the original publication and the second is of the edition we used. In extracts from newspapers, read 'inst.' (*instante mense*) to mean 'day of this month'.

When Emilia quotes the Bible, she always quotes from a King James Version, although sometimes she paraphrases when speaking from memory. My reference KJV is my great-grandmother's well-used BFBS edition that was published during Emilia's ministry.

The novel includes a sample of the following accounts and a glossary, a map of Colac and a family tree.

Garth Coverdale

List of Historical Accounts

Date	Place	Type	Author
c. 1864	Colac, Vic	Photograph	Anon
Nov 1865	Hawthorne, Vic	Register	Christ Church
Mar 1871	Colac, Vic	News	*Herald*
Mar 1871	Colac, Vic	Notice	*Herald*
Mar 1871	Melbourne, Vic	Article	Cartridge
1871	Colac, Vic	Letter	E. L. Baeyertz
Dec 1873	New Vienna, Ohio	Photograph	Anon
1875	Geelong, Vic	Testimony	E. L. Baeyertz
c. 1876	Dorking, England	Book	E. R. Cotton
Oct 1877	Melbourne, Vic	Picture	*Illust. Aust. News*
1877	Melbourne, Vic	News	J. Singleton
Jan 1878	Hobart Town, Tas	Report	*Willing Work*
Apr 1878	Launceston, Tas	Report	*The Examiner*
Apr 1878	Launceston, Tas	Letters	D. and E.
Aug 1879	Sandhurst, Vic	Report	*Willing Work*
Sep 1880	Ballarat, Vic	Report	Unknown
Dec 1880	Adelaide, SA	Letter	SABA
c. 1881	Launceston, Tas	Appreciation	E. L. Baeyertz
Apr 1883	Adelaide, SA	Editorial	*Truth and Progress*
Nov 1883	Gladstone, SA	Report	*The Areas' Express*
Dec 1883	Adelaide, SA	Letter	A. O. Chambers
Apr 1885	Colac, Vic	Report	Izaak
July 1885	Melbourne, Vic	Letter	YWCA
Sep 1889	Brisbane, Qld	Report	Unknown
Dec 1889	Melbourne, Vic	Letter	J. G. Paton et al

Date	Place	Type	Author
Mar 1890	Dunedin, NZ	Report	*Otago Witness*
June 1890	Nelson, NZ	Interview	*Evening Mail*
1890	Wellington, NZ	Report	Unknown
Aug 1890	Wanganui, NZ	Report	*Chronicle*
Sep 1890	Auckland, NZ	Interview	Unknown
Apr 1891	Los Angeles, Cal	Report	*Churchman*
1891	Toronto, Ontario	Interview	Unknown
1891	Boston, Mass	Report	Unknown
1891	Boston, Mass	Statement	J. A. Gordon
1891	Ottawa, Ontario	Reports	S. Watson
1891	Toronto, Ontario	Interview	*Press*
Dec 1891	London, Ontario	Report	Unknown
1892	Montreal, Quebec	Report	Unknown
June 1892	Dublin, Ireland	Report	*The Irish Times*
Mar 1893	Birmingham, England	Report	S. P. Wood
Mar 1894	Abergavenny, Wales	Report	YMCA
1894	London, England	Preface	S. Watson
1894	London, England	Conclusion	S. Watson
Oct 1897	Blackheath, England	Flyer	E. L. Baeyertz
Oct 1897	Blackheath, England	Report	*The Christian*
c. 1900	Edinburgh, Scotland	Report	S. Watson
May 1904	London, England	Photograph	A. Percival
Nov 1904	Perth, WA	Letter	E. L. Baeyertz
Apr 1905	Melbourne, Vic	Interview	Celia
Dec 1905	Clifton Hill, Vic	Report	J. Carson
Aug 1908	Nayland, England	Report	J. F.
July 1918	Newbury, England	Report	*The Christian*
Nov 2012	Colac, Vic	Photograph	A. L. Coverdale

COLAC, VICTORIA, 1864 OR 1865
NATIONAL BANK OF AUSTRALASIA

The photograph of the National Bank of Australasia, Colac, circa 1860–1869, held by the State Library of Victoria, is of albumen silver (11 cm x 7 cm). Reproduction rights are owned by the SLV. Used by Permission.

The photo appears to have been taken for the banking or building company immediately after construction but before any signs or neighbouring buildings followed.

HAWTHORNE, VICTORIA, 16 NOVEMBER 1865

MARRIAGES SOLEMNIZED IN THE DISTRICT OF BOROONDARA

This extract from the Marriage Register of Christ Church in Hawthorn (Births Deaths Marriages Victoria) includes the signatures of the bride, groom, vicar and two witnesses.

The official spelling of the suburb was Hawthorne until the District of Hawthorn was separated from the District of Boroondara.

COLAC, VICTORIA, TUESDAY 7 MARCH 1871

MELANCHOLY ACCIDENT

A MELANCHOLY ACCIDENT OCCURRED ON SATURDAY afternoon by which Mr. C. Baeyertz manager of the National Bank narrowly escaped a fearful death.

He left the town about 4 o'clock and proceeded to the racecourse paddock to shoot quail. While in the paddock Mr. Woodward of the Stoneyrises passed up the road and observing Mr. Baeyertz called to him and he came to the fence dividing the paddock from the road; he placed the stock of his gun on the ground and reached over to shake hands with Mr. Woodward when suddenly the gun went off, the charge entering between the left shoulder and breast and passing out at the top of the shoulder. He made some exclamation and then fell to the ground.

Information was immediately brought to town and so as soon as possible he was conveyed to his residence at the bank, and Dr. Rae being in attendance shortly afterwards, he prescribed for the unfortunate gentleman in the circumstances of the case admitted. A telegram was despatched to Geelong for Dr. Reid who arrived in Colac at 3 o'clock next morning having changed horses on the way. After an examination was made it was thought amputation would be unnecessary, but when daylight came, and the extent of the injuries could be better arrived at, the doctors, after consultation, decided that amputation was compulsory in order that life might be saved; this was performed on Sunday morning close up the joint of the shoulder, and the patient bore the operation with great fortitude.

On Sunday he was well as might be expected, but at night violent vomiting took place which had a very weakening effect. Yesterday he was very low. It appears that the charge when it entered the shoulder struck the bone and glanced off in almost opposite directions thus rendering the wound of a more jagged nature. This is the second accident the unfortunate gentleman has met with while shooting having on a previous occasion shot two of his toes off.

All those who are acquainted with Mr. Baeyertz will read the above particulars with profound regret, as he was a gentleman esteemed by all; as a business man he was strict to the letter, and as a townsman has given many instances of his enterprise. We sincerely trust he will soon be restored to health and strength and occupy his former position among us.

Since the above was in type the unfortunate gentleman has gone to his long home having expired at 11.00 p. m. last night. From an early hour this morning a gloom was cast over the town, and when it became fully known that death had ended his sufferings, one by one the inhabitants drew down their blinds or put out their shutters and it needed not a very perceptive eye to observe some melancholy event had occurred, one which was felt by every resident of Colac. Sales were postponed and for a time all business appeared to be suspended; and a feeling possessed many as if they had lost a dear friend.

Many an expression of heartfelt sorrow was given for the deceased gentleman, who young in years and strong in body and mind, was so suddenly called from amongst us, without we may say, a moment's warning; cut off in the soundest of health and in a career of usefulness. Truly, 'in the midst of life we are in death'.[1] As a townsman none other was higher esteemed; of a happy disposition he was a good husband and a kind parent, and those who were dearest to him will lose a warm protector. Much sympathy is expressed for the young widow, and two children, and we believe we but re-echo the sentiments of Colac, when we say that his melancholy death will be deeply regretted by everyone who knew him.

We transcribed this account and the next from microfilm of the *Colac Herald* generously made available by the Colac and District Historical Society. *Colac Herald* is still Colac's weekly newspaper.

[1] In The Order for the Burial of the Dead, the priest by the graveside would say, 'In the midst of life we are in death: of whom may we seek for succour, but of thee, O Lord, who for our sins art justly displeased?' (*Book of Common Prayer*, 1662/2015).

COLAC, VICTORIA, 7 MARCH 1871

THE MAGISTERIAL INQUIRY

A Magisterial Inquiry was held at the Victoria Hotel, this afternoon before C. Beal Esq., J. P.

Charles Baeyertz, sen., deposed:

I reside at Colac, and deceased is my son and was twenty-eight years of age last October.

W. Woodward deposed:

I am a grazier, residing at south Purrumbeet. Remember Saturday last. At about six o'clock I was going along the main road, and saw deceased in the Racecourse paddock near the roadside. I spoke to him, and he came over to the fence, and had spoken a few words, when one of his dogs 'pointed' at a bird, and he walked up to the dog, and asked me if my horse would stand fire. I said I would chance it if he did not fire in my direction. No bird got up, and he came close to the fence, placing the gun on the rail, and it went off, and shot him in the arm. He gave a jump, and said 'I am shot'. I saw his coat torn and pieces of flesh hanging out. He held on by the fence, and I got over and supported him. I saw a man coming, and got him conveyed to Colac. He was quite conscious after being shot.

Dr. Rae deposed:

I am a surgeon residing at Colac. On Saturday evening I was called to see deceased, who had received a gunshot wound in the shoulder joint. Upon examination I found it of such a severe nature that I deemed it necessary to call in another medical man. Dr. Reid of Geelong, came, and after consultation it was decided to amputate the arm, about eight o'clock the next morning. I closely attended him up to the time of death. I am of the opinion that Charles Baeyertz died from the effects of a gunshot wound. He was conscious to within two hours of his death. I have known him for the last four years.

The result of the enquiry was that deceased died from the effects of a gunshot wound accidentally received on the 4th inst.

This also is from *Colac Herald*.

MELBOURNE, VICTORIA, 11 MARCH 1871

QUAIL JOTTINGS

IT HAS NOT BEEN, I SHOULD SAY *IS* NOT, A VERY BAD season for quail this time, after all. Notwithstanding the almost utterly empty bags with which most sportsmen that I have any acquaintance with returned to their homes on the opening and following days, better things have come to us with the advancing year. Breeding has become much prolonged. Not only has the handsome little painted quail raised, as usual with us, several successive broods (these lay generally four eggs only), but several other species, notably our very best substitute for the home partridge, and which commonly rears a brood of over a dozen, have kept on, where undisturbed, pairing and diligently repeating their kind.

Even now, beginning of March, hundreds of small fledglings are to be found, more especially in quiet, well-grassed districts; and a Colac correspondent tells me that quite recently (middle of February) he found, to use his own words 'numbers of cheepers, unable to fly'. So who shall presume, after all, to fix dates for the close season for quail which shall be applicable to all years?

...

The pleasantest afternoon must have an ending, and the darkness came down upon us when, of course, the birds were well on the feed and readier found ...

But had we not enough ... and had the powder not for once as a rule proved straight, and the dogs worked well, and, in short, what on earth was there lacking to our happiness?

Cantering home afterwards, in the cool of the evening, upon the old stock-horse, I found myself arriving at two sage conclusions. One was ... the Game Act[1] has not by any means proved a failure ... Further, I proposed, seconded, and carried a private resolution, that little beggars as they might be, there certainly were worse ways of passing a nice cool afternoon in the month of February, than in shooting quail.

N. B.—Little thought I, when penning yesterday the 'quail jottings' above, that an old friend and comrade, than whom no sportsman ever knew a truer, and to whom I made allusion as my 'Colac Correspondent', was lying on a bed of agony, stricken down by an accidental discharge of his gun while pursuing his favourite pastime. Should it not teach the lesson to us, one and all, that however old and experienced we may be in the use of firearms, we cannot exercise too much care with them?

Cartridge

[Shortly after the above article was in type we learned with extreme sorrow that Mr. Charles Baeyertz, the Manager of the National Bank at Colac, a keen sportsman, and an occasional valued contributor to our columns, has died from the effects of the sad accident above mentioned. SP ED]

This is the top and tail of a long article in the sporting pages of *The Australasian* describing a day's shooting by Cartridge and friends that we found in Trove, the digital repository of the National Library of Australia.

[1] The *Protection of Game Act 1867* regulated the hunting season.

COLAC, VICTORIA, 1871

I HAVE A DREAD OF WHAT IS BEFORE ME

I HAVE A DREAD OF WHAT IS BEFORE ME. IT IS HARD TO leave all that is dear and go amongst strangers, appearing cheerful and happy when your heart is breaking!

Ah, I hope you will make a better thing of your life than I have done. I am a desolate, lonely woman, feeling that my life has been a grand failure, although I must always have the comfort of feeling some good has come out of it in the knowledge of Jesus Christ. I would not change to be the happiest wife in Christendom without Him.

Mrs. E. L. Baeyertz

This extract is from a letter collected by H. C. N. (see page 111) and published on page 151 of 'A Supplementary Chapter' to the 1910 edition of *From Darkness to Light—The Life and Work of Mrs. Baeyertz,* by Sydney Watson, published in London by Mrs. Baeyertz. Sydney Watson wrote many other books, mostly fiction.

NEW VIENNA, OHIO, DECEMBER 1873
THE CRUSADING WOMEN OF NEW VIENNA

THIS PICTURE IS FROM A TIN-TYPE TAKEN AT THE TIME BY A TRAVELLING ARTIST. THE WOMEN OF THE VILLAGE ARE LAYING SIEGE TO THE SALOON OF VAN PELT, 'THE WICKEDEST MAN IN OHIO'. THEY FINALLY CONQUERED HIM, THOUGH IT WAS A HARD STRUGGLE.

You can find this picture and caption with the story of John Calvin Van Pelt and the Women's Temperance Crusade in *Historical Collections of Ohio* (Howe, 1900, pp. 428–430). Many illustrations from that time show women gathering for prayer outside saloons. Some show snow, some show kneeling. The women started kneeling in the snow of Hillsboro, Ohio, on 22nd December 1873. In fifty days, the Women's Temperance Crusade had swept liquor traffic out of 250 places, Church attendance doubled and court attendance halved. 'The excitement soon died away, and at the end of a few months the crusade had passed into history' (Howe). Well, not entirely. Out of these crusades came the Women's Christian Temperance Union (WCTU).

GEELONG, VICTORIA, 1875

FROM DARKNESS TO LIGHT

I HAVE BEEN ASKED BY ONE OF MY FRIENDS TO WRITE A brief sketch of my experience, and I do it believing that the precious Saviour whose I am and whom I serve, will bless this simple testimony to His grace and power to save.

Nine years ago I came to Australia with the intention of staying a short while with my friends here as I had been through some very bitter trials in the old country, and my dear parents thought that a change of scene might help me to forget the past.

Before proceeding, I must tell you that I and my family for ages back were strict Jews, and I had been brought up by good, religious parents. How the memory of the old days comes over me as I write! Never shall I forget my father's earnest prayer, the last hour I spent under his roof. He gave me up to the God of Abraham, Isaac and Jacob, and prayed that the angel that redeemed them from all evil might bless me.

I landed in Australia upon a Sunday evening, and when I arrived at my destination I found a party assembled, and joined with all my heart in the mirth around me. For twelve months I went into every kind of gaiety Melbourne afforded—dress, balls, the opera in fact, pleasure of every kind seemed my one thought.

About this time I met a gentleman to whom I became deeply attached; but though our affection was mutual, the thought of marriage I could not entertain, as he, being a Christian, and I, *heart and soul* a Jewess, it seemed out of the question. However, time wore on, and I at last consented to marry him, though I knew it would involve leaving all who were dear to me, and that it would bring a stigma upon my family. Before we were married I exacted a promise from my husband that he would never use any arguments to make me believe, as I was determined to live and die a Jewess. I will

not dwell upon my married life; my husband was all in all to
me—I wanted nothing more. God blessed us with two dear
little children, and only He who gave me them knows the
agony of mind I endured in the thought, 'How shall I teach
these little ones what I do not believe myself?' For I had made
up my mind, simply out of love for my husband, that they
should be brought up in their father's faith.

Although I attended God's house regularly, my heart was
in no way changed, and I never thought of Jesus as my Saviour.
After my second child was born, I became earnestly impressed
with a desire to become a Christian. My prayer at that time
always was 'O God! if it be right, let me believe.' I could not
see that it was honouring the Father to honour the Son; and
although I really wanted to be a Christian, I did not seek God
with my whole heart; my husband and my children were all
that I desired.

And now there came a time of trial that I must pass over as
quickly as possible. By an accident my beloved husband was
taken from me in a few days. So terribly sudden was the blow
that I could hardly realize that he had gone forever; and, oh,
what a gulf separated us!—it seemed to me impossible. I knew
he had died in the faith of Jesus, and I—I was as far off being a
Christian as the first day I met him. I was very bitter and hard
in my grief, and felt that God had dealt cruelly in crushing
me so, taking all the youth and brightness out of my life.
It seemed impossible to live, and I felt nothing but the desire
to be with my loved one again. Many a day I have laid on his
grave in the damp, and prayed that God would take me; but
God 'while I was yet a long way off'.[1] took compassion, and
raised up dear friends who showed me that only *in one way*
could I ever hope to see my husband again. The desire to be
a Christian became so intense as to become a part of my life.
No half-heartedness about it. I began to seek the Lord with all
my might. 'When ye seek Me with your whole heart, ye shall
find me,'[2] is a promise I have proved.

One day I was reading the old, old story, when something whispered to my soul, 'He suffered all this for you', and the truth seemed to burst upon me like a flash of lightning. I had found the Saviour, *my* Saviour, and such a flood of love as came into my heart for Him I cannot describe. I went into my room and on my knees I sobbed aloud, not for sorrow this time, but for joy. Words fail me in attempting to tell you half my Saviour is to me. He is indeed my all; and I can say 'The life which I now live in the flesh, I live by the faith of the Son of God, who loved me and gave Himself for me'.[3]

It is now some years since I found my precious Saviour, and although my trials have seemed sometimes as though they would overwhelm me, I have never doubted from the moment that I first believed in Jesus, but have thanked God on my dear husband's grave, for taking him (oh, it is only for a short time), and giving me the rich gift of His Son. My Jesus is no far-away God to me, but a very near and present help. I trust Him for all things and He never fails me.

Should there be some who read this who have not as yet known the precious Saviour, I do most earnestly and prayerfully implore you to seek Him with your whole heart. In looking back, I see I never knew what real happiness was; there was always a want the Saviour alone can fill. And, dear unsaved reader, down deep in your heart there is the same aching want. Oh, I beseech you, receive that One who is able to satisfy and fill up your life. He the 'I am' who heard the groanings and knew the sorrows of the Israelites, has come and died upon Calvary's cross for *you*. He offers to save you; then pause and think *what* must be the eternity that awaits you if you reject Him. You will be lost—*lost*—LOST! not because of your sins, but because you deliberately put from you God's Christ (John iii. 19). You cannot be saved, you cannot be made fit for the presence of God in any other way than by taking Jesus as your *Substitute*. By reason of sin you are *'condemned already'*. As you enter on the duties of the day; as you go to your worldly amusements; as you lay on your pillow to rest; as you read this, remember you are *'condemned already'*. God has said so. Oh! that He may awaken you to a knowledge of this. Oh listen to God's Word—'The blood of Jesus Christ His Son cleanseth us from all sin'.[4] Do not then harden your heart against such love as His; take this precious Saviour, and the moment you do so His glorious, beautiful life is yours, and He will be henceforth the strength of your life, and your heart will be tuned to sing—

> *I've found the Pearl of Greatest Price;*
> *My heart doth sing for joy—*
> *And sing I must for Christ is mine;*
> *Christ shall my song employ.*[5]

Should this fall into the hands of any of Israel, whom I love, oh, let me ask you, have you ever seriously thought whether that despised Nazarene may not after all be your looked-for Messiah? Have you ever honestly asked the God of Abraham, Isaac and Jacob to show you whether that lowly, humble Son of Mary is really the One of whom the prophet Isaiah spoke when he said 'Behold, a virgin shall conceive and bare a Son, and shall call Him Immanuel'? If you will only read the Books of Moses you will see there in what character our Messiah was to come. All those slain lambs, those burnt offerings, those morning and evening sacrifices, the blood shed and sprinkled, and the scapegoat, all pointed to one who was to come to bear the sins of His people and make atonement for them by giving up His own life. You need a saviour—a Substitute—for you have sinned against God, and 'the soul that sinneth it shall die'. Jesus was God's Son all the miracles He did proved His divinity. Accept that crucified King of the Jews, and you will say with joy, 'I have found the Messiah, the hope of Israel'.[6]

Mrs. E. L. Baeyertz

In 1875, Emilia was living in Geelong. This testimony was reproduced as a tract in Melbourne (1875) and London, England (circa 1879) and in *The Pioneer* (August 1886), a church newspaper in Tasmania. She added the last paragraph to the versions with her *Three Lectures* (Baeyertz E. L., 1890) in

New Zealand, *Five Lectures* (Baeyertz E. L., 1891) in Canada and *Twelve Addresses* (Baeyertz E. L., 1897) in England. We took this text from the *Five Lectures*. Emilia stopped publishing her short form of *From Darkness to Light* soon after she published the expanded version by Sydney Watson (1894/1895).

[1] Luke 15:20.

[2] Jeremiah 29:13.

[3] Galatians 2:20.

[4] 1 John 1:7.

[5] This hymn is by John Mason (1683).

[6] Isaiah 7:14, Ezekiel 18, Acts 28:20.

DORKING, ENGLAND, C. 1876

THE BOYS' CLASS EXPANDS INTO A MEETING

AT LAST THE MEN BEGAN TO COME INTO THE BOY'S CLASS which was hardly suitable!

On one fine day, however, matters were brought to a climax thus. In paying a visit to a cottage, I was told by the woman who had opened the door to me that her husband wished to speak to me.

'My man do want to see you very much', she said. I wondered what the reason could be, but finding she was not communicative on the subject, I invited him to come to the room, at the close of the boys' class, on the following Sunday.

At the appointed place and hour he appeared—a fine looking specimen of a navvy he was, head and shoulders taller than most of his fellow-workmen, and with a stalwart breadth of figure and muscular power to correspond. As he raised his cap from his curly head, he said 'I can't come it at all; you'll do anything for our *bodies*, you help us go to hospital, and all that, but you won't help us about our *souls*!'

I had never seen him before, and was somewhat overpowered by the sudden gigantic apparition, and the sententious accusation.

'What do you mean?' I said. 'I go every week to your houses, and will read and pray with anyone that asks me; and God knows, I ask Him many, many times to *save* your precious souls.'

'Thank'ee', he replied, 'but you only ever reads to the 'oomen, not to us men; we are never home.'

'You should go to church,' I said, 'and the clergyman will preach to you.'

'Well, I ain't so very partial to church, but I goes; yes I do, I goes *sometimes*.'

'Every Sunday?' was my query.

'Bless you, no!' was the very decided reply; 'Once in *six*, I should say, *about* that, and then I can't understand nothin'—I comes out again *just* the same. Now, look'ee 'ere, Miss, why shouldn't we come to this 'ere room, and you tell us somethin' more about it?'

'Well, H——,' was my reply, 'if you like to come here *alone*, next Sunday, I will tell you the words of poor sinners, just like you and me.'

'That'll do', he said, 'that's what I want; but—' after a pause, 'why won't you have a meeting, and some singing?'

'H——, I see that you are determined to have it out with me. The reason is this: people say that it is not right for women to teach men.'

Down came the great fist with an overwhelming thump on the table, and, in a very decided tone, he said—'I *thought* that was it, and I have been looking my Bible right through, to see whether that be *true*; but it *ain't*. There was the 'ooman of Samaria, she told the men; and Mary Magdalene, she *ran* to tell the men; and Rebekah, she stooped down and—she was a young lady, you know—gave a pitcher to a thirsty servant man. And this is what I think, Miss: if a man *don'* know, and a 'ooman do know, she ought to tell he, and it is very wrong of you *not* to tell we.'[1]

With that very peremptory conclusion, he wound up his oration, and departed, leaving me both amused and mystified ...

Elizabeth R. Cotton

Emilia read *Our Coffee-Room* by Elizabeth Reid Cotton in about 1877. This extract and illustration are from the 1884 edition (pp. 48–50) in the Robert Evans Collection.

[1] John 4, John 20:2, Genesis 24.

MELBOURNE, VICTORIA, 3 OCTOBER 1877

EVANGELISTIC SERVICES IN MELBOURNE

EVANGELISTIC SERVICES IN MELBOURNE—MR. VARLEY IN RICHMOND PARK.

This wood engraving, published by *The Illustrated Australian News*, is held by the State Library of Victoria. Henry Varley is shown preaching from the middle of the Melbourne Cricket Ground in what was then called Richmond Park or Richmond Paddock and is now called Yarra Park. The grandstand in the background, which seated 2000, was built for a cricket match played earlier that year that has become known as the First Test Match between Australia and England.

MELBOURNE, VICTORIA, 1877

LOCAL CHURCH NEWS

MRS. BAEYERTZ, A YOUNG JEWISH WIDOW WHO WAS brought to the faith some years ago, is a flame of fire. She visits the factories, and has now over four hundred young women in her Bible Class at the Assembly Hall each Wednesday evening. With but few exceptions these have all received God's gift of eternal life.

For some months she has addressed crowded congregations at the newly erected Mission Hall where over a hundred have found the Lord under her ministry within a very short time, whilst regular Church attenders have been revived under her clear, earnest holding forth of the light of Bible Truth.

In the next few weeks, Mrs. Baeyertz has been invited to speak to women and girls at the Gospel Hall Blanche Street, St Kilda, followed by similar meetings at the Presbyterian Church Clarendon Street, Emerald Hill.

Dr John Singleton

This undated and unattributed article from 'a weekly paper' was selected, and possibly edited, by Betty Baruch from Emilia's scrapbook. Sydney Watson (*From Darkness to Light*, 1894/1895, pp. 63–64) quotes from a similar article by Dr Singleton, published in *The Christian* in London, England, on 31 January 1878.

HOBART TOWN, TASMANIA, 26 JANUARY 1878

HOBART TOWN

MRS. BAEYERTZ HELD A SPECIAL SERVICE AT THE Ebenezer Church on Sunday, for the benefit of the children of the Sabbath School, and the scholars of any other who might attend. The building was literally thronged with juvenile and adult worshippers—the latter predominating—so that access, after 3 o'clock, to the church was almost impossible, and unpunctual yet anxious hearers had to content themselves with standing in the entrance to the aisle passage and in the vestry.

Mrs. Baeyertz chose the subject of her address from that passage of the 8th chapter of St. Luke's Gospel contained within the 26th and 36th verses. Her remarks were of that tenderly impressive nature which have ever secured for that lady very large congregations and attentive auditors; and such was the simple earnest force of her short scriptural stories that a dead silence prevailed in the building, the children, in spite of the heat, being particularly impressed. The kindly sympathy for the little ones that the lady evinces, her simple way of moving the feelings, and the beautiful manner in which she imparts truths of morality and religion, will not be easily forgotten by those who have, as at a teacher's, sat at her feet and learnt, and they will, we hope, not be without their effect.

From *Willing Work*, 'A weekly record of Christian testimony and work in the Australian colonies, edited by C. Edwin Good and published by Melbourne Bible and Tract Repository and M. L. Hutchinson.' This extract was reproduced by Rev. Robert Evans OAM on page 76 of his book *Emilia Baeyertz—Evangelist* (Evans 2007).

LAUNCESTON, TASMANIA, 15 APRIL 1878

THE LADY PREACHER

A LARGE CROWD OF SUNDAY SCHOOL CHILDREN ASSEMbled in the pavilion, Public Gardens, yesterday afternoon, the announcement that Mrs. Baeyertz, of Melbourne, would deliver an address being sufficient attraction to fill the room to overflowing. This lady has been holding a series of evangelistic services in Hobart Town, and has drawn large numbers of people together, those attending in the first instance merely out of curiosity to 'hear a woman preach' being impelled to frequently repeat their visits by her simple yet earnest and forcible language. She has a very pleasing appearance, and speaks in a sufficiently distinct tone of voice to be heard by a large assemblage.

The service yesterday began by singing one of Moody and Sankey's hymns, the harmony being led by Miss Price, who presided at the cabinet organ. A very earnest prayer was then offered up by Mrs. Baeyertz, after which another hymn was sung. The preacher then read portions of the tenth chapter of St. Mark's gospel, the account of the rich young man who desired to inherit eternal life, but who when required to give up all his possessions and follow Christ went away grieved, forming the basis of her address. She pointed out in clear language that it is not by rigid observance of the commandments that we can obtain salvation, but by becoming new creatures. Her subject was well handled, and was illustrated by many anecdotes, which were pointedly put.

Upon commencing to read the scriptures, she reproached very severely some whom she observed laughing, and reminded them of the solemnity of the occasion. Her discourse was mainly devoted to laying before her hearers the terms upon which salvation can alone be obtained, showing how condemnation rests upon all, and she concluded by saying that she washed her hands of the blood of her hearers if they failed to seek that salvation. She could but show the way; she could not do more.

Altogether the service was a most profitable one. The lady invited any who felt seriously impressed to remain for further instruction, and a number of her hearers accepted this invitation. Several other announcements were made, but being uttered during the bustle caused by a large audience rising from the seats, they were not heard by the great majority of the congregation. Mrs. Baeyertz will deliver another address this evening in the Mechanics' Hall, to which all are invited.

From *The Examiner,* still Launceston's daily newspaper. Also in Evans (2007, p. 87).

LAUNCESTON, TASMANIA, APRIL 1878

VISITING PREACHERS

17 April 1878

To the Editor of *The Examiner*,

Sir,

Have our ministers in town become superannuated that we actually need women from a distance to come and preach to us? Our place got the name of being dead or somewhat like it, and it appears to be true.

I think Mrs. Baeyertz and others of the same stamp should be 'keepers at home,' their proper sphere, and endeavour to train their *children* in the fear of God. If she and others have time to spare let them visit our lanes and alleys, where their services (if they are Christians) might do great good.

D.

[There is work enough for all.—Ed.]

18 April 1878

To the Editor of *The Examiner*,

Sir,

It is quite true that 'there is work enough for all'; still it seems to me unseemly that women should be public preachers of the Gospel, and if I understand the New Testament aright St. Paul thinks so too.

D.

19 April, 1878

To the Editor of *The Examiner*,

Sir,

Are you not sad at the wrongs of 'D.'? Poor fellow! It is really too bad that one strolling preacher after another should intrude here, and wind up with a *woman*! What makes the matter worse is, that members of poor 'D's' church and congregation should patronise these objectionable people.

Suppose our ministers (some of whom would be much better 'superannuated') were to go and hear for themselves, and learn the secret by which these women draw such crowds of attentive hearers, many of whom will *stand* for two hours at a time fascinated by the beauty of these Gospel addresses. Let 'D.' only hear Mrs. Baeyertz once, and, if he is not too conceited to learn from a woman, his future sermons may be the better for it.

E.

SANDHURST, VICTORIA, 1 AUGUST 1879

MRS BAEYERTZ AT SANDHURST

THE SERVICES DURING THE PAST WEEK HAVE BEEN accompanied with increased blessing; and again we have to record with thankfulness the answers that have been given to the many prayers that have been sent up for this place.

On Sunday, the 20th, at 3 p. m., Mrs. Baeyertz gave an address in the theatre, as none of the other buildings were large enough to hold the crowds who sought to gain admittance to each service. Though the theatre holds about 2,200, it was densely packed, and more than half an hour before the time for the meeting to be commenced the doors had to be locked, and numbers were obliged to go away disappointed. Sixty or more remained to the after-meeting; about twenty of these were men; those who usually remained at the close of the former services had been mostly women and girls. After Mrs. Baeyertz had spoken to them a few words, several rose to testify that they were now enabled to rest on Christ. After these had left, Mrs. Baeyertz and the Christian workers went down amongst the anxious ones remaining, not a few of whom also professed their faith in the Lord Jesus before leaving.

On Wednesday, the 23rd, Mrs. Baeyertz held a meeting for women and girls only, in the large Hall of the Masonic building. Long before the hour arrived the place was thronged, and large numbers had to go away, not being able even to get near the doors. It is supposed that more than twelve hundred women and girls were gathered together in the hall; such a sight had never before been witnessed in Sandhurst. Many prayers went up from the hearts of the Christians present that the Lord would give a very great blessing, and that numbers might be won for Jesus. Mrs. Baeyertz addressed them on the word 'Come,' 'Come into the ark,' 'Come unto me and rest,'

'Let him that is athirst come,' interspersing her address with impressive and thrilling anecdotes.

At the close of the meeting nearly a hundred, it is thought, stood up to say they were seeking Christ. Before the after-meeting concluded a number professed to have accepted the Lord Jesus as their Saviour. When these had left, and Mrs. Baeyertz and her band of workers went down among the groups of weeping girls remaining, very touching were the scenes they witnessed; some of these dear young girls had come back to each service from the commencement of the meetings, unable yet to say, 'Jesus is *mine*,' but one after another of them were this night able to say with happy faces, 'I can now trust Jesus.'

On Thursday evening, Mrs. Baeyertz preached the gospel in the Presbyterian Church, Eaglehawk, the building being quite full. The meeting on Friday evening, in the Masonic Hall, was crowded as before. Mrs. Baeyertz's address was on the 'Seven cries of our Lord Jesus on the cross.' More than sixty remained behind to the after-meeting; after a few words addressed to them on 'Peace made by the blood of the cross,' several stood up to signify they were resting on Christ. The others remained in their seats; after these had passed out, and were spoken to personally, and as on each preceding evening, some were enabled to take Jesus as their Saviour.

Some most touching scenes were witnessed at these after-meetings; one evening a woman sat there with such a look of remorse and agony upon her face; as Mrs. Baeyertz sat down beside her, she was greeted with the words, 'I want Jesus, do you think He would take me?'

'I am sure He would,' was the answer, 'He is waiting to receive you.'

'But I have closed my heart against Him. My husband was suddenly killed by an accident in the mines, he left me in health and was carried back to me in his coffin, and I hardened my heart against the Lord. Then He took my baby from me, and still I hardened my heart. I had only one child left, a dear little boy; at last he got ill, and I said, "God shan't have my boy"'; and then lowering her voice she added, 'But God took him too, and again I hardened my heart. But I would take Jesus now, if He would have me.'

Mrs. Baeyertz talked with her for half an hour, she felt she could not leave her; but the woman went home that evening wretched, the light had not yet broken upon her. The next night she stood up amongst others to testify that she had come to the Lord Jesus, and had been received by Him.

A young Sunday-school teacher came to several meetings, bringing members of her class with her, showing great anxiety about *their* salvation, and rejoicing when three of them professed to be saved. She was also very energetic at the children's meetings. But a night or two after she came up weeping, saying she had never known Christ herself, and although she was a Sunday-school teacher, and made a high profession, came to the Lord's table, was believed by her pastor to be a true Christian, but that she now knew that she had never been born again. Her mother then came up saying, 'Thank God, my daughter is now awakened, she has not been converted; I knew she was not, for she never showed the fruit of the Spirit in her life.'

From *Willing Work*. Also in Evans (2007, pp. 102–104).

BALLARAT, VICTORIA, SEPTEMBER 1880

BALLARAT MISSION DRAWS TO A CLOSE

THE MISSION, WHICH HAS BEEN CONDUCTED BY Mrs Baeyertz over the past month, will conclude at the end of this week. No-one who has been to either the evening meetings or the afternoon Bible Readings, where over one thousand gathered each day to hear her, can deny that she has been a blessing to us all. As the crowds have been so great it was an act of providence that made our largest theatre available for the length of her stay with us, and even this was packed night after night with many being unable to gain admittance.

On Sunday afternoons, many who attended the meeting wisely brought with them their evening meal, counting it no hardship to be locked inside the building until the doors were again opened for the night service. Only in this way could they be assured of obtaining seats! So great was the press around the entrance doors, and so dense the crowd spilling onto the road, that our municipal authorities had no recourse but to close off the entire street to passing traffic. At the conclusion of one of the meetings, those who stayed behind for counselling were so numerous that it became impossible for the helpers to reach them all.

I take it upon myself to say that never before has our city been privileged to hear a servant of God whose endeavours on His behalf have been so overtly blessed. Not only the unsaved, but people from all our Churches, have received spiritual benefit as a result of Mrs. Baeyertz coming among us.

This extract from 'the Ballarat paper' was selected by Betty from the Baeyertz family papers. Sydney Watson (*From Darkness to Light*, 1894/1895, p. 70) quotes part of a similar article.

ADELAIDE, SOUTH AUSTRALIA, 8 DECEMBER, 1880

LETTER TO MRS BAEYERTZ

Dear Mrs. Baeyertz,

We cannot allow you to leave our shores today without giving expression to our sincere and grateful appreciation of your visit among us. As the Committee who have acted with you in the services you have held in this city we are sure that we speak, not only for ourselves but also for each worker who has taken part in the meetings, in saying that we are devoutly grateful to God for directing your steps into our midst.

We are equally confident that we are only expressing the thoughts and feelings of a very large number of Christians in Adelaide and suburbs in testifying not only to our esteem for you as a sister in Christ Jesus, but to our conviction that God has eminently endowed you with gifts for the setting forth of His precious truth both to Christians and non-Christians.

We are aware that you feel specially called to minister the Gospel of Salvation to the unconverted, and we rejoice to know that during these recent meetings it has proved to be the power of God unto salvation to many unsaved ones. We trust that you will still make the salvation of sinners through faith in Christ the distinguishing aim of your labours, and we pray and will pray that our gracious Lord and God may give you wisdom and power to win for His glory many thousands of souls from the thraldom of sin and Satan.

At the same time, we know both from experience and from the earnest and unanimous testimony of large numbers of Christians that your very clear unfolding of the foundation truths of the Gospel have been most helpful, stimulating, and edifying to the great bulk of believers. May you still be greatly honoured by God in ministering to the saints, though this be not your first aim. We rejoice to believe that your steadfast adherence to and love of God's Word has made the Bible a more precious volume to many of us.

On our part there have been grave shortcomings. We have had before today evangelists in our city, and we have not always been able to look on their work with full satisfaction. That was to your disadvantage on your arrival, and we did not enter with you on your work with that degree of expectant sanguine faith with which we ought to have co-operated with you. Your own faith has rebuked our lack of faith. We want to confess this before God as well as to you. Had we been more believing, doubtless the results would have been larger. Nevertheless, we are intensely grateful that so large a number of souls have been saved, and that so much real spiritual good has been accomplished.

You know—at least we hope you in part understand—how ardently we entertain the hope of your returning to labour afresh in and around Adelaide as well as in the country districts. Rest assured, we and others will earnestly strive to promote in every possible way the true and highest success of your second visit. Will you permit us to urge it on you that with the existing feeling and expectation it would be best if you could return to us as soon as the summer is over, say in May next? We will ask the Lord to send you back to us soon. Meanwhile our prayer is that He will more abundantly and graciously bless you than we have language to express.

Yours in the faith of the Lord Jesus,

The Committee

This letter from the South Australian Baptist Association was published in the January 1881 edition of *Truth and Progress*, the South Australian Baptist monthly, with this introduction: 'The subjoined letter was handed to Mrs. Baeyertz on the morning of her departure from Adelaide by the Committee which assisted in the direction of the services. Several of the members of this Committee waited on Mrs. Baeyertz and personally expressed the great joy which they in common with others had experienced in connection with her visit.' Also in Evans (2007, p. 123).

LAUNCESTON, TASMANIA, 1881

APPRECIATION OF HENRY REED

I FEEL IT A GREAT PRIVILEGE AND JOY TO BE ABLE TO contribute my reminiscences of my dear personal friend Henry Reed.

The first time I met him was when I went on a visit to Wesley Dale with my two children at his own invitation. On my arrival, he with Mrs. Reed came out to the carriage to welcome us. I can see him now, his tall figure and handsome face, kind eyes, and oh! the sweet smile and loving words of welcome. We all went into the large dining-room, and without any notice or words of warning, he went down on his knees and prayed. Yes, it was prayer; we were taken into the holiest and put right into our heavenly Father's care. As I came into contact day after day with that saintly man of God, I used to go from his presence to my room; and on my knees cry to God to reveal to me the secret of his wonderful life.

During my Christian course, I have come in touch with holy men of world-wide fame, but often I fancied they were austere, and I have felt uncomfortable in their company; but with Henry Reed, his personal character and holy walk with God were so winning and attractive that they drew you unconsciously to himself, and through him to Christ. I was always a better woman through contact with him.

In those early days, when I suffered much persecution because of the solitary walk as an evangelist which the Lord had marked out for me, I owe more than I can tell to the loving sympathy and saintly life of that blessed man of God, dear Henry Reed. I love to write his name. I stayed very often in his home, and can say after all these years that without any exception he was the most Christ-like man I have ever known. He was indeed 'righteous before God and blameless.'

Mr. Reed was most original and unconventional in all his ways; no one could copy him; and it was most charming to see him after some of my meetings at Wesley Dale, when he would go about amongst the people and urge them to decide for Christ.

'Why, Mary, you are going to decide; your mother is a Christian. John, come, give your heart to God; why, your father was converted through me before you were born. Now, James, now, that's right; come along; there is joy in Heaven to-night. What's keeping you back, Sarah?' and so on, like a father amongst these young people. Many of them had been born on his estate, their parents were serving him, and some had been converted through him. The souls he won to Christ will be known up there by-and-by.

He was thoughtful too at all times. Once I had to make a very early start to catch the train (thirteen miles distant), long before the household was astir. They all knew how nervous I then was about horses. The groom had brought out my luggage, and I was standing on the verandah waiting for the dog-cart, when presently the blind was drawn aside and Mr. Reed's dear face appeared at the window. He called to the groom, 'What horse are you putting in for Mrs. Baeyertz? Put in old Granny,' that being the name of a very quiet mare. Thus the fear and dread of that long drive fell from me.

Before my last visit to him at Mount Pleasant, I was told of the doctor's verdict, that he could not recover; and I went with a very sad heart. We were shown into the dining-room. When we entered he was standing at the window, but when the door opened, he turned round and I saw his face. Never shall I forget the radiant look as with that rare smile he said, 'Well, little woman, welcome once more to Mount Pleasant! Have you heard the news? Is it not beautiful?' I could not reply; but as was his custom, he dropped on his knees and prayed and praised. Oh, such nearness, just talking to God! And once more he commended us to our loving Father. I forget the details of that visit; all I know is that I left 'sorrowing most of all that I should see his face no more'.[1]

'The law of truth was in his mouth and iniquity was not found in his lips; he walked with God in peace and equity, and did turn many away from iniquity' (Mal. ii. 6).

> *Thanks for thy noble witness,*
> *Thanks for thy life's accord,*
> *Thanks for thy saintly valour,*
> *Heaven's dew upon thy sword.*

Mrs. E. L. Baeyertz

This is one of several 'appreciations' included by Margaret Reed in her biography of her husband (Reed, c. 1881, pp. 236–240). We found a copy in the A. N. S. Coombe Archive. This is a rare example of Emilia's writing that is neither a letter nor a talk. We haven't found the source of the concluding verse.

[1] Acts 20:38.

ADELAIDE, SOUTH AUSTRALIA, 1 APRIL 1883

EDITORIAL

AFTER A REST AT CHRISTMAS AND THE NEW YEAR, Mrs. Baeyertz began evangelistic labours at Nairne, which proved very successful—several persons being brought to the knowledge of the Saviour during the fortnight that she continued her services there. After finishing at Nairne, Mrs. Baeyertz paid a second visit to Mount Barker, where she found many who had been brought to the knowledge of the truth under her appeals twelve months before, ready to welcome her.

Questions have, at different times, been freely raised respecting the places where evangelistic work of this kind has been carried on, whether the fruit of the work is found in the way of additions made to the Churches, and whether the change is found to be durable. Our own impression as to the first point is that the Churches which give ungrudging aid and that enter with full sympathy into the work do reap fruit in the way of additions to the Church. Alberton, Kapunda, and Mount Barker may be adduced as instances of this.

But where on the other hand, a disposition is manifested to criticise, thwart, and opposed the Evangelist and the work, it is contrary to reason to expect much addition to the Church under such conditions. Not only the converts fail to be attracted, but such a spirit is itself subversive of spiritual success.

Our own conviction is that the Churches in South Australia in many of the denominations owe much to the labours of Mrs. Baeyertz (not to mention other Evangelists) during the last two years and that the membership has been greatly increased through her. Then, as to the durability of the change wrought in those who profess to find peace the only answer that can be given is that many who professed to find peace are found to be steadfast, consistent, useful Christians.

It must be confessed, on the other hand, that there are some who are drawn aside and who go back again into the worldliness and sin from which they seemed to have escaped. But what ministrations that the Church has ever known could we pronounce free from such a drawback? Does not the Saviour teach us that there are hearers from whose hearts the good seed is snatched away, and that there are others in whom the good seed is choked? The conversions that take place in the fervid atmosphere of an evangelistic revival will bear favourable comparison as to intelligent perceptions and as to durability, with those which are affected in the more ordinary methods of church work.

The visit of Mrs. Baeyertz to Mount Barker was not so marked as her first visit, but in a small population it would scarcely be reasonable to expect it. After leaving Mount Barker she visited Kanmantoo, where the success was as striking as in any place she has visited. We are informed that the entire neighbourhood seemed swayed by the power of divine truth, that the congregations were overwhelming, and that numbers were brought out of darkness into light.

During the past week Woodside has been visited, and our latest information is to the effect that a special messenger has been sent to Adelaide by some prominent members of the Wesleyan Church to endeavour to obtain from the President of the Conference an evangelist to direct and continue the work that has been there accomplished. We wish Mrs. Baeyertz a rich blessing in the populous district of the Burra, to which she is now proceeding.

From *Truth and Progress*. Reproduced by Evans (2007, p. 170).

GLADSTONE, SOUTH AUSTRALIA, NOVEMBER 1883

MRS BAEYERTZ AT GLADSTONE

THE LAST OF THE SERVICES IN CONNECTION WITH Mrs. Baeyertz's evangelistic work, at Gladstone, was held on Thursday, November 1st, in the Institute Hall. The building was crowded, and many were unable to gain admittance.

The method Mrs. Baeyertz adopted was one which she said she did not often do—viz., take a text. The words chosen were—'The Master has come and calleth for thee,' John xi. 28th verse.

We are willing to admit that the previous services held here were to us in a measure disappointing, the wholesale denunciation of many things which are enjoyable, and her teachings would, if pushed to its logical conclusions, destroy much which goes to expand the soul, and magnify the powers which the Creator has bestowed upon us. We are prepared to go on the question of expediency in these matters. 'All things are lawful to me, but not all things are expedient' This teaching disarms prejudice, and unless we are obtuse to a degree, the same end is achieved, and the teacher is exempt from the charge of intemperance.

In last night's service no charge of this kind could be brought. From the beginning to the end there was nothing whatever to shock the feelings of the most sentimental. It was marked by an intense earnestness, and yet withal a deep sympathy. Temperate in her reproofs, generous and kind to her opponents, practical in her teachings, and several of her points and passages were thrilling in the extreme.

We are persuaded if any fault is to be found it must be with the 'message' and not with the 'messenger.' A solemnity prevailed [through] the assembly, and it was with difficulty the people could be induced to leave. Mrs. Baeyertz went to Jamestown yesterday morning, leaving behind her many friends, and the sincerest wish we can express is that her visit will be productive of much good.

Truth and Progress (1 December 1883) reproduced this article from *The Areas' Express and Farmers' Journal* which was published twice weekly for the agricultural 'Areas' around Gladstone in South Australia. From Evans (2007, p. 174).

ADELAIDE, SOUTH AUSTRALIA, 1 DECEMBER 1883

LETTER TO THE EDITOR

Sir,

To do aggressive work and build up the various Churches, we need an Evangelist, and one that has proved his call to be one by the fruits following his teaching. If such a man can be found we should engage him for the Association work, but if we cannot find a MAN we can find the WOMAN who has proved her call to the work of an evangelist. And I would respectfully request that, with all the evidences before us of the fitness of Mrs. Baeyertz to do this work, an effort be made to engage her services for the Association, if it be possible to do so.

The testimony given from all the Churches where she has laboured is so conclusive as to the great good done that we should at once try and secure her before her plans are matured for leaving the Colony, as I believe she is contemplating doing after this year.

Hoping this will set the Churches a-thinking and acting,

I remain, yours truly,

A. O. Chambers

From *Truth and Progress*. From Evans (2007, p. 173).

COLAC, VICTORIA, 10 APRIL 1885

MRS BAEYERTZ IN COLAC

ON MONDAY EVENING LAST MRS. BAEYERTZ'S MISSION IN Colac was brought to a close. These evangelistic services, which were commenced on Wednesday the 1st inst., have extended over six days, and during that time this lady has conducted about ten meetings, including holiness, Bible reading and evangelistic services, the whole of which have been characterised by much religious awakening amongst the people, and numbers of her hearers will, no doubt, date their conversion from the visit of this gifted servant of God.

Mrs. Baeyertz's manner and style of delivery is easy, graceful and natural, her utterance being marked by great clearness and lucidity, so much so that the densest intellect is able to understand and grasp her meaning. With a voice not overstrong, she can, nevertheless, make herself heard in every part of the building; the singular gifts of perspicuity, deliberation, and power of elocution rendering every word intelligible, while throughout the service her listeners feel themselves, for the time being, refined, elevated, and chastened by her fervid and impassioned sentences. These qualities, together with the happy knack of telling a good story, or relating a soul-stirring anecdote, coupled with strong persuasive powers and argumentative ability of a high degree, are the main sources from which she has derived those qualifications which so ably fit her to control the popular mind, thus enabling her to draw the large masses that nightly assembled together, all eager to list to the voice of 'one frail woman.' This lady possesses little of the rant or clap-trap which, we are accustomed to hear from evangelists in general, and all, even those who may disagree with her on points of doctrine (and there are many who do), must admit that, as a teacher and expounder of the scriptures, she stands in the front rank.

Mrs. Baeyertz has expressed herself as being well pleased with the success which has attended her labours in 'dear old Colac', and considering that during her stay here 165 persons have professed to be saved through her instrumentality she has little cause to repent the visit she paid to this town. She stated at one of her meetings that in South Australia the average number of conversions was 100 a week, and in one town where she held a men's meeting, forty came out for Christ in one night.

Part of the past history of this lady is connected with this town, and though associated with sad memories, a recital of by-gone time will be read with increasing interest now. It will be remembered that her husband, Mr. Baeyertz, was at the period we speak of manager of the Colac branch of the National Bank, a gentleman loved and respected by all who knew him. He was a Christian man in the best sense of the word, a good husband, a kind father, and an estimable citizen; his wife at that time being a Jewess. In an unlucky hour Mr. Baeyertz went to the racecourse paddock to shoot quail. Seeing a friend of his coming along the road from Colac, he crossed over to speak to him, and when he came to the fence he placed his gun against it, when, from some unaccountable cause, the piece went off, the contents of it entering a little below the left shoulder.

He was quickly conveyed into Colac, where medical assistance was immediately obtained. But little hopes were entertained of his recovery, and although, after consultation with Dr. Reid, of Geelong, the shattered limb was amputated, the relief obtained was of short duration, and after nearly two days of intense suffering, borne with Christian fortitude, Mr. Baeyertz sank under his injuries and died. This sad event took place on the 6th of March, 1871, or fourteen years ago last month. The newly-made widow was inconsolable in her grief. Her husband, whom she idolized, had been cut off at the early age of 28 years, and with his death all the brightness and gladsomeness in her life seemed extinguished for ever.

She was at this time a Jewess, hating and despising Christ and Christian people. On her arrival in the colony she had thrown religion away, and entered into a life of gaiety and pleasure, dancing, balls, opera, and card-parties being her greatest bane. Before she was married to Mr. Baeyertz she exacted a promise from him that he would never attempt to turn her from her Jewish faith, and subsequently she on her part promised to bring up their children in their father's faith. Speaking of the loss of her husband on Friday evening, she remarked that it was the turning point in her life. She knew that he loved Jesus, and that he wanted her to love Him too.

'He often prayed for me,' she said, 'but I used to mock him while he was on his knees. When he was dying, he gave me a look I shall never forget, and from that moment I felt that there must be a Christ. Before he was cold, I vowed by the body of my dead husband that I would find Christ. I did not want Christ; it was my husband I wanted.'

'Three or four weeks before the truth was flashed into my mind, my relatives wrote to me to come back to them with my two children. In my then desolate condition I was yearning for that love which had been taken away, and I decided to go back. Oh, I now know that Jesus was near me then, that his loving arms were around me. As I took up my pen to write the thought struck me, "If I go back I will never see my husband again", and with that the pen fell from my fingers.' Believing that if she went back to her Jewish friends she would not have the opportunity of becoming a Christian, and so lose all chance of finding her husband in the next world, she determined to remain away from them.

It was some short time after this that she was visiting at Mr. Calvert's, where the great struggle from darkness to light took place. Whilst reading the Bible and praying for revealing grace, the truth flashed suddenly into her mind, 'He is Christ, and he died for me,' and then she wept for joy as if her heart would break. 'When my husband died' she continued, 'I thought it was the worst calamity that could happen, and I sorrowed for him for two years. Now, I can say, thank God for taking him from me. He did want me to believe in Christ, and if he does not know it now, he will by and by that his wife is saved.'

During the fourteen years that have elapsed since she embraced Christianity, she has never had cause to regret the decision then come to, her present life she says yields her such exquisite pleasures, such exquisite delights. It is now about ten years since she began to preach the gospel from the platform, and during that time she has been the humble instrument in God's hands of converting hundreds of men, women, and children. Mrs. Baeyertz belongs to no particular church or denomination, but any one skilled in the critic's art can easily perceive from the tenor of her addresses the sources from whence her theological opinions emanate. She is not afraid to speak out on such subjects as hell, damnation, or eternal punishment, not being, of course so fancifully fastidious as that clergyman was who on one occasion apologised to his congregation for having made use of such a 'vulgar word' as hell.

These subjects were freely dealt with on Saturday night, when she was discoursing on 'Dives' the rich man. This meeting was for men and boys only, the speaker dwelling at considerable length upon the responsibility which devolved upon husbands and fathers in relation to their wives and children. The terrible consequences attending those who dragged others down with them to hell were vividly described, and the fallacies of those who believed in the ultimate restoration of lost souls pointed out and explained away. She reproached those men who had not the moral courage to come out for Christ, and said that to go to the Soudan was a noble act, but what was nobler and required more courage was for a man to walk up to the penitent form.

On Sunday afternoon an evangelistic service was held, when twenty-seven were added to the number of the 'saved', and at the evening service the rush to the enquiry room was something marvellous. The proceedings terminated with a grand hallelujah meeting, at which several of the new converts gave their 'testimony'. The mission was concluded by a grand farewell gathering on Monday evening, at which the evangelist addressed herself especially to young converts and elder Christians, giving them some solid practical advice as to their future conduct in life.

At the termination of the proceedings, Mrs. Baeyertz made a statement to the effect that during her mission in Colac 165 persons had been personally dealt with by her, and that all had 'professed to be saved'. But she very properly added, 'I dare not say that they are all saved'.

Mrs. Baeyertz left by the 3.25 p. m. train on Tuesday for Melbourne.[1] A large number of her friends and admirers were present on the platform to give the lady a 'shake of the hand' and wish her 'God speed' and a safe journey home.

Izaak[2]

From *Colac Herald*. In the previous week's article (*Colac Herald*, 3 April 1885), Isaak told us that the 'revival services' were to be held at the Oddfellows' Hall. This hall was replaced in 1891 (*Colac: A Short History*, 1995) by the present building at the corner of Dennis Street and Gellibrand Street which is now Oddfellows' Restaurant. We also learn that 'she had studied, fought and prayed over the Bible and believed every word of it' and that she said, 'Strange that I a Jew should be sent to you Gentiles to tell you of your Saviour. In some places the knowledge of my history has influenced many to turn to God.' Those she spoke to after the meeting were presented 'with a tract containing the story of her conversion' (see page 22). We found these articles on Trove.

[1] When Emilia returned to Colac the following year, 'the Wesleyan Church was filled night after night', according to *The Southern Cross*, 4 June 1886 (Evans, 2007, p. 186).

[2] Isaac Hebb wrote his *History of Colac* as a serial in *Colac Herald* from 1888 under the name Izaak. This history has since been reproduced as a book (Hebb, 1888/1970). Decades later, he wrote a history for the Anglican Church in Colac (Hebb, 1930).

MELBOURNE, VICTORIA, JULY 1885

'LET HIM THAT HEARETH SAY, COME'[1]

Dear Sister,

During the ensuing month (July) we [YWCA] intend, as an 'association', to hold a fortnight's special mission services. These services will be conducted by Mrs. Baeyertz, the converted Jewess and lady evangelist, whom we all know and love. As we were praying last month for a special outpouring of the Holy Spirit, we hope during these mission services to see the result in a great ingathering of souls.

And now, dear sister, what is your part in the great work of winning other lives to Jesus? You have heard for yourself the Master's loving invitation, 'Come unto Me.' Gladly your heart responded with the cry, 'Lord Jesus, Thou hast bid me come take me just as I am, and save me now.' Then, in that glad hour, you knew for the first time what it was to 'come' to Jesus.

'Let him that heareth say, Come.' Will you not obey the loving command, and carry the message to some other weary soul? Look around you in your own home circle. Is there not someone close at hand waiting for you to bid them 'come?' Ask Jesus Himself to direct you, and you will not long be left in doubt. Have you ever tasted the joy of carrying the message to some weary, waiting soul—to one who has been longing for it as the parched traveller in the desert longs for a draught of cool water? Then we are sure it will thenceforth be your highest ambition to be constantly employed in carrying the Master's invitation. Will you try this month, dear sister, to make a special effort to win one soul for Jesus? Also, we would ask you to help us by your prayers (and in any other way open to you) to make our first Young Women's Christian Association mission a great success.

Mrs. Baeyertz will commence the mission services on Sunday night, 12th July, in the upper hall of the Young Men's Christian

Association building, Russell-street (as we cannot have the Assembly Hall on account its being otherwise engaged), and will hold meetings on Tuesday, Wednesday, and Thursday nights of each week, also on Monday and Friday afternoons at half-past three. Hoping to see all our members, if possible, at these meetings.

We remain, your loving sisters in the Lord,

S. C. and E. W. Booth.[2]

P. S. Replies gladly received.

Robert Evans (2007, p. 180) found this Monthly Letter of the Young Women's Christian Association in *The Spectator and Methodist Chronicle*, 17 July, 1885, p. 349.

[1] Revelation 22:17.

[2] Sarah and Lila Booth were sisters who together ran the YWCA in Melbourne.

BRISBANE, QUEENSLAND, SEPTEMBER 1889

A VISITOR FROM THE SOUTH

SHE CAME TO BRISBANE UNKNOWN TO US, AND DUE TO heavy rain, her first meeting was not well attended. But as her addresses have created interest, more and more of our people have been attending them till finally the large Opera House has been unable to accommodate the immense crowds that are now flocking to hear her. Such congregations as are packing that building are said never before in the history of the colony to have assembled to hear an evangelist. Every class is represented, men coming from both the Upper and Lower Houses of Parliament as well as those from the back slums.

Her methods are somewhat singular at least in this respect, that Mrs. Baeyertz holds one lot of meetings for women and girls only, and separate meetings for men and boys. She is a Jewish lady who came to the colonies intending to remain a very short while, but by a series of providential circumstances her intentions changed remarkably and she is now a devoted and much-sought-after evangelist for the Lord.

On the conclusion of her three weeks in our midst, Mrs Baeyertz will visit Ipswich to conduct meetings there. We join our readers in wishing her God Speed as she embarks on her mission to the country areas of our colony.

This account from an unknown paper was selected by Betty from the Baeyertz family scrapbook. For a longer account in the C. N. Baeyertz Collection in New Zealand, see Evans (2007, p. 217). *The Brisbane Courier* published many short reports and announcements about this mission.

MELBOURNE, VICTORIA, 27 DECEMBER 1889

CIRCULAR LETTER

Brethren,

Mrs. Baeyertz, the bearer of this letter, has long been known to us as a devoted and gifted servant of our Lord Jesus Christ.

She has faithfully served the Churches of Victoria and of the other Australian Colonies during the past thirteen years as an evangelist of exceptional power.

Her meetings have invariably been crowded, and the spiritual results of an abiding character. There is not a city, and scarcely a town or hamlet, in Victoria, where men and women won to Christ through her instrumentality are not to be found.

In addition, it gives us pleasure to say that our sister has, since her conversion from Judaism to Jesus, maintained a high level of Christian consistency, and of whole-souled consecration.

We affectionately commend her to the Churches of Christ, wherever in the providence of God she may be led, as a sister worthy in every way of their confidence and esteem, and as one eminently qualified by the great Head of the Church to be their helper in the work of the Lord.

John G. Paton, Missionary, New Hebrides

H. B. Macartney, jun., St. Mary's Vicarage, Caulfield

Henry A. Langley, Minister, Church of England, St. Matthew's Prahran, Archdeacon of Gippsland

A. J. Campbell, D. D., Presbyterian Church of Victoria

Samuel Chapman, Collins Street Baptist Church, Melbourne

John Watsford, Wesleyan Minister, Richmond, Victoria

Samuel Knight, Brunswick Street Wesleyan Church (late of South Australia, to which this letter is equally appropriate)

Allan Webb, Albert Street Baptist Church, Melbourne

Alfred Bird, Baptist Minister, Hawthorn, Melbourne

Wm. Christopher Bunning, Baptist Minister, West Melbourne

D. O'Donnell, Congregational Church, Malvern

W. Lockhart Morton, jun., Presbyterian Church, Malvern

John MacNeil, Evangelist of the Presbyterian Church of Victoria

Silas Mead, LL. B., M. A., Flinders Street Baptist Church, Adelaide (in whose church she held services continuously for over two months with great success, accompanied with many signs of God's blessing).

This circular letter (Paton, et al.) was presented to Emilia at her private farewell from Melbourne. The text is from a footnote by Sydney Watson (1910, pp. 83–84).

DUNEDIN, NEW ZEALAND, 27 MARCH 1890

LOCAL AND GENERAL

A SOCIAL GATHERING OF THE MEMBERS AND FRIENDS OF the Young Women's Christian Association was held in the Garrison Hall on Friday night in honour of Mrs. Baeyertz, who has been conducting an evangelistic mission in Dunedin for the past few weeks. Tea was provided in the hall by ladies of the association at about half-past 6 o'clock, nearly 350 persons partaking of the repast. After the material wants of all had been satisfied Mr Brunton's choir rendered a number of sacred selections in their usual tasteful manner.

Mrs. Baeyertz subsequently addressed the meeting on Christian work, pointing out that all might and ought do some work for Christ. She indicated that people might work for Him by visiting the sick at the hospital, by making up bouquets of flowers and taking them to that institution, by teaching at the Sunday Schools, by 'winning souls to Christ', and by holding intercourse with men and women, and in other ways.

She also said that if God called women to preach, let her go, but take care that no women went out on her own account. When she did that God's name was dishonoured; but wherever a woman was really called by God to preach she was never in a hurry to obey the call.

We found this article from *Otago Witness* (p. 32) in PapersPast, the digital newspaper archive of the National Library of New Zealand.

NELSON, NEW ZEALAND, 24 JUNE 1890

INTERVIEW WITH MRS BAEYERTZ

BELIEVING THAT SOME FEW PARTICULARS RELATING TO this lady and her mission will prove interesting to our readers a reporter from the Mail office recently waited upon her, and was received in a most courteous and friendly manner ... Mrs Baeyertz ... was interrogated as follows ...

'I see, Mrs. Baeyertz, that you hold meetings for men only; isn't that rather an innovation for a lady missioner?'

'I dare say it is, but don't you run away with the idea that I have anything different to say to the men to what I have to the women.

'If you care to hear, I will tell you how I came to address them separately. I firmly believe that through all my work God has led me step by step. It was in Adelaide that I commenced this innovation, as you call it. I was at the time holding a mission, and assisting one of the ministers. The church was full whenever I spoke, but like it is everywhere else—I suppose it is very much the same in Nelson—there were very few men present, so the minister consulted with me. "Can't we do something", he asked, "to get the men to come? What do you say to holding a meeting for men only?"'

'"The very thing", I replied, "about which I have been seeking guidance, I'll do it." And I did, and found it a great success, and that was how I adopted the plan. It has this great advantage, too, that among the poorer classes, where both the father and mother can't very well get away at the same time, one can come one night and one another.'

'Do you find that the same men come again and again?'

'Yes! I don't say it boastingly—I hope you will believe that—but if I once get them to come I know they will return. I never now consider my mission made until I have held my first men's meeting, for, until they come, I feel I have not got hold of the people. I don't know exactly why it is—perhaps because I have an absent son who is very dear to me—but the men seem to engage my sympathies, as I know they have many temptations to meet and overcome.'

'Are the young as well as the adults attracted to your meetings?'

'Well, to tell you the truth, I don't get hold of the young as much as I do the middle-aged and old persons. I have often wondered what was the reason of this, until I was told that I appeal to the will more than to the feelings or to mere sentiment. Whether this is so or not, I don't pretend to say, but the people of Nelson will soon have an opportunity of forming their own opinion on the subject.'

'Yours has been a rare experience; trained in the religion of the Old Testament, and subsequently adopting that of the new. Do you find the two creeds in any degrees similar, or widely divergent?'

'... Christianity does not seem to me a new religion as compared with that in which I was reared. Both Christianity and Judaism have exactly the same principle as their basis, that of atonement and sacrifice. I'll tell you what I do feel—that carefully as I was nurtured in it, I never understood my own religion until I became a Christian. It was not until I began to read the Old Testament under the light shed upon it by the New that all its truths and all its beauties were laid open to me. You cannot realise what a revelation it was to me when I began to study it anew with the new aid to understanding it.'

'Are you one of those who believe in the ultimate restoration of the Jews to their old land?'

'I do believe it! My feeling on the subject is much stronger than that. It is more of a conviction than a belief ... '

From an interview in *The Nelson Evening Mail* found in PapersPast. Emilia supplied the whole interview to Sydney Watson who relied heavily on it for his biography.

WELLINGTON, NEW ZEALAND, 1890

A JEWISH LADY EVANGELIST IN NEW ZEALAND

MRS. BAEYERTZ, A CULTURED AND GIFTED SPEAKER, WHO being Jewish, is as one would expect well versed in Bible truth, has been favoured, despite unpropitious weather, with very large attendances wherever she has travelled in our islands. No building in Wellington was large enough to contain the crowds coming to hear her. One would have expected that the Opera House would be sufficiently spacious, but there too, many men and women stood throughout the services, in the aisles, side rooms, even on the stage. A very great number were only able to gain a foot-hold as far as the doors, and so were not able to be admitted.

The speaker shows a thorough mastery of every scriptural subject on which she discourses, and the large audiences are kept enthralled during the whole course of each address, no sign of weariness or inattention being seen anywhere.

Any slight prejudice against her sex appearing on a public platform disappears as soon as she begins to speak. Her mission is purely evangelical and unsectarian, and it is her custom at the end of every meeting to issue a most earnest appeal to those who have never closed with God's offer of mercy, to do so at once. Time after time numbers of people have remained behind to be spoken to for further counsel and instruction.

Endeavours have been made to induce Mrs. Baeyertz to extend her visit beyond the brief return she has promised to our city, but as she is urgently in need of a few days' rest, and will be eventually setting out with her daughter overseas, this is not possible.

We join with her many admirers to wish her journeying mercies, as well as blessings from above on all her future endeavours.

Selected by Betty from the Baeyertz family scrapbook.

WANGANUI, NEW ZEALAND, 23 AUGUST 1890

LOCAL AND GENERAL

THIS EVENING MRS. BAEYERTZ WILL SPEAK ON THE subject which has always drawn large audiences, a subject on which she is specially qualified to speak, namely, the Jewish Passover, as she must necessarily have been familiar with it from her earliest years. She will show the striking typical teaching of the Passover, pointing as it so clearly does, to the atoning work of the Lord Jesus Christ. Coming too from the lips of a Jewish lady, it is not to be wondered at that large audiences have always been present to hear this address.

Speaking of this, the Wellington correspondent of the *Lyttleton Times* says: 'Mrs. Baeyertz, the lady missionary, is very well spoken of as an elocutionist of the first order, remarkable for simplicity of diction, impassioned earnestness of style, and great clearness of voice. Her account of the Jewish and Christian Passovers is said to be the most masterly description ever heard here upon a lecturer's platform.'

From *Wanganui Chronicle*; reproduced in Evans (2007, pp. 227–228).

AUCKLAND, NEW ZEALAND, SEPTEMBER 1890

INTERVIEW WITH MRS BAEYERTZ

A PLEASANT-LOOKING WOMAN ABOUT MIDDLE-AGE, with a kindly face, bearing the hallmark of gentlewoman. Such is Mrs. Baeyertz, the Jewess and present evangelist now lecturing in Auckland. Her eyes are brown and very expressive they lighten and soften, or get wide with indignation, and sparkle with enthusiasm as she talks, according to her mood. … There is singularly little to betray her Semitic origin in her looks, except that she is dark and short, as the chosen people generally are. Our reporter was granted an interview with her yesterday afternoon at the house of Mrs. Stone, where she is at present staying. … There is nothing about Mrs. Baeyertz to indicate her vocation. Unlike many of her brother and sister workers, she does not adopt any badge or costume. A simple black dress made in a manner neither ultra-fashionable nor antediluvian, she looks what she undoubtedly is, a highly cultured English lady, with strong emotions and impassioned feelings. Both these characteristics have been merged into a religious fervour, which even the most superficial observer cannot fail to notice immediately she begins to speak.

'You want to interview me?' she began. 'I think you had better let me get my scrap-book. It has all my previous interviews in it, and you will see at once what to ask, and we will get on quickly.'

The book being produced, with its help the interview was prosecuted with great dispatch.

'About your birthplace?'

'I was born in North Wales, and spent my childhood there. My parents were strict Jews, and I was brought up most carefully in the Judaic faith. My girlhood I spent at home. I was a delicate child, and my mother kept me by her instead of sending me on the Continent for my training, as had been the case with my sisters. So things went on till twenty-four years ago, when I came out here to join a married sister in Victoria. Then followed a gay time. I went out to theatres, balls and operas almost every night. In fact, I lived the life of a careless society girl, fond of gaiety.

'It was during this time I first met Mr. Baeyertz, who was a bank-manager at Colac. There was reciprocated affection, but I could not entertain a thought of marriage, for at that time, you must remember, I was heart and soul a Jewess and such a thing seemed quite impossible. It was a long time before I consented, but at last I did. I made him promise, however, he would never try and change my view. Then after a time came a dreadful blow. He died and all the world seemed dead to me.'

'Had you any children?'

'Yes, two. It was the first great trouble when I realised I must bring them up to a faith I did not believe in. For I loved my husband, so that I determined they should be brought up in his faith.'

'Had this anything to do with your becoming a Christian, do you think?'

'Yes it was after the birth of my second child that I first wanted to become a believer. It was very hard. I could not believe that honouring the Son was honouring the Father, though I really wanted to do so. But it was not till after my husband died that the struggle really began.'

'And then?'

'Well, *then* I really wished it with all my heart and soul, and one day it came to me in a flash.'

'But the old religion is a very beautiful one too, is it not—I mean the Jewish faith?'

'Yes, it is something like the Unitarian faith, only there is no inner life: the soul is not alive. When a man or woman is converted then the soul begins to live and work just as the body lives and works.

...

'You have stated elsewhere, Mrs. Baeyertz, that some time elapsed between your conversion and your adoption of mission work. What was the cause, if one may put it so, of your starting evangelising?'

'A very dear friend of mine was really the outside cause, a lady of the Y. W. C. A., who asked me to address some of the girls. But, of course, it was the Spirit.'

'Did the gift of eloquence come to you at once, or was it a matter of training?'

The converted Jewess is extremely modest, and scarcely allows that she is eloquent, but attributes her power of diction and beauty of expression to the early home training she was fortunate enough to have. Her mother was a splendid reader, and used to read Macaulay's essays and Shakespeare to the little delicate daughter every day.

'Mr. Varley, an evangelist whom we had lately among us, told us that the millennium is at hand. Do you hold the same views?'

'Most undoubtedly I do. All the troubles that are now disturbing the whole world I regard as the beginning of the end. There will, I fear be civil war and all sorts of troubles, for I certainly do think this is the end.'

With regard to the meetings for men and boys only, Mrs. Baeyertz says that she adopted the idea of advertising in that way in order to get the men and boys to come, as she had noticed how few came to the general meetings as a rule. 'And,' she added, 'it has always been a very good success.'

'How do you find Auckland compares with other New Zealand towns?'

'In what way? In the matter of religious life it is the best city I have yet visited. I have had the largest women's meetings here I have had in all the 14 years of my mission life. The men and boys too gave me the finest meeting I have ever had anywhere in the colony.'

'And in other ways?'

'Well, you can't say too much on how I admired its beauties. I am in raptures with it.'

It was quite pleasant to see how enthusiastic the little woman got over her praises of the Harbour and the various beautiful views.

'How do you think the working man is off here? Do you think his position really good?'

'Good? Why, who can doubt it? It seems dreadful to me to see these strikes, and to think of the poor, starving creatures at Home striving to pay their coppers a week to *relieve the distress here*. It really seems quite wicked.'

'With regard to your expenses, Mrs. Baeyertz, how do you manage?'

'I trust in the Lord entirely. I have no guarantee, and make no charges. I have never failed yet. If it doesn't turn up one way, it does in another. I get sums of money, I often don't know who from.'

'Does your daughter travel with you?'

'Yes but takes no active part in the mission. She is my private secretary. My correspondence is a very large one.'

The sympathies of the evangelist are very strong with men, for she realises how many temptations they have to overcome.

It was with regret on the reporter's side that the interview closed, for the evangel of this lady is cultured and refined, and religion from a true gentlewoman, as she is, seems doubly worthy of respect.

From an unknown paper; reproduced in Evans (2007, pp. 229–232). Joanna Woods supplied Robert Evans with a copy of this interview that she found in the C. N. Baeyertz Collection in New Zealand while writing her biography, *Facing the Music: Charles Baeyertz and The Triad* (2008).

LOS ANGELES, CALIFORNIA, APRIL 1891

PACKED TO THE DOORS

A MONTH AGO IT WOULD HARDLY HAVE SEEMED possible for a lone woman, a converted Jewess, to have come into this city, unknown and almost unheralded, and begin a series of Bible readings and doctrinal sermons to a few score people in the unfinished Y. M. C. A. Hall, and in two weeks' time pack to the doors the largest church in the town with over four thousand people. Yet such is the case, and Mrs. Baeyertz is the woman. Nor was it newspaper notoriety. Almost nothing appeared in the papers; the growth came from the interest excited by the merits of the woman herself. Her profound knowledge of Scripture; her spiritual perception of its truths; her soundness in the faith of Christ; her aptness, grasp, pathos, boldness, hard common sense, freedom from cant, made one feel that they were listening to a Jewish prophetess. The Scriptures are a new book to many through her teachings, and the unity of the Old and New Testament in testifying to the Lord Jesus as the Messiah who is to restore all things is fully established in their minds.

... Mrs. Baeyertz's closing meeting at the Simpson Tabernacle, where she addressed over 4,000 people on the Easter subject of Dead unto Sin and Alive unto God (Romans vi).

... her phenomenal success here, or on the marvellous escape from a panic in the crowded assembly by the repeated cry of 'fire!'

... created a deeper and more lasting impression than any evangelist or lecturer over here, not excepting Moody
...

We compiled these extracts from *Los Angeles Churchman* from three sources: Sydney Watson (1894/1895, pp. 97–98) in England, who quotes from a clipping in Emilia's scrapbook, Betty Baruch (1998, p. 11) in Victoria, who quotes from a clipping in the Baeyertz family scrapbook, and Robert Evans (2007, p. 239) in NSW who quotes from a copy of a clipping in the C. N. Baeyertz Collection in New Zealand. They may all be quoting overlapping parts of exactly the same clipping in one well-travelled scrapbook!

TORONTO, ONTARIO, 1891

A PLEASANT LITTLE TALK

I HAD A PLEASANT LITTLE TALK ONE EVENING THIS WEEK with Mrs. Baeyertz, the Australian lady evangelist, who by her earnest speech is drawing large audiences to Association Hall.

I found Mrs. Baeyertz a guest at the home of Mr. Henry O'Brien, the well-known philanthropist. She is a pleasant-faced, brown-eyed woman, of quick, impulsive movement, with a physique suggestive of perfect vitality, and a full, smooth, English voice and accent.

'It is just twelve months since we left Melbourne,' she said. 'My daughter came with me. Oh, I couldn't think of travelling so far without her.'

'How does Canada compare in your eyes with Australia, Mrs. Baeyertz?' I asked.

'Canada is more like Australia than I thought possible, considering the difference of climate. You are English here, just as we are,' she said. 'I landed in San Francisco, and came through the American cities, and I cannot tell you how different they seemed to me. When I crossed to Canada, it seemed like coming home.'

'Tell me something about Melbourne,' I entreated.

'It is a large city—an essentially English city. The Sabbath is well kept. We have no Sunday papers, and the municipal government is chiefly in the hands of active Christian people, as it is in Toronto,' she added innocently.

'Now, Sydney is altogether different. Sydney is largely influenced by a sceptical element. I think, perhaps, the chief difference between the people of Australia and Canada is, that the former are more susceptible to influence than the latter.'

'It is probably a climatic difference. We are not so easily warmed up,' I said, smiling.

'I do not know. But I certainly find that Canadians are not so easily impressed,' she answered. 'The Australian climate is very mild, but very healthy. Yes, it is quite true; we have no rheumatism there.'

'Did you stop at the Hawaiian Islands on your journey out?'

'Only for a day, and it was lovely. It seemed to me like a little Eden dropped in mid-ocean. A grand missionary work has been done there in the past, and now nearly all the natives are Christians. But the beautiful gardens, the fragrant flowers, and white houses, how delightful they were. And how odd it seemed to see the native women riding leisurely down the roadway, clad in bloomer costume, and sitting astride their steeds.'

'Then the Hawaiian women are in advance of us,' I said; and Mrs. Baeyertz laughingly assented.

Our talk turned to graver subjects presently, and she told me of her Jewish training, etc. ...

The lady gave the gentlest of suggestions to the good people of Toronto. 'You have so many fine Christian men and women in your city,' she said, 'if they were only just a little more united. In Melbourne we work together, and accomplish much more than if we were to work in separate or rival organizations.' ...

A lady interviewer

From the content and context, we can tell that this 'chat' was recorded during Emilia's first Toronto mission. Sydney Watson (1894/1895, p. 123f) copied 'some of that interview' from Emilia's scrapbook.

BOSTON, MASSACHUSETTS, 1891

CONSECRATION

SHE TOOK HER PLACE AT THE READING-DESK, conducted the devotional exercises, announced that she would speak in the evening to women and girls, and then made 'Consecration' her theme, based on Romans xii., 1—'I beseech you, therefore, brethren, by the mercies of God, that ye present your bodies a living sacrifice, holy, acceptable unto God, which is your reasonable service.'

'This is a beautiful holiness chapter all through', she said. 'It is a very practical thing, the presentation of the body ... '

'Consecrated hands must not touch questionable things; after playing a game of cards once, I was in darkness for six weeks. Holiness consists in a practical life, and in a life of unbroken communion with God; to have communion with Christ we must be like Him in character. We want to be holy, because we are made for companionship with the Lord Jesus Christ; we get to be like Christ by living with Him. Quoting from 1 John, third chapter and second verse—"Beloved, now are we the sons of God, and it doth not yet appear what we shall be; but we know that when He shall appear we shall be like *Him*, for we shall see *Him* as He is."' She pronounced *Him* with such a marked emphasis as to give the passage a fresh meaning. 'This blessed truth refers to the Lord's second coming. People are not asked to consecrate themselves to the Lord until they are converted.'

Mrs. Baeyertz then read copiously from the Old Testament, showing the need of entire consecration. 'About ten years ago', she said, 'the Lord taught me the secret of deliverance, and He has enabled me to enter into a blessed life, a life lived with Jesus. The God of the Old Testament to me is the God of the New Testament—just the very words spoken under a new dispensation. Just what He says of the Jews of old is binding on us. I don't think there is enough fear in the hearts of God's children, a fear of grieving the Spirit. What is said to the Jews of old about fear is helpful to us; we can live a life that will bring us into a living touch with Christ Jesus; he watches the life, and the man or woman who lives in obedience to Him loves Him best; we must obey the Word of God. The very first step in this holy life is consecration; obedience is the path of holiness, as it is the way to God's will; what we want more and more is the opening of God's Word. There is the privileged side of consecration; if people knew what consecration is there would be more joy, more songs in the night.'

This report is from 'a local daily' (Watson, 1894/1895, p. 109f).

BOSTON, MASSACHUSETTS, 1891

A HEBREW PROPHETESS

WE COUNT IT AMONG THE MOST SIGNIFICANT SIGNS of the times that so many women are moved by the spirit of God to tell out the story of redemption, and to lend their help in the work of the gathering of the harvest of souls.

At home and abroad as missionaries and evangelists, as Bible readers and tract distributors, the number of Christian women who are doing the Lord's work is constantly increasing. The psalmist's prediction seems to be literally fulfilled before our eyes—'The Lord giveth the word: The women that publish the tidings are a great host'.

…

We believe, in spite of the seeming prohibition of Paul, that the Spirit of God calls and commissions women to be evangelists, and to tell out the story of the cross. What else can be the meaning of the words of Joel, reiterated by Peter on the day of Pentecost, 'And it shall come to pass in the last days, saith God, I will pour out of My Spirit upon all flesh: and your sons and your daughters shall prophesy, [and your young men shall see visions, and your old men shall dream dreams:] And on My servants and on My handmaidens I will pour out in those days of My Spirit; and they shall prophesy'. 'Prophesy' means not to foretell necessarily, but to *forthtell*, to witness for Christ unto the people.

…

We rejoice that in these days of lax theology and feeble preaching of the doctrines of grace, such a witness has been raised up; so sound, so clear, so fearless in her setting forth of the utter ruin of human nature, and salvation alone through the vicarious death of Jesus Christ, 'who is over all, God blessed for evermore'. We wish her great success and in her future missions, and pray that God will greatly use her, as in the past, to strengthen Christians, and to win the unsaved.

Rev. Dr. J. A. Gordon

From *The Watchword* (Watson, 1894/1895, pp. 105–106). Dr Gordon quotes from Psalm 68:11 (Revised Version), Acts 2:17–18 and Romans 9:5.

OTTAWA, ONTARIO, 1891

THIS REMARKABLE FOURTEEN DAYS

'TOTALLY DEVOID OF SENSATIONALISM, OF QUIET DIGNIfied manner, and exercising a marked influence over her hearers; such was Mrs. Baeyertz, the Jewish Evangelist. She addressed over 2,000 persons last night in the Dominion Church.'

'Nearly all the Protestant clergymen of the city were present, either on the platform or in the audience.'

'The fact that Knox Church was well filled again last evening to hear Mrs. Baeyertz, while outside the rain was coming down in torrents, is the best evidence that this earnest convert from Judaism has a hold on the affections of the people, not usually gained by one coming among us entirely unknown.'

'For more than an hour Mrs. Baeyertz kept her audience spellbound. In simple, yet beautiful language, with an utterance refined and sweet, yet so distinct as to be perfectly audible in the farthest corner of the building, she presented the truths of the Gospel.'

The next day, the afternoon meeting was held in the Dominion Church, and so densely was it packed, that orders had to be given to close the doors, and admit no one else except Mrs. Baeyertz, who had not arrived. This was done, and presently gave rise to a most amusing incident. When Mrs. Baeyertz did arrive, in company with the president of the Y. M. C. A., under whose auspices the meetings were being held, she was admitted, but he was shut outside, and it took some time to persuade the door-keeper that his place was upon the other side of the door ...

Night after night the interest seemed to deepen, the crush at some of the meetings being so great that hundreds were turned away; night after night individual cases of conversion were manifest, and the diverse character of those who remained to the after-meetings, was, in itself, a proof of the adaptation of Christianity to all sorts and conditions of men. Ladies and gentlemen of rank and influence, working men and women, old and young, rich and poor, remained to the after-meeting with but one thought, 'What must I do to be saved?'

That a thorough work was done in the soul of almost every seeker, was due, in a great measure, to Mrs. Baeyertz's excellent method of dealing with that class. She puts the Word of God into their hands, and waits for the Spirit to burn it into their souls, believing that the Spirit and the Word are the two great agents in the regeneration of a soul.

Sydney Watson

Sydney Watson summarised 'scores of columns' in 'the Ottawa press'. These are extracts from his summary (*From Darkness to Light*, 1894/1895, p. 118f).

TORONTO, ONTARIO, 1891

MRS BAEYERTZ

MRS. BAEYERTZ IS OF THE HEBREW EXTRACTION, AND was once an adherent of the Jewish faith. She is a middle-aged lady, of striking presence—erect and commanding in figure, though not tall; with a dark countenance, brown eyes, firm chin, and characteristic nose. Her face is one that would arrest attention in a crowd. It is full of character—strong, eager, and expressive; and when lit up by the fire of her emotions while she is speaking, it is quite beautiful.

But Mrs. Baeyertz's power is not in her presence. She is a most effective speaker. Her voice is one of rare sweetness and power, and she uses it like an experienced orator. She has a good command of choice, nervous English, and she speaks with directness, simplicity, and clearness, avoiding subtleties of argument and obscure allusions. Earnestness and burning zeal stamp all her utterances, and there is no doubt that she speaks from the depths of profound religious conviction, a fervent love for human souls, and an intense devotion to the cause she is seeking to promote.

Mrs. Baeyertz is evidently proud of her Jewish extraction. Twice she referred to it last evening, and both times with an emphasis of voice and manner which was singularly impressive. 'I am one of God's chosen,' she said, 'one of the seed of Abraham, the friend of God; and yet I have had need to be born again before I could be saved and gain eternal life. How much more do you Gentiles need to be born again!' And once again she said, 'I was brought up a strictly religious Jewess. My father was an orthodox Jew. On the day of atonement I fasted, and did all I could do for the atonement of my sins, and I lived up to the strict tenets of my faith. I will never allow anyone to speak in my presence disrespectfully of Judaism. I love it, and respect it. Christianity is not antagonistic to Judaism, but it is supplementary to it, and a fulfilment of it. To the Jews of old it was said that the life was in the blood, and that the blood on the altar makes atonement for sin. This is just what Christianity teaches: life is found in the blood of Jesus Christ through atonement.'

Speaking of the new birth, she said, 'There is no mystery about the new birth. Birth means life, and when we are born again, it means that we have received another life in addition to the life received from our parents. This is life eternal. It is impossible to be born again apart from Jesus Christ. We must get into direct contact with Christ in order to receive the gift of eternal life. What I love about the Christian religion is that it does not depend upon creeds and doctrines for its life, but upon a living and loving Person. Creeds and doctrines may have made Christendom, but they never made one Christian; only the living Christ can do that. Apart from the new Birth we cannot love God. Heaven itself would be unbearable to the soul that did not possess this eternal life; it could not endure the celestial atmosphere of God's presence.'

From *Toronto Press* (Watson, 1894/1895, p. 100f).

LONDON, ONTARIO, DECEMBER 1891

MOST REMARKABLE PERSONAGE

MRS. BAEYERTZ, THE CONVERTED JEWESS, IS PERHAPS the most remarkable personage who has ever visited London. As an evangelist having the powers of attraction for the masses, she outrivals even the great Moody. Only a dozen days ago she came here almost unheralded, and the Victoria Hall was thought large enough for any audience that would assemble to hear her. But how great was this mistake! From being a lady almost unknown, in less than two weeks the name of Mrs. Baeyertz has become a household word. Instead of filling a small hall, she has alone attracted a crowd twice over what one of the largest churches in the city could accommodate. In truth no unprejudiced mind can doubt that she is a sincere woman fulfilling a Divine mission.

...

Last evening the meeting was announced to be held in St. Andrew's Church, to begin at *8 o'clock*. At fifteen minutes after the city bell rang out the hour of six, two men walked up to the church steps and sat down. Then others came alone, and in twos and threes. At 6.45 the doors were swung open, and nearly a hundred people poured in immediately. At 7 o'clock the body of the church was filled. Fifteen minutes more and the galleries, too, were crowded. And still people came from all directions, hurrying past each other in the hope of securing a seat, only to be disappointed in finding the aisles, the pulpit stairs, and the lobbies literally jammed. And then, after a fruitless endeavour to search out even a place to stand where to be within hearing of the great woman, all comers after 7.20 were compelled to face about.

...

Women climbed up the pulpit stairs, and the edge of the platform was seized on with avidity. One young lady thus seated made a head-rest out of the back of the reporter's chair, a fact of which he was constantly reminded by being tickled in the neck with bonnet feathers, while in attempting to write he was compelled to prod another lady in the back with his elbow.

From two sources (Baruch, 1998, p. 12; Watson, 1894/1895, pp. 126–127) who both quote the unknown and undated 'London paper'.

MONTREAL, QUEBEC, 1892

WOMEN EVANGELISTS

THE PROPRIETY OF EMPLOYING WOMEN EVANGELISTS, which has lately been discussed a good deal in Christian circles in the United States and Canada, seems to have been pretty effectually settled in the affirmative in Montreal, by the recent visits in close succession of three or four very eminent women speakers. There was, first, Mrs. Booth Clibborn, of the Salvation Army, a woman who inherits the singular powers of her remarkable parents, who had also the privilege of calling out Lady Henry Somerset, otherwise silent in Montreal. Then there was Miss Blanche Cox, another of the Salvation Army heroines, whose thrilling tales of devotion were calculated to renew the lives of many. And lastly, with the same message of complete personal consecration, came Mrs. Baeyertz, the converted Jewess.

Facts are often more convincing than argument, and few who heard any of these holy women could doubt that God had given to them, as well as to consecrated men, the evangelistic power of drawing and deeply infecting large audiences with their own spirit of Christian consecration.

The Protestant community of Montreal is known to be very conservative in religious matters; and nearly all of the many evangelists who have laboured here unite in the statement that Montreal Christians are about the least impressionable people to be found on the continent. Even Mr. Moody had to acknowledge that a comparative defeat attended his labours in Montreal, and he has since shown considerable reluctance in renewing them. It was scarcely to be expected that an almost unknown evangelist, and a woman at that, would in one short week turn the tide of Christian sentiment here from a cold indifference, if not aversion, to an overflowing enthusiasm, such as has rarely occurred in this city ...

Whence, then, is the power which drew the thousands towards St. James's Methodist Church, which was taken for the occasion, being the largest church in Montreal, last Sunday evening, and which on Monday evening filled that large church with two thousand five hundred Christians, admitted by ticket? Where is the sober believer in the New Testament who will venture to ascribe this attracting power to other causes than that which drew the crowds to hear the Apostles on the day of Pentecost?

From Watson (1894/1895, pp. 129–131), who describes his source as 'a press leader entitled "Women Evangelists" which appeared in the Montreal papers'.

DUBLIN, IRELAND, JUNE 1892

MISSION IN THE CHRISTIAN UNION BUILDINGS

THE MISSION IN THE CHRISTIAN UNION BUILDINGS, where Mrs. Baeyertz has been conducting meetings twice daily every day except Saturday, has come to an end. From her first address on Martha, Mary and Lazarus, when her topic was 'The Master has Come and Calleth for Thee', it was evident that no ordinary Bible teacher was amongst us.

Her experience as an Orthodox Jewess has laid a fitting foundation for the exceedingly clear and beautiful exposition of Holy Scripture with which Dublin audiences have been favoured. The gospel has been earnestly and faithfully preached, and special mention must be made of her teaching on the subject of holiness. Mrs. Baeyertz avoided the error of those who regard holiness, or as it is styled 'the blessing', apart from righteousness of life. At the same time she kept clear of insisting upon righteousness of life apart from an inner experience of wholehearted surrender to Christ.

During the mission almost 200 persons came into the inquiry room to receive help, but this number very inadequately represents the total good done. The Dublin mission will long be remembered, and an earnest desire is being felt that Mrs. Baeyertz should, before too much time passes, visit our city again.

From *The Irish Times*; collected in the Baeyertz family scrapbook.

BIRMINGHAM, ENGLAND, 23 MARCH 1893

MRS BAEYERTZ IN BIRMINGHAM

REMARKABLE SUCCESS HAS IN THIS CITY ATTENDED THE labours of this lady evangelist. She has concluded a fifteen days' mission in the Baptist Tabernacle, Longmore-street, and though there has not been that thronging and overflow in the attendances which in other places have characterised her missions, the results have been great. At her first and last meetings as many as one in twelve of those present were apparently led to decision, while over three hundred in the fortnight have given in their names as having received Christ. Many of these are joining the church at the Tabernacle, and others will be recommended to the care of the churches they have previously attended.

Mrs. Baeyertz's addresses have been simple, clear, and pointed expositions of the way of salvation, and in their delivery she has indeed been endued with 'Power from on High.' The afternoon Bible readings, notably those on the 'Clean Heart,' the 'Perfect Heart,' and the 'Secret of Victory,' have been greatly helpful to Christians.

She begins a mission in Edinburgh on April 9, where the prayers of God's people will follow her.

Charles S. P. Wood, Pastor

Quoted by Evans (2007, p. 252) from *The Christian,* 'a Weekly Record of Christian Life and Testimony, Evangelistic Effort, and Missionary Enterprise' published in London, England, by Morgan and Scott (according to their advertisement) (Watson, 1910, p. 156).

ABERGAVENNY, WALES, 1 MARCH 1894

MRS BAEYERTZ AT ABERGAVENNY

VERY GRACIOUS HAVE BEEN THE MISSIONS HELD IN THE past in this town, but none has excited such interest or awakened such concern as the mission just held by this Jewish lady. The interest has increased day by day, and the buildings have been taxed to the utmost, very many at times being unable to gain admission.

The Sunday services were held in the Town Hall, the meetings during the week being held in the various chapels, kindly placed at the disposal of the Y. M. C. A. for the purposes of the mission. The men's services were greatly appreciated, and attracted large numbers, particularly on Sundays, and resulted in several men confessing Christ.

The first week-night service was held in the Wesleyan Chapel, which was crowded out, and as the interest deepened the attendance increased so much as to necessitate an earlier migration to Frogmore-street Chapel (the largest chapel in the town) than was originally intended. The first night, when Mrs. Baeyertz gave her address on the Passover, this was overcrowded. The afternoon Bible readings have been a rich treat. They were well attended by the ministers and Christians of the town, and were much appreciated for their invigorating, strengthening, and helpful spiritual influences.

The last Sunday's services will be long remembered, both for the numbers who crowded the Town Hall, and by the exceedingly powerful and solemn address on 'The Master is come and calleth for thee.' Many were convicted. The following meeting being the last, such great numbers attended that Frogmore-street Chapel was too small, and an overflow meeting was held at the Presbyterian Church. Many were moved to tears in the after-meeting, and during her address on Romans vi. The Christians felt it was a time to reckon themselves 'dead indeed unto sin, but alive unto God, through Jesus Christ our Lord.' The holiness meeting afterwards was a rich experience to all present.

The Y. M. C. A. has had the privilege of sending to the various ministers the names of over 200 individuals who passed through the inquiry room, and also the names of about seventy children, who desired to follow Jesus, to the Sunday-school superintendents.

Thos. Tom King, President,
Winfred Rose, Vice-President,
Abergavenny Y. M. C. A.

From *The Christian*; in Evans (2007, pp. 259–260).

LONDON, ENGLAND, 1894

AUTHOR'S PREFACE

IT WAS IN FEBRUARY, 1893, THAT I FIRST met Mrs. Baeyertz, in Winchester, during a very gracious mission held at the Soldiers' Home in that city. Again, on her return visit for another mission we met. She was evidently intensely surprised to see me on this occasion, and said at once, 'I have been asking the Lord to guide me to you, for I want you to write the story of my life and work.'

That is how I came to take up my pen for these pages. Mrs. Baeyertz supplied me with notes, press reports, and various other matters, out of which the present volume has been compiled.

There has been no attempt to colour a story which had in it all the material for very vivid depicting. I have allowed the facts of a romantic career and a marvellous work to speak for themselves. If any special effort has been used in the writing, it has been that of putting a strong check upon the pen rather than of yielding to the seductiveness of the material in hand for brighter colouring.

While frequently quoting from the various world-wide press notices of Mrs. Baeyertz's work, I have sought to avoid repetitions that would only weary, and have inserted that which seemed most likely to interest the reader, and to best introduce the subject of these pages to those to whom she is as yet a stranger.

By far the most flattering comments of the press I have kept back altogether, assured that such a course was safest, wisest, most God-honouring, more in accord with the spirit of His children, Mrs. Baeyertz included.

In his own inimitable way, in a preface to one of his books, C. H. Spurgeon once wrote:—'The *preface* is merely a porch to the house; no one ought to be long detained in it.'

Following humbly in that great man's footsteps, the writer would not presume to keep the reader long in the porch.

Yours, in His service,

Sydney Watson

The text is from Watson's Preface to *From Darkness to Light* (1895, p. v). This photograph of Emilia at about the age of 58 is from Watson's Frontispiece.

LONDON, ENGLAND, 1894

CONCLUSION

THUS FAR OUR WORK OF TRANSCRIBING THE STORY OF a life and its work is finished. We have striven to write those things which should best glorify God. It was impossible but that, with the task that lay before us, the *personality* of the worker should be exhibited, but we trust that amid it all the *Power* of the Master has been the most prominent feature of these pages.

As will be seen by those who have read this short record of her work, Mrs. Baeyertz has been wonderfully owned of God, both in leading souls to Christ and in the all-important work of reviving Christians. At present she has given up any idea of immediate return to Australia, work having opened up largely in Great Britain, and, as God has shown us, He has a message and a mission through her whose story fills these pages.

Sydney Watson

From Watson (1895, pp. 138–139).

BLACKHEATH, ENGLAND, OCTOBER 1897

MRS E L BAEYERTZ
A JEWISH CHRISTIAN LADY EVANGELIST

The mission described in this flyer is typical of Emilia's missions at this time. This ephemeron survived only because someone who attended that 1897 mission at Rink Hall pasted the flyer inside the front cover of a copy of Watson's 1895 edition of *From Darkness to Light*. Others have cared for that copy and made it available to be scanned and transcribed for The Online Jewish Missions History Project. We offer grateful thanks to all of those people.

ORDER OF

FROM OCTOBER 10

Sundays and Week Evenings.

Sunday,	October 10th, at	3.30,	"Mary, Martha and Lazarus."
"	"	7.0,	"Unpardonable Sin."
Monday,	October 11th,	7.30,	"My Conversion from Judaism."
Tuesday,	October 12th,	7.30,	"Atonement"—from Genesis
Wednesday,	October 13th,	7.30,	"Women and Girls."
Thursday,	October 14th,	7.30,	"Men and Lads."
Friday,	October 15th,	7.30,	"Passover" (with table spread Modern Jewish way).
Sunday,	October 17th,	3.30,	"The Conditions of Effectual Prayer."
"	"	7.0,	"The Master is come, and calleth for thee."
Monday,	October 18th,	7.30,	"Jewish Day of Atonement."
Tuesday,	October 19th,	7.30,	"The Lord's Coming; how to get ready for His appearance."
Wednesday,	October 20th,	7.30,	"Impossible to renew them again unto repentance. Whom?"
Thursday,	October 21st,	7.30,	"Great White Throne."
Friday,	October 22nd,	7.30,	"The Lord's Coming to the earth. Return of the Jews to Jerusalem. Ushering in of the Millenium."
Sunday,	October 24th,	3.30,	"Perfect Heart."
"	"	7.0,	"Come."

SERVICES.
O OCTOBER 25TH

✣ Bible Readings. ✣
DAILY AT 3 P.M.

Monday,	October 11th,	"Secret of Failure."
Tuesday,	October 12th,	"Consecration."
Wednesday,	October 13th,	"Fruit-bearing."
Thursday,	October 14th,	"Seven Steps in the Blessed Life."
Friday,	October 15th,	"Clean Heart."
Monday,	October 18th,	"Worry."
Tuesday,	October 19th,	"Christian Joy."
Wednesday,	October 20th,	"Temptation."
Thursday,	October 21st,	"Always."
Friday,	October 22nd,	"Secret of Victory."

Last Day of Mission.

Monday,	October 25th, at	12.0,	"Five Talents or One."
"	"	3.0,	"Baptism of the Holy Ghost."
"	"	7.30,	"Holiness."

A Hearty Invitation and Welcome to All.

SANKEY'S HYMNS WILL BE USED.

Collections to Defray Expenses.

At the request of well-known local Christian friends

MRS. BAEYERTZ

has undertaken to conduct the SPECIAL MISSION now announced. For thirteen years she laboured in the Australian Colonies with a great blessing. Carrying with her the affectionate commendations of a large number of Clergymen and Ministers of various denominations—headed by the venerable Dr. John G. Paton, Missionary to the New Hebrides —"to the Churches of Christ, wherever in the providence of God she may be led, as a sister in every way worthy of their confidence and esteem," she has since then conducted many Missions in the United States, Canada, and several large cities in Great Britain with the same results.

The inhabitants of Blackheath and neighbourhood are cordially invited to avail themselves of this opportunity of hearing the Gospel of the Lord Jesus Christ; and Christians of all denominations are asked to pray that God's abundant blessing may rest upon these Services, to the increase of spiritual life among believers, and in the conversion of many souls.

Sundays at 3.30 & 7 p.m.   Week-Days at 3 & 7.30 p.m.
NO MEETINGS ON SATURDAY   BRING YOUR BIBLES.

BLACKHEATH, ENGLAND, 28 OCTOBER 1897
BLACKHEATH

MRS. BAEYERTZ HAS CONCLUDED A SIXTEEN DAYS' united mission at Blackheath. Afternoon and evening meetings were held daily in the Rink Hall, and from the first were very full. At the afternoon Bible readings the numbers, beginning at two or three hundred, rapidly rose to 750 and upwards. At the evening meetings the large hall was packed to the doors and beyond the doors, the passages and outer porch being crowded with those who could not find seats, and who stood for an hour and a half listening with quiet and deep attention. Night after night, after the Gospel meetings, the room behind was filled with anxious inquirers, and large numbers have professed to receive Christ. The results of Mrs. Baeyertz's mission here have been of a nature to reach far beyond anything seen on the surface.

From *The Christian*; in Evans (2007, p. 283).

EDINBURGH, SCOTLAND, CIRCA 1900

THE OUTCOME OF A LITTLE INCIDENT

A VERY INTERESTING INCIDENT HAPPENED AT Mrs. Baeyertz's mission in Edinburgh a short time ago, showing how God works through 'little things' to bring about His own ends.

A man was left by his master in charge of the house while the family were away and, feeling very dull and lonely one afternoon, he began to look about for something to pass the time away.

Pulling open one of the drawers in a kitchen table, he saw a dilapidated copy of a book, which turned out to be *From Darkness to Light—The Life and Work of Mrs. Baeyertz*. He began to read it, and soon got so deeply interested that he could not put it down until he finished it.

Soon after, one of his mates came to see him, and he gave him the book, telling him how deeply it had influenced him.

'Why!', said his friend, 'I believe that is the very lady who is preaching up at Chalmers' Territorial Church every day, just now', and, rummaging in his pocket, he produced a handbill of the meetings. Comparing this with the book, they both decided to go and hear her that very night, and the result was that both were savingly converted. But it did not stop there, for they brought their wives, and they too were converted to God.

Sydney Watson

Sydney Watson first tells this story in his 1904 edition of *From Darkness to Light*. What the man found in the drawer was an earlier edition of the same book that was first published in 1894. Emilia's mission to Chalmers' Territorial Church must have been undertaken between those years.

LONDON, ENGLAND, 5 MAY 1904

MRS BAEYERTZ

From *The Christian*. Robert Evans reproduced this illustration on the cover of his biography (Evans, 2007) and also allowed us to include this scan of a print of microfilm of newsprint of a lithograph of a photograph taken by Anthony Percival of Edgeware Road, London W.

PERTH, WESTERN AUSTRALIA, 17 NOVEMBER 1904

TO MY FRIENDS WHO HAVE WRITTEN

SO MANY LETTERS HAVE REACHED ME BY THESE LAST three mails that it is quite impossible to reply separately. I thank you all for that love and faithful prayers that have followed me to this land. Your letters have also been a comfort and cheer. Although I am glad to be here, I hope, if God spare me, to return in a few years. This lovely climate, with its perpetual sunshine, has already done wonders for me, and I feel stronger and better able to work for my beloved Master than ever. Two missions have been held already, and whole families were converted in Fremantle. God's children have had a glimpse of a better life than before experienced, and many we know have entered in.

I go to Kalgoorlie next week, and invitations are coming in from all parts. The need is appalling. Do pray for me to be 'sent forth by the Holy Ghost as a flame of fire.' Oh for a mighty revival!

I am constantly meeting those who were converted when I was in Australia twenty years ago. Many are ministers, and it is a great joy to have my spiritual children scattered all over the land, preaching Christ. It is a joy, but the joy in *Himself* is greater; it is this that makes life worth living.

Mrs. E. L. Baeyertz, Perth, Western Australia

See Evans (2007, pp. 333–336) for more of this correspondence in *The Christian* which began with a letter from Emilia dated 27 August.

MELBOURNE, VICTORIA, 20 APRIL 1905

AN INTERVIEW WITH MRS BAEYERTZ

SLIGHT AND PETITE, HER DARK EYES GLOWING WITH enthusiasm as she talks of her mission it is difficult to believe that Mrs. Baeyertz has already accomplished no less than thirty years' work since her conversion from Judaism. Her face shows little sign of age, her dark hair is still unflecked with grey, and her figure quite of youthful contour. It really seems that work and enthusiasm have kept her young.

Mrs. Baeyertz was to leave for Geelong in an hour, when called upon, but made time for a little chat. She talks in a bright, cheery way, for as she says her religion is love, and therefore happiness. A member of the Church of England, Mrs. Baeyertz is not particularly enamoured of dogmas and ceremonial, for she is of the opinion that they serve rather to hide and to deaden the simple truth.

'Religion as religion is a dead thing,' she explains. 'Christ is life, and it is Christ I teach simply and clearly.' The beauty of the Christ-life is touched upon, and Mrs. Baeyertz declares there are hundreds trying to lead it today, simply, quietly, unostentatiously, and this is the religion which is a living, glowing thing, not the religion of rituals, of ceremonies, and of antagonistic denominations. 'I am always coming across people who teach the spiritual life. Why, here at the Y. W. C. A. there is one who leads the most perfect Christ-life. She is all for others, most absolutely selfless; I noticed it when I was here many years ago. I have been struck afresh by it now.'

'No, I am not an Australian. I was born at Home, but came to this country as a young girl, and lived with my relatives. I married a Christian but it was not until after his death I was converted. It was by reading the New Testament, which I had refused to do before, and there I found the revelation of Christ. It was so marvellous, so wonderful, that I could not but believe. It was like new life, and that is what I have always felt, that I found life. It is not only a God, but a near friend and guide that is with one always.

'I worked quietly for a year or two at Geelong, where I lived. Just in the ordinary way with the little affairs of the church, for I shrank from making myself conspicuous. Then somehow the Young Men's Christian Association heard of me, and they sent an invitation for me to come up to Melbourne to speak to them. I prayed for guidance, and felt impelled to accept the call—and that is how my evangelical work started.

'It has always been the same. I have always gone where I have been spiritually directed. I make no plans, nor arrange anything, and it is wonderful how I have been directed. I worked thirteen years in Australia and it gave me great happiness to hear various clergymen who spoke at my welcome yesterday, refer to the permanence of the effects of my work. More than one said that some of his best church members had found Christ through my missions long ago.

'I am the only Jewess who has ever felt led to take up the work of an evangelist. There are plenty of converted Jews so working, and there are many converted Jewesses, but none working publicly, as I am.

'After working in Australia, I went to New Zealand and held a most successful mission. The Bishop of Nelson sat upon the platform at my meeting, and encouraged the work. Then I felt led to America.

'I went without invitation, without introductions, just sustained by faith. The day before I arrived there I shut myself in my cabin and prayed for guidance, after which I felt quite safe and sure, although I had no means to return to Australia, nor to go on. When we arrived at San Francisco I called upon the secretary of the Y. M. C. A., but he said that they had never had a woman to speak to them, and that at that time he had no work to offer me. I went away, a little cast down, but in a few days he sent for me, and asked me to undertake a mission. It appears the secretary of the Y. M. C. A. of New Zealand had written to him of me and my work, and told him if possible to secure my services. The letter had arrived after I called. I went all through America, and Canada. In Canada we could not find halls large enough to accommodate the people; at Montreal and London in particular. At London I again had the support of a bishop on the platform.

'My wish was to go to England, and my way was made plain by an invitation from Dublin to conduct a mission. I went and ever since I have been working in Great Britain—fifteen years; and I think I am known from end to end. During my last mission there the halls were again not large enough to hold the people, and when I was at Norwich the Rev. Hay Aitken, who I think is known to all church people, had quite a hard struggle to get through the crowds, in order to be on the platform with me.

'I had not the slightest idea I should ever come to Australia again. It was solely a question of health that decided it, not for myself, although I needed a change and a rest, but of my relatives, with whom I made my home. Perth was recommended, and we settled there for a time. I came to Victoria in response to an invitation to conduct a mission, which I start tomorrow at Geelong. It is really only a visit to Australia, for we expect to return to England, though as I tell you I make no definite plans, but am led from day to day.'

Mrs. Baeyertz's teaching is undenominational, but it is what she describes as 'true, pure Christianity, without denomination'. She believes in the religious value of beautiful music, also in the spiritual effect of some of the beautiful pictures of Christ. She incidentally tells how Count Zinzendorf, the head of the Moravian mission, which is doing such splendid work, was converted through gazing on a picture.

Celia

This article in *Table Talk,* Melbourne's society magazine, was accompanied by a photo of Emilia seated and wearing the hat she wore for Mr Percival in London. From a microfilm at the State Library of Victoria.

CLIFTON HILL, VICTORIA, 7 DECEMBER 1905

CLIFTON HILL

THE LAST MISSION HELD BY MRS. BAEYERTZ IN
Melbourne was at Clifton Hill, one of the northern suburbs.

Much prayer was offered in all the churches and in many homes that the spirit of indifference, which has always been very evident in previous missions held, would be removed. The Hill is acknowledged to be one of the hardest places in and around Melbourne to move, but the blessing that attended Mrs. Baeyertz's labours in other places was manifested here.

The oldest workers say they have never seen the place so moved. Night after night there were such crowds that the largest building procurable was not capacious enough, and although the stewards filled every available space—the pulpit steps on both sides being packed—scores of disappointed people were turned away. And what shall we say of the after-meetings—such deep conviction of sin, such definite reception of Christ! It has been soul-inspiring. Among the numbers who turned to God were men and women who up to this had no thought about their souls, and who for years had never entered a church. Many times we had to adjourn to the church, as the inquiry-room was too small for the number of seekers.

A most encouraging feature of the meetings was the number of young men who came out for Christ. At one meeting alone there were thirty and we were stopped again and again in the streets by those who had found the Saviour, and who told us they were trying to get their friends and companions to come to the mission.

About twenty-five years ago Mrs. Baeyertz was mightily used of God in a district not very far from here, and it was most delightful to see those who were converted then seeing their children, and in some instances their grandchildren, brought to Christ through the same honoured instrument. One minister was heard to say, as an envelope with fifty names was handed to him: 'Ah! These cards mean something, as we ministers know what is lasting. We are always coming across those who were converted through Mrs. Baeyertz in the old days and these will be the same, we are sure.'

Over 300 persons were dealt with and professed to trust the Saviour, and ministers and workers are organizing meetings to help these babes in Christ. We are devoutly thankful to the Lord for sending Mrs. Baeyertz to us, and unceasing prayer will go up for her life to be spared for many years to witness for her Master.

John Carson, Minister, Baptist Church, Clifton Hill, Melbourne.

From *The Christian*; in Evans (2007, pp. 345–346).

NAYLAND, ENGLAND, 18 AUGUST 1908

MRS BAEYERTZ AT NAYLAND, SUFFOLK

IT IS NOT EASY TO ADEQUATELY PRESENT IN WRITING ALL that transpires during a mission, but it is safe to assert that never in late years has the whole district been so powerfully influenced for righteousness as during the sixteen days' mission held recently by this Jewish lady evangelist. It requires something very attractive to induce some village-dwellers to come under the sound of the Gospel, but here was a distinct novelty in the shape of a lady speaker, and she a Jewess; curiosity was greatly excited, so the people came to the services in considerable numbers; many came night after night, from ten, even twenty miles distance, till the tent was packed.

Again and again the same people made these long journeys, so highly esteemed were the addresses of Mrs. Baeyertz; nothing like them had been heard before. There was a power behind it all, the power of the Holy Spirit at work among the people; souls came to Christ, backsliders were won back, Christians refreshed and strengthened, and the whole valley quickened and renewed by the Spirit's power.

From *The Christian*; in Evans (2007, p. 365).

NEWBURY, ENGLAND, 11 JULY 1918

MRS BAEYERTZ AT NEWBURY

AT THE INVITATION OF THE Y. W. C. A., MRS. BAEYERTZ recently conducted a mission at Newbury, where the power of God has been manifested in a wonderful way. From the first day the Bible-readings were well attended, and many testify to the fact that through the unfolding of God's Word and its searching application by the Holy Spirit, their lives had been lifted to a higher level. One said: 'My Bible has become a new book to me.'

People came from miles around. One woman, whose father had been to one of Mrs. Baeyertz's missions nineteen years ago, walked four miles with a friend. Both were converted and went home rejoicing.

From *The Christian*; in Evans (2007, p. 415).

COLAC, VICTORIA, 11 NOVEMBER 2012
THE GRAVE OF CHARLES BAEYERTZ

This photograph was taken by Amanda Coverdale at the Colac Cemetery.

The Works of Mrs Baeyertz

EMILIA MAY HAVE WRITTEN THE CONFERENCE PAPER 'CONSECRATION' in 1874 (see page 113).

She wrote her tract *From Darkness to Light* (Baeyertz E. L.) (see page 22) in 1875. Within five years, this tract was in use in London, England, for Jewish evangelism.

Emilia contributed to the 'Appreciations of Henry Reed' (Reed, c. 1881, pp. 236–240) (see page 43).

Throughout Emilia's ministry, both church and local papers bore witness to the subject and content of her talks. Robert Evans (2007) has collected and reproduced many examples.

Emilia used music sparingly in her meetings. Even so, R. K. Thomas of Grenfell Street, Adelaide, printed *Hymns for Mrs. Baeyertz's Evangelistic Services* in 1881.

Henry Brett of Auckland, New Zealand, produced *Three Lectures* (Baeyertz E. L., 1890) for Emilia. The three lectures are 'The Great White Throne', 'The Jewish Passover' (see page 121) and 'Holiness' (see page 135). A leaf of plates adds illustration. Her testimony 'From Darkness to Light'(see page 22) is included. The new owner of a bookshop in Goulburn, NSW, advertised these 'pamphlets' for sale in *The Goulburn Herald* 13 & 15 May 1891 @ '6d. each or wholesale at great reduction'. The *Three Lectures* are now listed in the catalogues of the Rabbi L. A. Falk Memorial Library at the Great Synagogue and in the Mitchell Library, both in Sydney, NSW.

In Toronto, Ontario, in Canada, Emilia had *Five Lectures* (Baeyertz E. L., 1891) 'printed for the author by Hill and Weir, Temperance Street'. These five lectures are 'The Two Offerings of Cain and Abel', 'The Clean Heart', 'Seven Steps to the Blessed Life in Psalm 32' (see page 147), 'The Coming of the Lord' and 'The Overcoming Life'. The two Forewords (see page 145) were by Thomas Wardrope, the Moderator of the General Assembly of the Presbyterian Church, and Robert Stewart, the President of YMCA of Ottawa, Canada.

In England, Emilia commissioned Sydney Watson, a prolific novelist, to turn her story, with the help of her publications and scrapbook, into her biography. *From Darkness to Light—The Life and Work of Mrs. Baeyertz* (Watson, 1894/1895) was printed by Guy and Co. Ltd., of 70 Patrick St, Cork with a photo of Emilia and a Preface (see page 90). The book declared that one could obtain it, and *Ten of Mrs. Baeyertz's Addresses* (Baeyertz E. L., c. 1894), from 26 Fore St, London., E. C., which just so happened to be the shop of Rosenthal, Aronson & Co, run by Emilia's brother, Saul (Miskhel, 2011). In a copy of a later printing, held by the Presbyterian History Society in England, mention of *Ten* had been replaced by *Twelve*.

By 1897, the *Ten* had been 'Enlarged' to *Twelve Addresses* (and an illustrated plate) (Baeyertz E. L., 1897). Some British libraries have copies. The five new addresses found in neither the *Three Lectures* nor the *Five Lectures* were 'The Parable of the Ten Virgins', 'The Baptism of the Holy Ghost', 'The Unpardonable Sin' and 'Worry'. 'Worry' includes a quote from *The Wisdom of Folly*, a poem by Ellen T. Fowler published in 1895.

Emilia created many ephemera, now lost, similar to the flyer for *A Sixteen Days' Mission in the Rink Hall, Blackheath* in 1897 (see page 93).

On her last Australian tour, a New Edition of *Twelve Addresses* (Baeyertz E. L., 1904), could 'be obtained from Mrs. Baeyertz, Post Office Perth and YWCA Melbourne'. This 'New' edition was produced by 'Printers and Publishers: Varley Brothers, Melbourne and Sydney' at 326–328 Flinders Lane, Melbourne. The Varley Brothers were Thomas and Charles (Hauser, 2006)—and appear to be unrelated to Henry Varley, the evangelist. By this edition, Emilia had omitted the plate and her testimony, abridged 'The Great White Throne' and added to 'The Coming of the Lord' mention of the First Zionist Congress of 1897.

The *Six New Addresses* (Baeyertz E. L., 1904), printed by City Printing Company Limited, 221 Murray St, Perth, Western Australia, were 'Tears', '"Impossible to Renew Them Unto Repentance"', Whom?', 'The Personality of The Holy Spirit', 'Is There a Hell?', 'The Young Ruler and Bartimeus' (see page 151) and 'The Jewish Day of Atonement' (see page 155).

Also in Perth, Emilia published a second edition of *From Darkness to Light* (Watson, 1904/1905) without the author's name. There is a copy in the Baillieu Library at Melbourne University. This edition includes reports from

Langholm and Hawick in 1900 and 'The Outcome of a Little Incident' (see page 98).

Extracts from Emilia's letters from Australia were published in *The Christian* newspaper in London (see page 100). These have been reproduced by Robert Evans (2007, pp. 333–336).

H. C. N. (whoever he or she was) of 43 Huntingdon St, Barnsbury, London, N., wrote a long article, 'Mrs. E. L. Baeyertz The Jewish lady Evangelist'. This was published in *The Christian* of 5 May 1904, accompanied by a lithograph of Emilia (see page 99).

In 1910 or 1911, Sydney Watson produced, and Guy and Co Ltd of Cork printed, a *New, Revised and Enlarged* (and as far as we can tell, Final) *Edition of From Darkness to Light*. The 'Enlargements' include the *Circular Letter* by Paton, et al. (pp. 83–84) (see page 59) and 'A Supplementary Chapter' (pp. 142–154) by H. C. N. that includes some events since 1894 and extracts from a few of Emilia's letters (see page 20). Watson also added some poetry. A copy of this edition in the Robert Evans Collection is our principal reference.

From Darkness to Light was then available from Mrs. Baeyertz at her home at 42 Leigham Court Road, Streatham Hill, London, where one could also buy the *Twelve Addresses*, *Six Addresses*, *Can God's Children Expect Answers From Prayer?*, *Rest—Deliverance from Worry*, *My Authority as a Woman for Preaching the Gospel* and *A Postcard Photograph of Mrs. Baeyertz*.

Emilia published at least twenty of her addresses. Many others have not survived. As Robert Evans (2007, p. 13) points out, her published addresses are not whole: they are not long enough and omit her striking illustrations. For example, one of her longest recorded addresses, 'The Jewish Passover', omits most of her description of the meal and reports only her conclusion.

As you read the following five or six of her addresses, imagine her voice and the response of her listeners then, and yourself now.

CAULFIELD, VICTORIA, JULY 1874
CONSECRATION

'I beseech you therefore, brethren, by the mercies of God, that ye present your bodies a living sacrifice, holy, acceptable unto God, which is your reasonable (intelligent) service. And be not conformed to this world; but be ye transformed by the renewing of your mind, that ye may prove what is that good, and acceptable, and perfect will God.' [1]

In every true believer's heart there should be the desire that *in* him and *by* him may be carried on uninterruptedly the Lord's will and purposes. But in order that it may be so, it is necessary for him to understand his position as an heir of God, and also what is required of him as a responsible agent.

From God's word let us view our glorious position *in Christ*. We possess a life which is perfectly pure and holy in its character, for it *is Christ* (Col. iii. 4). 'When Christ our life shall appear, then shall ye also appear with Him in glory.'

This 'new-creation-life' never sins (1 John iii. 9). Heaven will add nothing to it in the way of holiness; for it is *perfectly holy*, even now fit for the presence of God (Luke xxiii. 43).

But we have another life, 'the flesh' or the 'old man'. This characterised us before our conversion to God; it is incurable, and incorrigibly bad; and never will be any better; it is incapable of improvement; all it can do is to sin; it is a corrupt fountain which can only pour forth corrupt water.

Now, with these two natures, how can we be holy? Practical holiness is the full and free development of the new life, unhindered by the contrary action of the flesh; so in order to be holy, the flesh must be kept practically in the place which God gave it in the cross—the place of death. We are called to *reckon* it dead, and it is simply obedience to do so.

Then the question suggests itself, '*Can* a believer so keep the flesh in subjection as not to sin?' Certainly he may—it is what God expects from him. 'These things write I unto you, that ye sin *not*.' Shall I then ever attain to such a state on earth as never to sin again? Scripture again replies, 'If we (believers) say that we have *no* sin, we deceive ourselves, and the truth is not in us;' and 'If we say that we have not sinned, we make God a liar, and His word is not in us' (1 John i. 8, 10).

The soul that bows to the Word seeks to walk in holiness in the footprints of his Lord, yet knows very well that he will never attain to *perfect* practical holiness while on earth. He looks onward to the day of his Lord's return, and groans for the time when his mortal body shall be manifested in life. He knows full well that it is only 'when Christ appears' that he shall be *like Him*, and not before. He therefore waits with longing, earnest desire the fulfilment of the words of the Lord Jesus, when about to leave His disciples to go to the Father: 'If I go and prepare a place for you, *I will come again* and receive you unto Myself, that where I am there ye may be also' (John. xiv).

The risen and exalted Christ in glory is the only perfectly 'Holy One' before God. We are to follow after Him, treading in the footprints of His humiliation, never expecting *absolute holiness* till *with* Him in glory.

The great secret of holiness is submission of heart and mind to revealed truth, and to the will of God.

If we wish to walk as children of God, then we ought to *know* that such is our relationship to God. If we would walk as strangers and pilgrims in this world, then we must *know* our heavenly position in Christ Jesus risen and exalted. If we would walk in grace towards others, then we must *know* the manner in which God has acted in grace towards us. If we would go through this world as dead to it, then we must *know* that we are *dead with Christ* and *risen with* Him. If we would reflect Christ in our lives, then we must *know* Christ as *He is* and *was*, and gaze on Him *where* He is.

> *Only by gazing, I become like Him;*
> *His name shines out through me, He dwells within.*

CONSECRATION

> *My calling is to live with Him alone;*
> *Unlike all others—lacking what they own,*
> *Content to be by all the world despised,*
> *Knowing that I by Him am loved and prized.*
> *Content to be like Him, and call Him mine,*
> *In fellowship ineffable, divine;*
> *Happy to lose the brighter portion here,*
> *That I may gain the weight of glory there;*
> *Happy to know that He does all in love,*
> *To bear the cross below, the crown above;*
> *Happy that not my will, but His be done,*
> *Happy in prospect of the rest of home.*

In order that we may realise this, and walk worthy of our high calling, there must be an *entire surrender* of ourselves to God. This is plainly taught in the Word, both in the Old and New Testaments. In Exodus xxxii. 26, 29, we see how God called upon all those who were really on His side, to separate themselves from the rebellious idolaters—'Who is on the Lord's side? Let him come unto me.' 'Consecrate yourselves to-day to the Lord ... that He may bestow upon you a blessing this day.' So now He calls upon all His people, those who are on His side, to come out clearly, boldly, and distinctly from all (excepting necessary) association with such as, by unrepented sin or worldliness, are dishonouring Him.

The command is distinct—'Wherefore come out from among them and be ye separate, saith the Lord, and touch not the unclean thing; and I will receive you' (2 Cor. vi. 17). God calls us to come out and be separate; that is, to give up our whole lives to Him, consecrating ourselves in regard to every form and manifestation of sin, as fast as discovered to us by the Spirit. And not only must we turn away from the old sinful life to the Lord, but having done so, we must gird on the sword of the Spirit, and turn *in His name and in His might* upon our iniquities and slay them, even though they have been and are—so far as the flesh is concerned—as dear to us as the life itself of a brother (Exod. xxxii. 27). There may be a sin as dear as a right hand, but our only safety lies in cutting it off and casting it from us.

Many make a great mistake in thinking that a consecrated life is one without conflict. This is not the case; far from it. It is only then that we begin to understand what is meant by the Saviour's words: 'If any man will come after Me, let him deny himself, and take up his cross and follow Me' This taking up of *our* cross seems to give the true idea of the term self-denial, or denying self; that is, enduring positive pain in abandoning old habits, thoughts, tempers, affections, and associates, for the sake of entering on a pathway of unspeakable joy in the following of Christ. The crucial agony lies in the mortification of the flesh, and not in the following of Christ, as thousands vainly imagine.

It would be no compliment to the bridegroom, if his bride should enter into a matrimonial alliance with him as an unpleasant duty, and regard the relationship itself as a life-long crucifixion. Nor is the common idea of cross-bearing one whit more complimentary to Christ. The most joyous moment of life, up to that time, is supposed to be the one when the bride loses her own life and name in that of the bridegroom, at the altar. And certainly the most blissful moment of our lives, up to the moment when we give all to Jesus, is that of giving ourselves over into His hands, *unconditionally* and *for ever*. This done, the Lord needs no inducement to take entire possession of us. He takes *abiding* possession of us for Himself, And now what a change! *Self* no more—God evermore the object. Now, instead of *trying* to make something of ourselves, we receive the Heavenly One to be everything, to be all in all to us. We have exchanged *self* for God, and oh! what gain by the transaction!

How often Christians are kept in a very low spiritual condition by parleying with some idol. They see and recognise the evil of certain things, and turn away, but turn to them again, because they are there—not put away. The weak point, or the point of failure, with many of the Lord's people is, at the point of taking the sword, in the name of the Lord, against cherished sins—aye, against *all* sin, as it is made manifest by the Spirit.

Either our darling lusts must die, or our darling lusts will kill us. 'For if ye live after the flesh ye shall die; but if ye, through the Spirit, do mortify the deeds of the body, ye shall live' (Rom. viii. 13).

The testimony of one of the Lord's feeble, but trusting servants, may serve to show forth the praises of Him who has delivered her out of great darkness and spiritual bondage into glorious liberty, and peace, and joy in the Holy Ghost. For several years after my conversion my experience was of the most melancholy description. There was, it is true, life in the soul, but *few* would have imagined that grace had begun its work, so little did it affect the walk and conversation.

Romans vii. 15 to 23 was truly a picture of *my* mind, and my daily and hourly cry was this—'Who shall deliver, me?' I *tried* to pray, *tried* to love my Saviour, *tried* to get peace; but all in vain. When a soul is *trying* to love Christ, in order to get peace, it finds but sorrow and failure. At last, through means of one of His dear consecrated servants, the Lord showed me that what was needed was an entire abandonment of *self*, a yielding of *all* to Jesus; *all* my vows and professions; *all* my legal and faithless strivings; *all* unbelief. I saw it clearly, and oh! how gladly I gave up my all.

> *I came to Jesus as I was—*
> *Weary, and worn, and sad;*
> *I found in Him a resting-place,*
> *And He has made me glad.*[2]

How thankful I was now to let Jesus do what I had been vainly *trying* to do for myself for so many years. Never shall I forget the sense of rest and peace I then enjoyed, and still increasingly enjoy. There was nothing exuberant in my joy: it was as the peaceful lake after the omnipotent 'Peace, be still.' There have been often since then the surface heavings, but they are soon calmed by the sweet whisper, 'It is I, be not afraid.'[3]

For many months now, with but brief exceptions, I have experienced something of the unspeakable joy which arises from soul-union with my Lord. He is no longer *Baali*. I now call him *Ishi*, by my God's command (Hosea ii. 16).[4]

> *Ishi, Ishi, is the jewel!*
> *Mine He is while ages roll,*
> *Angels taste not of such glory—*
> *Ishi, Ishi, of my soul!*
>
> *How I love Thee! none can utter*
> *Of its wondrous depth and power;*
> *Growing deeper, growing stronger,*
> *Day by day, and hour by hour.*
>
> *Ishi, Ishi, night and morning!*
> *From my lips that holy name,*
> *All the while my soul exulting,*
> *Beareth on the self-same strain.*
>
> *Earthly loves are very lovely,*
> *Passing, passing fair they seem;*
> *But they come and go before us,*
> *Like some bright and happy dream:*
>
> *Thou art a reality,*
> *From which, like dreams, I never wake;*
> *Those I cast aside as nothing,*
> *Ishi, Ishi, for Thy sake!*

None but inspired writers cans fully tell the blessed results of *self-abandonment*, or show what consecration really is. It is indeed a life of faith, wherein we cease to limit the power of the Holy One of Israel, and find there is no limit to the possibilities of such a life, for '*all* things are possible to him that believeth.'

To the believer the difference between this new life and the old one is so great that he could never express it. The *one* desire of his heart seems to be, to do the will of God. He is so certain that *God's* will is best that he desires his own to spring forward to meet it, as soon as known. By faith he now *reckons* himself and all that he possesses to be the Lord's, to use or dispose of as He shall please. There is indeed in his experience much evident failure, many dark and cloudy days, consequent upon unbelief, for we must remember that the crucifixion of the flesh is a painful process; it is hard to die to sin, hard to let one's-self die, by simply letting the matter alone, as done in Christ.

And how changed does then become the Word of God! It seems indeed 'the joy and rejoicing of the heart'. With Job each believer can truly say, 'I have esteemed the words of His mouth *more* than my necessary food'.

> *The treasure I've found in His love,*
> *Has made me a pilgrim below.*[5]

Our earnest prayer ought to be that *all* Christians may know the joy of those who are *wholly* the Lord's; then what is termed 'the higher Christian life' will be known, and should be known, as 'the *common* Christian life'.

Oh, that all believers would give up at once *all* the lying vanities of the world; *all* vain, legal, and faithless strivings; *all* vows and professions; *all* unbelief; and simply and trustfully rest in the love of the Heavenly Bridegroom; then would they have a heretofore unknown joy in life and in worship, and strange, new power in unwearying work for Christ.

A Lady

The *Caulfield Addresses* (Macartney H. B., 1874, July) were delivered at St Mary's Church of England in Caulfield 'by Ministers and Laymen of Different Denominations'. Hussey Macartney appended 'Consecration' to the published proceedings with this prefix, 'The following paper, written by a lady at the Editor's request, was not read at the Conference, for want of time.'

The proceedings of the conference include papers, on the subjects of 'Consecration' and 'The Right of Holiness purchased by the Cross, co-equally with the Right of Salvation', that were each 'written by a lady at the editor's request'. The current vicar of St. Mary's, Rev. Dr. Mark Durie, has suggested to us that Emilia may have been one or both of those 'ladies'. There is no proof either way from style or content. The Holiness and Salvation paper was read to the assembly by Hussey Macartney, jun., the convenor of the conference. This paper, which 'is perhaps the first Christian sermon [written] by a woman delivered to a mixed audience in Australia' (*150 Years*, 2008), is different in emphasis from Emilia's address 'Holiness' which was first published sixteen years later (see page 135). On the other hand, this 'Consecration' paper refers to Hebrew concepts and describes experiences so similar to those of Emilia at just the right time that we believe that she was the author. For the dates to work, 'several years' must be allowed to describe 'three years'. See page 74 for a précis of one of Emilia's many later talks on Consecration.

[1] Romans 12: 1–2.

[2] From 'I Heard the Words of Jesus Say' by Horatius Bonar.

[3] Matthew 14:23, Mark 6:50, Mark 4:39, John 6:20 and Job 23:12.

[4] *Ishi*: my husband; *Baali*: my master.

[5] From 'A Song for the Wilderness' by J. N. Darby (1849).

AUCKLAND, NEW ZEALAND, OCTOBER 1890

THE JEWISH PASSOVER

NOW I WANT JUST TO LOOK FOR A LITTLE WHILE INTO this subject of the Passover, and I will begin by telling you how the Passover is kept to-day amongst the Jews.

You know that, as I read to you in this chapter,[1] God was going to pass over the land, to redeem the Israelites out of Egypt, where they were in bondage; and God said, 'In all generations this night is to be remembered amongst you,'[2] and wherever Jews exist now they look back to this night as the most remarkable in the whole of their experience, because it was the night when they were delivered from bondage and slavery, and led out, and, as you know, ultimately reached the promised land.

Of course, until I came out to these Colonies, I kept the Passover regularly every year with my family; and I must tell you there was no synagogue where I was born and brought up, so all the fasts and feasts had to be observed in the house. My father was a strict Jew; a good, upright just man, and a man who loved the observance of the Jewish religion; and we were all brought up in the Jewish faith, in all the observances of that religion. You must remember that all the fasts and feasts and the Sabbath always begin at sundown. For instance, the Jewish Sabbath begins on Friday night and ends on Saturday night, just as the sun goes down. And so the Passover begins in the same way.

It is always customary amongst the Jews, at every feast or fast or religious service, to have a white table-cloth spread upon the table, and upon this to place the prayer-books or whatever may be needed. On the Passover night a cloth is laid in the evening, and upon the table are placed the prayer-books, which generally consist of books as big as this one (holding up her Bible), printed in Hebrew on the one side and English on the other.

At the end of the table would be a dish with a white finger-napkin, and on it layers of Passover Bread—the unleavened bread—and then on top of that the finger-napkin would be folded over; and there would be a plate, and on this plate was what is most interesting for you to know—a lamb-bone burnt black in the fire. It is typical of the lamb that was slain. They roast or burn it in the fire as an emblem of what we read here.

Then there is a mixture known very well to the Jews, which the host or master of the house makes. It is a symbol of the bricks and mortar which the Jews were obliged to make in Egypt. This mixture is always eaten at a certain stage of the supper with horse-radish. This horse-radish is cut, and strips placed upon the plate. These are dipped into the mixture and handed to each of the family at certain intervals, with a piece of the Passover cake. At each corner is a decanter of simple, home-made raisin wine, non-intoxicating, generally made by the mother of the house.

At certain intervals a prayer is said; and so the feast goes on until the prayers are all said and the Psalms are all chanted. But at a certain stage of the supper it is most interesting to know that a wine-glass of wine is poured out and set by itself on the table. Then the eldest son rises and gets a seat and sets it down empty, and it is left empty. He goes to the door, throws it wide open, and then the whole family bow and pray that the Messiah may come. That is always done at the Passover feast. So that all over the world, at our Easter, it is a very remarkable thing that while we are thinking of Christ on the Cross, the Jews are commemorating the Passover in this way; and at a certain point in the Passover supper they are praying for the Messiah to come, and their prayers will be answered, for He will come.

We will see now how it was instituted originally, and you shall notice what is the one thing that is lacking in the observance, and perhaps you will find one thing lacking in your own life.

The first thing to notice in the Passover is this—God brings Egyptians and Israelites on one common platform. He shows us that there is no difference. All have sinned and come short of the glory of God.[3] And as God looks down upon this meeting tonight, He sees you who are unsaved, condemned already. The wages of sin is death,[4] and God has shown us plainly in His word that there is no difference. It does not matter whether you are enlightened or ignorant, whether you are refined or unrefined, whether you are a church member or have never joined a church; if you are an unconverted man tonight there is no difference in God's sight, because all have sinned and come short of the glory of God.

You would have thought the Jews, the chosen people, would surely have been let off, but they have to die just the same as the Egyptians have to die. The only difference is this: the one died in the person of a substitute, the other died in their own person.

God says to Moses, 'Go down to the children of Israel and tell them to take a lamb.' This lamb had been kept for four days, and on the evening of the Passover they were to take this lamb and slay it. And if you will come with me into the court-yard we will look at the scene. The first-born son comes along, leading a white, innocent lamb, and as he stands there he represents the family; remember that God is going to pass over the land, and the first-born is going to die; he represents the family, and the lamb represents him. In every household there is a lamb, and where there is a first-born he must take it out, and do just as this one does. He takes the knife and slays the lamb. Now comes a question, and I want you to think about the answer. The lamb is slain, but is that first-born son saved? Jehovah is going to pass over the land at midnight, and He has told them what to do; would you think that as that first-born son stands there he is safe? No, I think he is in greater danger than ever, because there is something more to be done.

But let us for a moment leave him. Come to Christ. See that Lamb of God, of whom this lamb was the type. What does the Apostle Paul say? 'Christ, our Passover, is slain for us.'[5] And what does Peter say? 'For as much as ye know that ye were not redeemed with corruptible things, as silver and gold, from your vain conversation received by tradition from your fathers; but with the precious blood of Christ, as a lamb without blemish and without spot.'[6]

What does John the Baptist say? 'Behold the lamb of God, which taketh away the sins of the world.'[7]

Now come up to the Cross. Jesus has been taking this very Passover supper that I am telling you about—John xiii. He has just been sitting round the board with His disciples, and He says, 'My soul is exceeding sorrowful, even unto death.' Then He tells then, 'One of you shall betray Me.' And so John, who is next to Him, looks up and says, 'Master, is it I?' And they all say, 'Is it I?' And Judas, not to look peculiar, joins in and says, 'Is it I?' And Christ said, 'He to whom I shall give a morsel'. That custom is always kept up amongst the Jews. The Lord gives the morsel of unleavened bread; and Judas went out.[8]

I have often followed Judas as he went out, going down those stairs in the bright moonlight. It was in an upper room where the feast was, and Judas went down step by step, until he came into the street. And as he went on through the bright moonlight surely he must have thought, 'Well, He was a kind Master.' And Peter and John—never could he look them in the face again. But the devil possesses the man; and it is an awful thing to be under the power of the devil. He goes on, carried on by this awful power until he comes to the place where the priests are seated, and says, 'What will you give me if I betray Him to you?'[9] and they counted him out thirty pieces of silver, which he takes, and they go to the garden where Christ is and take Him.

Do you know what the Unitarians say? I will tell you. They say that Jesus never said He was God. On two occasions

He used the very name He Himself gave Moses. When Moses said, 'Whom shall I say sent me?' Jehovah answers, 'Say I Am sent you. I Am that I Am.'[10] That is what He calls Himself.

And when we come to the New Testament, what does He say? The Jews came to Him one day, and He says to them, 'Your Father Abraham rejoiced to see My day, and he saw it and was glad.' Then said the Jews unto Him, 'Thou art not yet fifty years old, and hast Thou seen Abraham?' Jesus said unto them, 'Verily, verily, I say unto you, before Abraham was, I Am.'[11] That is the name of God.

Now they had come to take Him in the Garden, Judas leading the train. Jesus seeing them asks, 'Whom seek ye?' They say, 'Jesus of Nazareth.' He says, 'I Am.' And what was the result? The soldiers went backwards and fell to the ground, because He used the name which was never used except by Jehovah. And twice we find him saying that He Himself was Jehovah—'I Am.'[12]

Now Judas has betrayed Him, and He is handed over to the power of the Jews. You know how Pilate sought to deliver Him, and how he washed his hands, and said, 'I am innocent of the blood of this just man.'[13] Did you ever notice that everyone who had a hand in the death of Jesus, left his testimony on record that He was just, innocent, righteous? Pilate had to leave his testimony, and Judas had to leave his testimony. After betraying Jesus, Judas is in such agony that he is beside himself, and he comes back to the priests and throws down the money on the table. What a sight for those men! He comes in wild, haggard, and heart-broken, throws the money down on the table, and says. 'I have sinned in that I have betrayed innocent blood.'[14]

But, ah! Jesus came into the world to die. He was the Lamb that was preordained from the foundation of the world. 'Behold the Lamb of God which taketh away the sin of the world.'[15]

There He is hanging on the Cross. I wish some of you could get the sight I got of Him twenty-two years ago. It was while reading the account of the crucifixion in John that it all came before me. I saw Him upon the Cross. I heard them taunting Him, and saying, 'If Thou be the Christ, come down from the Cross. He saved others, Himself He cannot save.'[16]

Yes, as He hung upon the cross He was meeting all the powers of hell. He looked down to earth to see if there were any that did pity, if there were any that did notice.

'Is it nothing to you, all ye that pass by? See how Jehovah hath wounded me in the day of His fierce wrath!'[17] No, there were none to pity. Where was Bartimeus, whose sight had been restored? Where was John, the beloved disciple? Where were all those loved ones? They had all forsaken Him and fled. Earth had no friends for Jesus, and in His agony He looks up to Heaven.

I saw a picture in Melbourne of Jesus on the cross, and an angel stooping down and kissing Him on the forehead. It is all very well for the artist's fancy, but there was no one from Heaven who came down to comfort Jesus then. Heaven had no friends for Jesus and earth had no friends for Jesus. The flames of hell will never make a man love God. But I am amazed sometimes how men can sit down and look up at Christ on the Cross and not be drawn in love.

Ah! Dear sinner, if the Cross of Christ will not draw you to God I do not know what will. He Who hung upon that Cross. He Who was the great I Am, He Who by His Word could call Lazarus from the grave, could come down from the Cross. And if He had let His awful, almighty power beam forth one moment upon these people, what a scene it would have been! But there was the hiding of His power, and He hung there till at last that cry went forth from His breaking heart which has filled the universe, 'My God, My God, why hast Thou forsaken Me?'[18]

Do you know why? Can you look up with love tonight and say, 'For me, Lord Jesus, Thou hast died!' Can you look up tonight and say 'As far as I am concerned, that death was not a waste; as far as I am concerned, that death has made me free?' Can you look up tonight and say, 'He loved me, He gave Himself for me!' Many of you can. But many of you cannot.

He hangs there until all the debt is paid; until He has made your peace with God, and then He cries with a cry of a Conqueror, 'It is finished!'[19] And they came round to break the bones of those who had been crucified. They break the bones of one of the thieves, and he is soon out of torture. They break the other thief's bones, and he soon dies; and then they come to Jesus and lift up the hammer.

'No!' 'Not a bone of Him shall be broken' was the prophecy thousands of years before, and the hammer would drop, and they cry. 'He is dead already.' And then to fulfil the Scripture, one of the men takes up a spear and pierces His side, out of which comes the water and the blood that cleanses us from all sin. And when Jesus rose again, what is the first thing that He says to His disciples? 'Go and preach the Gospel to all the world beginning at Jerusalem';[20] as though He would say, 'Go to the man who put the crown of thorns upon My head and tell him that I will give him a crown of glory. Go and tell the man who pierced My side that the blood of Jesus Christ cleanseth from all sin. Go and preach the Gospel to every creature.'

It is very well known as a fact that it was the custom to bury the crucified at the foot of the cross. But Jesus was not to have that burial. The moment he paid the debt, that moment man's hands were done with him, then God commenced to honour Him, and He has never ceased honouring Him, and will never cease honouring Him. He was buried in the rich man's tomb.

Isaiah liii. 9: 'And they appointed His grave with the wicked, but, with the rich man was His tomb.' Loving hands take Him down from the cross. Look at that white face they are wiping so tenderly, and leaning over. That is the face of Jesus. He is really dead. There is no life in that body. And now comes the question. The Lamb has been slain—the Lamb of

God that taketh away the sin of the world. But are *you* saved? Scores of you, I am afraid, in this building tonight, are not saved, and as far as you are concerned up to this moment, it is no matter to you that Jesus died. You believe in Him, perhaps, with head belief; but he has never had any power over your lives yet. You have never come into contact with Him. There is something else to be done.

Perhaps if we go back and see what these Israelites did, it will help us to see what we ought to do. What is the first thing the first-born son had to do after he had slain the lamb? God says, 'And ye shall take a bunch of hyssop, and dip it in the blood that is in the basin; and strike the lintel and the two side posts with the blood that is in the basin; and none of you shall go out of the door of this house until the morning.'[21]

What is hyssop? Hyssop was just a common weed-like grass. It grew anywhere. So that the first-born son had only to go outside and pick the hyssop, and he could do what he was told. What good was the hyssop? I will show you. Supposing this is the blood in the basin, and I have a little bit of green hyssop in this hand. I dip the hyssop in the blood, and I take it out and splash or sprinkle the door post on one side. I dip it again, and sprinkle it on the other side, and also sprinkle the lintel.

After that was done, what did they do with the hyssop? Did they tack it up against the post so that God might see the hyssop and the blood? *No.* God says, 'When I see the blood.' Hyssop is just like faith, and they think that this that links them on to Jesus Christ is some very rare specimen that is to be found in very few, and they are lucky people who have got faith; but *they* cannot find it.

Why, it is all nonsense. Everyone of you have got faith, and I believe have got faith enough to save you. You have faith in me or you would not have come to the meeting tonight; if you did not believe I was going to preach you would not have come to these seats. Exercise the faith you have got. When

God says, 'Believe in the Lord Jesus Christ, and thou shalt be saved,' God will not withhold the power from you.

Very well, they have sprinkled the door post and lintel. Anyone inside this house is perfectly safe. Suppose some of the Egyptians said to the Jews, 'We believe God is going to pass over the land, and you Israelites know what will save you, because He has told you what to do. We will come and take shelter with you.' They would be just as safe in the house as the Israelites, because of the sheltering blood.

I would like to take you for a moment into two houses. In one the mother of the house is looking sad and miserable. Suppose they are just taking supper. We say to the mother, 'Why are you so sad tonight?' And perhaps she will say, 'Are you a stranger here? Don't you know that Jehovah is going to pass over Egypt, and that the first-born is to be slain?'

'Yes', we say, 'we heard that; but we heard Moses tell the Israelites that the lamb was to be slain instead of the first-born, and that Jehovah when He saw the blood would pass over the house.'

'Yes,' says the mother, 'that is very true; but you know we cannot be certain. Nobody can know they are safe until after twelve o'clock. I cannot tell whether my boy is safe until it is all over.'

In the other house there is a grand contrast, The mother is smiling and happy, because the Lord is going to deliver them from being slaves in Egypt. We say, 'Why do you look so bright and happy? Don't you know that Jehovah is going to pass over the land tonight?'

'Yes', said the mother; 'but did you not see the blood on the door-posts and lintel?'

'Oh, yes', we say, 'but you know you cannot be sure.'

'Sure!', she says with indignation, 'We believe in the word of Jehovah, and we are under shelter of the blood. How can we be more sure than that?'

In which of those houses do you think the first-born is the safest? Some will say, 'Inside the house in which is trust.' No such thing. He will be just as safe in one as in the other. Because it was not their estimate of the blood, or their feelings or thoughts about Jehovah; but it was the blood that was sprinkled that made them safe.

Now, for a moment, it is midnight, and Jehovah begins that awful journey. He begins, say, down in Egypt, perhaps at the beautiful palace of Pharaoh. There gleam those beautiful pillars in the moonlight, but there is no blood to be seen down there, and so God says, 'All the first-born must die.'

Then go down to the land of Goshen, to a tiny cottage perhaps. What is that dark splash on the door-post and lintel? Blood. There is no angel of death to go in there because they have died. The best way to keep out of death is by dying. There is the token. The first-born son had died in the lamb. The sprinkled blood was a token to God that he had died. Jehovah said, 'When I see the blood I will pass over you' and so there was not a house in Goshen where there was one first-born dead. They had to die because they were sinners.

The only difference was this, that in Israel they died in the person of a substitute, and in Egypt they died for their own sins. And that will be the difference with every man and every woman within the sound of my voice tonight. You must either die in the person of your substitute and accept the Lord Jesus Christ as your own personal Saviour, and take Him as your substitute, or else you must consent to die for your own sins. The Lord help you.

There is such a thing as appropriation. I want to explain what it is. Suppose I went to a shop and bought a present for one of you here, and I said to the shopman, 'I will pay for this'—say it is a book; and suppose the shopman says, 'What shall I do with it—shall I send it to your address?' And I say, 'No; keep this book until a person calls with a card answering this name.' By and by, of course, it is delivered to the person with that card.

Now, salvation belongeth to the Lord ... It belongs to the Lord Jesus Christ because He bought it. And who did he buy it for? For the one who answers the description for whom He died. Who is that? The sinners and ungodly, those are the ones for whom he died. You have only to claim your salvation, and God says it is bought for you. Christ bought salvation and paid for it. God is reconciled to every sinner in this building. Does that save you? No, and I will tell you why? You are not reconciled to God. If you would come tonight and be reconciled to God, you have nothing to do but receive the reconciliation. Jesus Christ has reconciled man and God by His death. He died on the Cross, and by His death put away sin by the sacrifice of Himself, and now God is reconciled to every sinner. And the reason sinners are not saved is because they won't come each for herself and himself, and be reconciled to God.

Now, just to close. You see the Israelites went into their houses, they were taking shelter under the blood. Mark you, they could not see the blood. They could not come out of the doors and see if it was all right. If they had gone out to see, it would have been at the risk of their own lives. God says you must stay under shelter of the blood. The words, 'take shelter under' and 'trust in' are synonymous. So as I stand here, I take shelter under, or trust in the blood of Christ. You say, I cannot see blood anywhere. Well, but Jesus Christ has gone to Heaven—by His own blood He has sprinkled the lintels and the door-posts of Heaven. I have no need to see the blood. God sees the blood. He looks into my heart and sees I am trusting in my soul's salvation in nothing, absolutely nothing, but the precious blood of the Lord Jesus Christ, and so I am as safe as God can make me. And any of you in this meeting tonight, who will simply trust or take shelter under the blood of Christ, you are as safe as God can make you.

Why do you not accept this glorious salvation? What need is there for you to go back tonight an unsaved man? What need is there for you to go back to the weary, lonely life of not being friends with God,—not having God for your friend—when Jesus died to reconcile you? Why not receive the reconciliation tonight? What were the three places where the blood was to be put up? On the right hand to keep out sin, on the left hand to keep out sin, and on the lintel so that Jehovah, looking down, could see the blood. But there was one place where the blood was not to be put, and that was on the ground. I fear that many of you have got no blood sprinkled on the door-posts, no blood on the lintel, but I fear you are trampling it under your feet.

I will tell you, just in closing, one verse from the 10th of Hebrews, which I think is a terrible verse, and just shows what God thinks of Christ-rejecters. It says there that in the old days men died at the mouth of two witnesses, and then it says, 'Of how much sorer punishment, suppose ye, shall he be thought worthy, who hath trodden under foot the Son of God, and hath counted the blood of the covenant, wherewith he was sanctified, an unholy thing, and hath insulted the Spirit of Grace.'[22] Just as though it were possible to trample the body of Christ under their feet. You say I cannot do that; Christ is in Heaven. No, but God regards a Christ-rejecter just as though he had done it; trampled under foot the body of God's dear Son!

Think what a sin that must be. Many men say, 'We do not need the blood, the atonement of Christ; there is something good in us that if developed will lead us back to God.' ... Very well ...

God, the Holy Ghost, witnesses to the blood of Christ, and if you go away from this meeting unreconciled you are insulting the Spirit of grace because He is the witness to the blood; and you unsaved men and women, you commit an unpardonable sin for which there is no forgiveness in this world or the next. If you reject Christ once too often, God save you and help you, through this big meeting, even if you do not come into the inquiry meeting, wherever you are, by the side of your bed tonight—God will help you to say, 'Jesus,

I accept Thee as my Saviour. I die tonight in the person of my substitute. Make me Thy child.'

God grant that hundreds of you may do this tonight, and come and stand beside this Jewess under shelter of the precious blood for His dear name's sake.

Mrs. E. L. Baeyertz

First published in *Three Lectures* (Baeyertz E. L., 1890). This text is taken from *Twelve Addresses* (1904).'

[1] Ezekiel 12.

[2] Ezekiel 12:42. Emilia paraphrases or misremembers some of the quotes in this address.

[3] Romans 3:23.

[4] Romans 6:23.

[5] 1 Corinthians 5:7.

[6] 1 Peter 1:18.

[7] John 1:29.

[8] Matthew 26, Mark 14:34, John 13:26.

[9] Matthew 26:16.

[10] Exodus 3:13–14.

[11] John 8:56–58.

[12] John 18:1–9.

[13] Matthew 27:24.

[14] Matthew 27:4.

[15] John 1:29.

[16] Matthew 27:42.

[17] Lamentations 1:12.

[18] Psalm 22:1, Matthew 27:46, Mark 15:34.

[19] John 19:30.

[20] John 9:36, Psalm 34:20, John 19:33, Luke 24:47.

[21] Ezekiel 12:22.

[22] Hebrews 10:29.

AUCKLAND, NEW ZEALAND, OCT 1890
HOLINESS

THE LONGER I LIVE, DEAR FRIENDS, AS A CHRISTIAN, AND the more I go about the world, the more I find Christians are crying in secret for something more than they have. They are saved. Their conscience has been quieted as far as penalty and punishment go; but oh, how few Christians are really satisfied! How few Christians are resting! And yet there are secrets in God's Word that are hidden from the wise and prudent, but are revealed to babes—secrets that would gladden many weary hearts once they are known to them. I know all about it, because I have passed through it step by step, and I would like, before I speak to you, just to take a few minutes in giving my own experience of this life, because it will be a help to some of you. And I always think there is a greater power in a personal witness.

When I was first converted, nineteen years ago, I found that although I was saved my character was not changed. All the old sins used to have dominion over me, and I thought that was all right. I did not know any better. But twelve months after I was converted I sought what is very often called 'the blessing'.[1] I did not like the term. But I sought the blessing, and I got it. And it came to me in this way: With a great rushing of feeling. I was lifted out of myself. I hardly knew whether I was in the body or out of the body, so great was my joy and rapture, and then, as time went on, I found I was delivered from sin. Gradually, however, I slipped back to the life, and there I lived just as I did when I was first converted. Then, again, I began to seek 'the blessing'. Four or five times did I get the blessing and it was always the same way, with a great rush of feeling. As long as the feeling lasted I was kept from sin.

I venture to say, if the secrets of many hearts were known, this is what some of you are saying: 'That is just like me. I have got the blessing, and I have lost it', and you keep on losing it as long as you go in for 'the blessing'. But I will tell you something better tonight. It's not a blessing to be got and lost, but a life to be lived. I just told God I could not live any longer dishonouring Him as I was doing.

I am naturally very impatient and irritable. The least little thing would put me out, and I called to Him in earnest prayer and anguish, and I told God He could do what He liked with me; that I could not live any longer leading such a wretched life. I said, 'Lord, tell me the secret'. The Bible is plain on this point, that there is deliverance from this kind of life, and that Christians can have rest of heart and deliverance from sin.

I said, 'Lord, deliver me from my sin, and let it be a constant thing'. I did not look for any manifestation. I simply wanted deliverance from sin. Nobody but God knows what I went through. I used actually to be afraid to go on my knees and pray. All I knew was this: I was such a sinner. And I do not believe people will get into this blessed life by simply holding their hands up, saying, 'Save me'. There is a work to go on in the soul of Christians just as in the soul of the unconverted, in order to get into this life, and that is the reason I have been holding these afternoon meetings, because at every meeting I have been trying to lead up to this meeting tonight.

At one time I was very ill. I was threatened with paralysis through overwork. And I remember I told the Lord over and over again, 'You can do what you like with me, only save me from sin'. Even while threatened with paralysis, I was not so anxious about healing as I was about deliverance. However, the Lord healed my body apart from any doctor, and He led me into this blessed life, and I will tell you how. It was not by any manifestation or feeling; but one day in a prayer-meeting while I, with others, was exercised about this truth, the Lord enabled me by faith to take hold of the promise of His word. And His promise was: 'You shall be clean'. There was no change I know of. I was not conscious when I rose from my knees of anything. I did not feel one single thing. I got up from my knees and trusted and kept on trusting. I believed God. And I found in the very circumstances where a few days before the temper would rise, now Christ put His own, gentle power within me, and I could look around and say, none of these things move me. It was just glorious, and yet not one bit of feeling. I believe if God had given me feeling I would have rested in that feeling and not have learned the lesson.

I would have you understand that it is not so much a blessing to be got and lost as it is a life to be lived. Of course, there is an entrance into this life, just the same as in the case of those who have been converted. They do not go away and say, 'I got the blessing at the meeting the other night'. No! They say, 'I was converted'. You begin a new life altogether. You come into a new relationship with Christ, and then you go away and live. It is a life to be lived. I do not expect to live any other life until Jesus comes. I would not dare to stand up here and say there has been no failure. God knows I would not be speaking the truth if I did. Of course, there is failure in everyone's life, if people would only be honest and say so; but the blood of Jesus Christ cleanseth us from all sin.
(See 1 John i. 7–9.)

Let us look at this chapter in Romans. We read in the sixth chapter, 'dead to sin'. What I want to speak tonight about is 'dead to sin'. We read three times over in this chapter that we are free from sin. Now, there is nothing prized so much as freedom. We prize freedom beyond words. As in the old days, the Turks used to persecute the Christians and take them as slaves, and the relatives of those Christians used to collect money to purchase their freedom. Now, sometimes, it would so happen that the Christians, when they heard their freedom was purchased, and the money was paid, had got so used to their slavery that they would not take the trouble to go free and they would stay in bondage. At other times their masters kept the money, and never told the people that their freedom had been purchased at all, and so, of course, they remained. Others, again, got free.

I want to tell you tonight that your Master has purchased your freedom and you are free. Whether you experience it or not, it does not alter the fact. You tonight are free from sin. There is no necessity for any child of God to yield to sin. And any child of God who yields to sin yields because his own will consents, and not because he is under any necessity to yield to the temptation that is brought to him.

When we say we are crucified with Christ, what does that mean? It means freedom from the power of sin. The cross means the utter surrender of our own will, to let God do what He pleases with us. It means death. The cross does not mean troubles and griefs, and difficulties and trials. It always means death, and I will show you how directly. There are two senses of death I want you to notice. And the cross, if it means anything to us, means the absolute surrender of our whole will, so that God may have all His own way with us; that we may have no liberty of choice, but just do God's will.

In this sixth chapter of Romans we read at the tenth verse that Christ 'died unto sin once'. Now, I want to show you a very important truth. We read that Christ died for our sins. I am speaking to Christians. What does that mean? He died for my sins, and in dying for my sins He wrought out atonement for me which, when I believe in Him, is imputed to me, and through the death of Christ I am justified in God's sight. But, mark you, that *only* won't give you deliverance from the power of sin, and that is what you want. So we want to go a step further and see where is then the secret of deliverance from sin.

We read in this most wonderful verse; speaking of Christ it says, 'For in that He died, He died unto sin once: but in that He liveth, He liveth unto God. Likewise reckon ye also yourselves to be dead indeed unto sin.'

Now, how could Christ die unto sin? In what sense could the Lord Jesus Christ die for sin? He never sinned. He could not sin. He was absolutely sinless and holy, and it was an utter impossibility for Christ to yield to sin. Then in what sense did He die to sin? In this sense: When He was alive, as in the Garden of Gethsemane, as on the Cross, sin could make Him suffer; sin could pain Him; sin could be a sorrow to Him, and you know when He bore our sins on the cross, although He never sinned, He was made sin. When He died He died to all that sin could make Him suffer.

Now comes the wonderful word 'likewise'. 'Likewise reckon ye also yourselves to be dead indeed unto sin'. Why is that 'likewise' there? For this reason: that the life which Christ has put into each of us is the resurrection life, and He takes His people up with Him on to the cross, and we died on the cross with Him. He takes us down with Him to the grave, and we are buried with Him, and then we are raised with Him.

Death is the secret of deliverance from sin. It is the greatest power of deliverance of any truth in the whole word of God. You see, it does not say in the Bible sin is dead, but it says we are to reckon ourselves dead to sin. If sin were dead, there would be no need for me to reckon myself dead to it. If sin were dead, it would be an utter impossibility for me to yield to sin, whereas no Christian can say it is an utter impossibility for him to yield to sin. A temptation might present itself, and you might yield.

It says, 'As Christ died unto sin once, likewise reckon ye also yourselves to be dead indeed unto sin.' You may say you cannot do that, and the chapter says, 'Sin shall not have dominion over you', and you say that it has dominion over you. I know the tears which you have shed in secret over that chapter. I dare say many people here have wished that that chapter was not in the Bible. I know you want to reckon yourselves dead unto sin. I tried to reckon myself dead. I prayed and still I could not; and afterwards God showed me the secret.

Now all of you who have your Bibles just turn to it and you will see the secret. In the eleventh verse we have, 'Likewise reckon ye yourselves to be dead indeed unto sin, but alive unto God, through Jesus Christ our Lord.' Now, in the fourteenth verse we have the promise, 'For sin shall not have dominion over you, for ye are not under the law but under grace.'

But what comes in between? People miss out those twelfth and thirteenth verses, and say 'I cannot reckon myself dead, and sin does have dominion over me'. The whole secret lies in the twelfth and thirteenth verses, 'Let not sin therefore reign in your mortal body, that ye should obey it in the lusts thereof. Neither yield ye your members as instruments of unrighteousness unto sin, but *yield yourselves unto God*, as those that are alive from the dead, and your members as instruments of righteousness unto God.'

And I will tell you the whole secret of failure in your life. The reason you cannot reckon yourself dead is this: you have never wholly and absolutely surrendered as to the satisfaction it yields to self to give way to sin. Oh! the struggle to give in. I will tell you why: because it makes you take a low place. You have to make yourself of no reputation. Unless we are willing to give up the satisfaction it yields, we will never learn the secret of deliverance. That is one point.

Then there is another other. If there is anything in the heart or life contrary to the word of God, you cannot expect to know anything about this glorious blessed life. God taught me years go, 'WHATEVER IS NOT OF FAITH IS SIN', and if I did anything my conscience condemned me for, although it might not be what people called sin, it was sin to me— because I had not faith about this particular thing.

There is another point that must be yielded. If you want this blessing, the will must be yielded to God. You must be willing to give up every doubtful thing, so that you can tell God, 'I will obey.'

Now turn to Joshua. Joshua had led the children of Israel out into battle. They had been delivered from their enemies. All of a sudden everything was changed. The people began to fly before their enemies, and they were beaten. Joshua was in a dreadful way, and he cried to God, and all the elders of Israel put on sackcloth and ashes upon their heads, and they all began to weep and cry. Presently, the voice of God came to them, 'Up; wherefore liest thou upon thy face? Israel has sinned ... and have taken of the accursed thing.' (See Joshua vii. 10–11).

Perhaps some of you have been praying, 'Lord, bless me! Deliver me! Let me enter into this blessed life!' and perhaps God has to say the same thing to you tonight as He said to Joshua. There is a time to pray and a time for action. I know this. I might have prayed to this day and might not have received this blessed life. It is not the time to pray now; it is the time for action. Israel had sinned. There was one in the camp who had sinned, and that was the reason they could not stand before their enemies.

God said, 'Neither will I be with you any more except ye destroy the accursed thing from among you.' What was it? They found out afterwards that one man had coveted a Babylonish garmet and a wedge of gold and had taken this forbidden thing and buried it deep down under the earth under his tent. Nobody had the least idea about it, but God's eye could look right down underneath that earth and see that forbidden thing. And so it may be with you. Deep down in your hearts are these things that are forbidden, and nobody knows anything about it; but God knows, and there are some of you Christians in this meeting tonight, and you know very well, as sure as you are sitting on those seats, that you have got a condemned conscience about something. There are things in your life and in your hearts that you know are contrary to the Word of God. God says you must give up the accursed thing. Will you do so? I cannot hold out hope for you to enter into the blessed life unless you are prepared to give up whatever it is that is hindering you. I do not know what it is. But God's Holy Spirit will show you.

His eye is as a flame of fire, although it is full of love and tenderness and God will search you through and through and through; and the Holy Spirit will tell you while you are sitting on those seats, what is the accursed thing in your life. In the case of some of you, even at this moment, there is something coming up to your mind, and you are saying, perhaps, 'Is that it? Oh, that is a little thing. God does not mean that.'

That is it, my brother and my sister. Just now, what the Holy Spirit is showing you in answer to your pleading prayer. That is just the very thing God wants you to give up. If you give it up, and give yourself, just as you are, wholly, entirely and absolutely to God tonight, He will give you the power to reckon yourself dead, and before this meeting is over you will find power will come, and you will be able to reckon yourselves dead. And then what is the result? Turn to the 6th chapter of Romans and see what is the result. 'Sin shall not have dominion over you.'

The idea of Christians who go to dances and who play cards, and join in those doubtful amusements—the idea of them going to a holiness meeting, and praying to God to deliver them! Why, it is mocking God! You can have the world if you want it; and ultimately such Christians MAY be saved and go to Heaven (see James iv. 4; and i. 22), but they never will know anything of deliverance from sin or communion with God. One day they will say they are safe, and another day they will be full of doubts and fears. The wonder to me is they can hold on at all.

I will put the truth before you just as it is and leave it with you. If you want to, you can enter into that life tonight, but you have to yield up every doubtful thing; cut yourself away from all the past that has been bad; lay yourselves down on God's altar and say, 'Lord, I want to reckon myself dead indeed unto sin. I want to obey Thy Word, so that sin will not have dominion over me.' God is proving you tonight; He is proving you in this meeting. Do you love Him enough to give up your idols and the doubtful things of your life? You know exactly what you have to do. If you on your part yield yourselves up to God, and tell Him He can have 'all His own way with you', and give up the doubtful things, and do not take them up again, then deliverance will come, and God will make you 'strongest on the very weakest point of your character.'

I do not feel I want to go on urging you; I leave it with you. I have told you about the life, and exactly what the results will be if you enter in, as far as I am able.

Now I come to this point. All of you who tonight are prepared to yield yourselves unreservedly to the Lord Jesus Christ, to give up all the doubtful things, to come out from the world and be saved, so that you may be at His disposal to use you, stay behind to our prayer meeting, and I will come down there, and we will join together in earnest pleading prayer that He may come and reveal the Truth to you while you are on your knees, so that you may go away from this meeting and commence a new life altogether, and I will tell you what it will be.

It will be just as different to the old life that you have been living in the past as it was when you were first converted. If you come into this blessed life, you will see what deliverance you will have to-morrow, and when temptation and trial come to you, you will just shout the shout of victory, because tonight God will give you the power to reckon yourselves dead, and sin will not have dominion over you. Now, the Lord help you and bring you to a decision on this point, for His Names sake. I will close with three questions the Lord put to me long, long ago:

'Lovest thou Me more than these?'

'Wilt thou come into such close union with Me as to make a separation from the world absolutely necessary?'

'Wilt thou be satisfied with My smile of approval, and leaving all others, cleave only to Me?'

What shall the answer be?

Mrs. E. L. Baeyertz

This is one of Emilia's *Three Lectures* (Baeyertz E. L.), first published in Auckland in 1890, with the reference to 'nineteen years ago'. This was updated to 'twenty years ago' the following year in Canada then left alone in subsequent editions including *Twelve Addresses* (Baeyertz E. L., 1904).

[1] Also in Auckland, *New Zealand Herald* (27 September 1890, p. 5) reported that 'in a lucid and forcible address Mrs. Baeyertz defined holiness and how the blessing might be acquired; her views being of the orthodox type uttered in nearly all the pulpits of this city ... There were in the address none of the unsavoury features of "American Holiness" with which the Auckland public have been made painfully familiar, and in announcing the after-meeting which closed her impressive address, Mrs. Baeyertz said, significantly, that she wanted no "ranting", shouting, clapping, screaming, and thumping at her meetings, and would have none of it. But instead quiet, order, reverence.'

TORONTO, ONTARIO, NOVEMBER 1891

FOREWORDS TO FIVE LECTURES

I ESTEEM IT A PRIVILEGE TO BE ASKED TO WRITE A FEW lines by way of introduction for the book being issued by Mrs. Baeyertz. It was my good fortune to be present when the addresses which it contains were delivered during the special services held in Ottawa. I was much benefitted, as were all those who attended day after day and I desire to commend to the Christian people the careful perusal of its pages.

One cannot read or hear Mrs. Baeyertz's addresses without feeling that it is not so much she who speaks as the Holy Spirit who speaks through her. The promise is that He will guide into all truth, and certainly light has been shed upon the sacred page, and passages of Scripture hitherto obscure have suddenly opened up in a wonderful manner as she expounds the Word.

While Mrs. Baeyertz's earnest words made a deep impression on the unsaved and were the means of leading many to Christ, her exposition of Bible truths caused Christians to study the Bible for themselves, and the interest thus created has done incalculable good.

My earnest desire and prayer is that the book will be a blessing to many, and that it may be used by Him as the previous one[1] has been to lead souls to Christ.

Robert Stewart, President, Y. M. C. A., Ottawa, Canada

From *Five Lectures* (Baeyertz E. L., 1891).

[1] The 'previous one' refers to *Three Lectures* published in New Zealand the previous year.

THESE ADDRESSES BY MRS. BAEYERTZ CONTAINED IN THIS little book I had the pleasure of hearing. They are well worthy of being presented in this more permanent form; and Mrs. Baeyertz has done well in acceding to the wish of the many hundreds who earnestly desired the publication of them. They will, I am sure, be read with interest and profit by thousands, although their form on the printed page conveys but an inadequate idea of the power that accompanied their delivery. It is my hope that they may be widely circulated, and it is my conviction that they will help those who read them to a fuller understanding of the great truths which they set forth. May He to whose grace they testify bless them to that end.

Thomas Wardrope, Moderator of the General Assembly of the Presbyterian Church, Canada, November 2, 1891

From *Five Lectures* (Baeyertz E. L., 1891).

TORONTO, ONTARIO, NOVEMBER 1891

SEVEN STEPS TO THE BLESSED LIFE IN PSALM 32

IN THE 1st VERSE OF THIS PSALM WE FIND THE BLESSED-ness of the man whose sins are forgiven, but in the 2nd verse we have the blessedness of the man in whose spirit there is no guile, that is, one whose heart is cleansed. There are *seven* steps to this blessedness.

In the 3rd and 4th verses we have *conviction of sin*, for the Holy Ghost as really convicts Christians of sin, as He does the unconverted, and our spiritual life depends upon our yielding submission to the Holy Spirit, for He is within us as a Personal Presence, with a mind and will of His own. He is Christ's inner Self, and if He is not hindered will at once let us know when the least little wrong-doing is allowed. If we refuse to obey and turn away from the sin, the 4th verse will be our experience. The *first* step, then, is *conviction*.

In the 5th verse, the *second* step is *Confession*. Now, it is most important to know what confession is. It is not merely saying 'forgive us our trespasses, etc.' There is no confession in *that*, for confession always involves real sorrow for sin; and to confess, we tell out in detail the sin to God with genuine repentance and a heart longing for deliverance.

In this same verse, we have the *third* step, *forgiveness*; and when we confess, the forgiveness follows. Turn with me to 1 John i. 9. We have exactly the same truth, 'If we *confess* our sins, He is faithful and just to *forgive* us our sins, and to *cleanse* us from all unrighteousness.' There we have *confession, forgiveness, cleansing*.

We confess to God, and who is He faithful and just to? He is faithful to Christ who is in Heaven, as the High Priest of His people, and just to the one who confesses; so that, by virtue of that precious blood, the forgiveness is instantaneous with the confession. When should we confess? At night when we are tired and weary, and have forgotten the shortcomings of the day? No. Confession should be instantaneous with the consciousness that the sin is committed. If it be an evil thought or unkind word, the Holy Ghost makes us know at once He is grieved; then, if we instantly confess to God, 'He is faithful and just to forgive.'

The 4th verse describes exactly the state of the backsliding sinner, and it all comes from 'keeping silence', as stated in the 3rd verse. Scores of backsliding Christians would be delivered from their backsliding by obeying the conviction of the Holy Ghost, and taking the *second* step which is described in the 5th verse. Instant *confession* brings instant *forgiveness*, and instant forgiveness brings instant and restored communion. But this is not the whole of that wonderful verse in 1 John i. He is also faithful and just 'to cleanse us from all unrighteousness'. Our failure lies simply in our getting forgiveness without going on to be cleansed from unrighteousness. We should ask the Lord to take the sin actually away. He will do it, then, you will come to abide in Christ habitually, and you will have days and days and days that are not clouded by conscious sin (though I do not forget there was an offering for the sins of ignorance).

Do not be discouraged in this life; God is very pitiful and of tender mercy, and loves us with the yearning mother love. He never scolds. Think of a mother teaching her little child to walk; as often as the child falls, she does not scold and punish. No, indeed, but lifts up the little one and encourages it to try again; and God does the same with us when we are trying to walk in the paths of righteousness, and fail. Jesus Christ puts His loving arms around us and lifts us up, and we are enabled to go on in this blessed life.

Turn back, now, to the 6th verse of the Psalm, where *prayer* is mentioned. This verse is wrongly translated; it says here, 'pray unto Thee in a time when Thou mayest be found'. God can always be found of His people. The correct translation is, 'pray unto Thee in a time of finding out sin', which just corresponds with what we have been looking at in John.

In the 7th verse, we have *protection*, or the protecting love of Jesus. He loves us as the very apple of His eye. How He encourages us to trust. 'Fear not, I am with thee; I will help thee; I will strengthen thee; I will never fail thee or forsake thee.' 'Leave thy fatherless children, I will preserve them alive. Let thy widows trust in Me.' And to the fatherless is He not the Father—our Father?

The 8th verse tells of *guidance*. It should read, 'I will guide thee; Mine eye shall be upon thee.' We are absolutely sure of guidance when our wills are yielded to the Lord. We must give up all idea of guiding ourselves, by an utter surrender of everything, and an absolute trust in Him. Let Him know our wants day by day, and our need of guidance, then leave all in His dear hands.

> *Fear not, care not,*
> *Only follow*
> *His way, this day*
> *And to-morrow.*

The 9th verse is wrongly translated. It is not 'lest they come near', but 'to keep them near'. God does not will His children to be *restrained* and *reminded* by bit and bridle, like the horse and mule, which are devoid of understanding. Yet when we do require these reminders, how gentle they are, and how thankful we should be for them.

The *seventh* and last step is in the last verse: *joy*. The Psalm closes with rejoicing, and how can we help rejoicing in the Lord, when we find His Word proved true in our daily life, and He such a Saviour? Now let me impress this thought: never let unconfessed sin remain upon the conscience; it corrodes and eats in, as acid does upon metal; it causes backsliding and all the sorrow that involves. It is sad, but too true, that Christians can smother conscience and drift away into sin. If you wish to be one 'Unto whom the Lord imputes not iniquity', yield yourself to the Holy Ghost. Confess your sin and put it away, don't make the mistake of trying to feel forgiven but lean upon the word in 1 John i. 9.

So the *seven* steps to this blessedness are, in the 3rd verse, *conviction*, 5th, *confession* and *forgiveness*, 6th, *prayer*, 7th, *protection*, 8th, *guidance* and 9th, *joy*.

Mrs. E. L. Baeyertz

The 'Seven Steps' were published in *Five Lectures* (Baeyertz E. L., 1891) and in *Twelve Addresses* (1897).

PERTH, WESTERN AUSTRALIA, 1904

THE YOUNG RULER AND BARTIMAEUS

READ IN MARK X., FROM THE 17th TO THE 22nd VERSE; also from the 46th to the end. We read of one who came running and kneeled to Jesus. There we have earnestness and reverence. Some people say, what does it matter if a person is only in earnest? Well earnestness is all very well, but it is certainly not everything. Note his question—'Good Master, what must *I do* that I may inherit eternal life?'

We can do *nothing*, and our only inheritance is eternal death. Notice—the Lord takes him up on his own ground, 'Why callest thou Me *good*? there is none good but one, that is, God.'

Did our Lord mean by this that He was not God? No, indeed. He knew what was in Man, and reading that young man's thoughts, He knew that he looked upon Him, that blessed One before whom he was then kneeling, as a *mere man*—a teacher, who could, perhaps, show him how he could develop some goodness in himself by which he could inherit life, and as a mere man, *apart from His deity*, He was not good.

And you who think you honour Christ by saying He was a good man, and yet say He was not God, you may keep your ascriptions of goodness to yourselves; He will have none of them. What awful blaspheming for a mere man to say, 'I am the light of the world'; 'He that believeth on me hath everlasting life'; 'Before Abraham was I am'; 'Glorify thou Me with thine own self with the glory which I had with Thee *before the world was*'; 'In the beginning was the Word, and the Word was with God, and the Word was God; all things were made by Him, and without Him was not *anything* made that was made. In Him was life', etc., and I tell you, you will never have eternal life unless you *receive* Christ, who is God over all blessed for ever, for He alone has life to impart to dead souls, and He says, 'Ye will not come to Me that ye might have life.'[1]

Notice: 'He that believeth not God hath made him a *liar*, because he believeth not the record that God gave of His Son, and this is the record, that God *hath* given to us eternal life, and this life is in His Son."—1 John v. 10–11.

Do you see that God has so ordained that this life, which alone makes us His children, is in Christ, so the acceptance of Christ as a mere man puts God's record of His Son on one side makes *God a liar*, and deters all who do this from ever receiving the life which fits us for heaven?

We who believe are in Him 'even in *His Son Jesus Christ; this is the one true God* and eternal life.'—1 John v. 20.

To go back to the young ruler, Mark x.—'Jesus, beholding him, loved him.' Why did He love him, surely not for any goodness in himself? No, but for the same reason that He loves you, sinner, because He is love, and *because* He loved him, He puts the test to him—'One thing thou lackest'.

What was the one thing? *Eternal life*. All his righteousness had failed to give him life. He certainly had come to the right source for life, but now for the test—'Sell whatsoever thou hast and give to the poor ... and come take up the Cross and follow Me.'

Why did Christ put *such* a test to him? Perhaps as He read that young ruler's heart he might have found such thoughts as these there: The Master is poor; I am rich; He will welcome me; I can give Him wealth, influence, and social position; but the Lord struck at the heart of it.

Come, follow Me! Follow Him; that would mean poverty, reproach, humility, social obscurity; it would mean to give up his eloquent home in Jerusalem, and as he still kneels at the feet of Jesus, he counts the cost, and he makes his decision. The price is too much to pay even for eternal life, and he went away grieved, for he had great possessions.

The elegant house has passed away, the wealth has gone, the social position—all gone; but he lives to regret, with unavailing remorse and anguish, the awful decision of that hour. He came into contact with Christ, heard His words, shared His love, but will never benefit by His precious death.

Take care, sinner, lest you sin away your day of grace and reject the Saviour, for a time comes to each one when the Holy Spirit brings a pressure to bear upon souls and when God treats a sinner's rejection of Christ as *final*.

Now look at the contrast, from verse 47. Blind Bartimeus sits by the highway side begging, but he hears that Jesus of Nazareth is passing by, so he lifts himself up and, with a great cry, calls out, 'Jesus, thou Son of David, have mercy on me'; but the crowd around told him to be quiet, not to make such a noise. Oh, no; I can't be quiet, thinks Bartimeus, *I'm blind*, I'm blind, and Jesus can give me sight. Oh, I can't go to Him; I can't see my way, but I'll call louder; perhaps He will hear me although I'm only a poor blind beggar.

So he cried out again, 'Thou Son of David, have mercy on me,' and Jesus *stood still!* (Of course He did. No needy one ever cried to Him in vain when He was on earth, and He is the same Jesus now) and commanded him to be called.

Then the crowd changes, and they go to the blind man to tell him the good news of comfort, 'Rise, He calleth thee', and he rose. There was just one thing to hinder him obeying that call as quickly as he wanted to—the long cloak that he used to wrap around him; every hindrance must go, and as that was the only one, we read, 'he casting away his garment, rose and came to Jesus.'

Now he stands face to face with that blessed One; but, alas! alas! he is blind; he can see nothing, but the loving voice reaches his ear.

'What wilt thou that I should do unto thee?'

Now comes the supreme moment of his life. 'Lord, that I might receive my sight.' And Jesus said, 'Go thy way, thy faith hath made thee whole.'

In obedience to the Lord, he takes one step to go, when, lo! a miracle!—those blind eyes were opened and *he saw Jesus!*

That sight was enough. 'Go!' Oh, no; 'entreat me not to leave Thee, nor to return from following after Thee', and he followed Jesus in the way.

The young ruler was called to come and he went away sorrowful. The blind man was told to *go* but he followed, satisfied with the sight that had burst upon his vision, and he followed and joined in the cry, 'Hosanna; Hosanna in the highest?'

One saw no beauty in Him that he should desire him; to the other He was the altogether lovely one.

Ah! dear sinner, you have eyes in your heart, and with these eyes we see Jesus. May He open your blind eyes and lead you to receive Him as your Saviour, and you shall then know the pardon and rest and peace with God that has been purchased through the atoning death of Christ.

> *Nothing in my hand I bring,*
> *Simply to Thy Cross I cling;.*
> *Naked, come to Thee for dress;*
> *Helpless, look to Thee for grace;*
> *Foul, I to the fountain fly:*
> *Wash me, Saviour, or I die.*[2]

Mrs. E. L. Baeyertz

First published in *Six New Addresses* (Baeyertz E. L., 1904).

[1] John 8:12, 6:47, 8:58, 17:5, 1:1, 5:40.

[2] From 'Rock of ages, cleft for me' by Augustus M. Toplady (1776).

PERTH, WESTERN AUSTRALIA, 1904

THE JEWISH DAY OF ATONEMENT

WILL YOU LET US TURN TO THE 16th OF LEVITICUS? Before I tell you of the first institution of the Day of Atonement as it came direct from the hands of God, let me tell you how it is now kept up among the Jews.

Every fast and feast of the Jews begins at sundown. So in the evening, *Yaum Kippour* is ushered in by the Jews going down to their synagogues, where a very solemn service is gone through. They return home after that and early the next morning they return to the synagogue again, where they spend the whole day, sometimes from seven o'clock in the morning, in fasting and prayer, and by fasting I mean that not one morsel of bread, and not one drop of water, is taken from sundown one evening to sundown the next evening, and all through the day the prayers are kept up—they confess their sins, they weep, they smite upon their breasts. Then towards the end of the day the *shauphor* (or ram's horn of consecration) is blown. The service closes with the intoning of the additional prayers, and then, when it is all over, they go away to their homes, believing that through their prayers, their fasting, and their confession, their sins are all forgiven.

For how long? Until the next Day of Atonement, when the same thing has to be gone through again.

Now let us look at the Day of Atonement, as instituted by God. The word 'atonement' is not to be found in the New Testament at all, but it is translated there 'reconciliation', whereas it is mentioned thirty times in the Book of Leviticus, and sixteen times in this chapter alone. What is atonement? Atonement necessitates a sacrifice.

Firstly: It is God's judgment upon, and death of the sacrificed animal.

Secondly: It is the sprinkling of the blood in the holiest by the priest.

Thirdly: It is the confession of the sins of the people and putting all the confessed sins upon the head of the scapegoat. All this was fulfilled in the death of Christ upon the cross.

Now, will you picture to yourselves the Tabernacle in the wilderness, made of easily moveable materials? In fact, it was a tent, modelled according to the fashion which God gave to Moses in the Mount. All round this was placed a fence of fine white linen, supported by many pillars. The space thus enclosed around the Tabernacle was called 'The Court of the Tabernacle', the gate of which consisted of hanging curtains, and corresponded to the door of the Tabernacle, both of which faced the east.

All around, as far as the eye can reach, are to be seen the tents of the children of Israel, forming one huge camp, and from each camp may be seen a standard or flag flying in the air, upon which is the name of the tribe to which they belong. Every man must declare his pedigree.

On this day no one was allowed inside the Court of the Tabernacle (verse 17), nor was any manner of work done by any of the people (verse 29). They are all at the doors of their tents. They dare not do anything. If anyone did work he was to be cut off from the children of Israel. Every eye is directed to one spot. Let us see what this object of such intent interest is. Aaron, the high priest, comes forth on this day, wearing his garments for glory and for beauty (Ex. 28).

First of all there is the *ephod*, the foundation being blue, purple, scarlet, and fine-twined linen. It had two shoulder pieces composed of two onyx stones, with *six* names of the twelve tribes of Israel on one, and the remaining *six* on the other, and the high priest was to bear these names before the Lord upon his shoulders, for a memorial, continually. The shoulder is the place of strength, and that is where Jesus bears His people.

The next thing was the breast-plate, suspended from the ephod by a chain of gold. It consisted of twelve of the most beautiful precious stones, in four rows—the diamond, the ruby, the emerald, the topaz, the sapphire, and so on; and engraven on each stone was the name of a tribe; and as Aaron moved about on this Day of Atonement the people could look on and say, '*My* name is written there'. The breast-plate was worn on the heart, the place of the affections; and that is where the Lord Jesus carries us.

Then there is the curious *girdle*, and the *long blue robe*—the heavenly colour—and all around the hem of the robe were pomegranates, embroidered by the women of the congregation, of blue, of purple, and of scarlet, and bells of gold between them; 'a golden bell and a pomegranate, a golden bell and a pomegranate'. The bell was for sound, that Aaron might be heard when he went into the Holy Place before the Lord. The pomegranate meant fruit. And, as it is said, '*one* bell and *one* pomegranate', it is to teach us that God expects as much fruit as sound. How is it with our lives?

Then there is the beautiful *helmet* of gold, with 'Holiness to the Lord' engraven upon it.

Now, let us see what next is done on this Great Day of Atonement. Eleazar and Ithamar, the two sons of Aaron, bring a bullock right opposite the gates of the outer court, and slay it before all the congregation.

Remember that this is the Day of Atonement, and there can be no atonement without sacrifice and substitution. Then they hand some of the blood in a bowl to Aaron, and he goes through the gate, and up that courtyard, all alone, for there is to be no man in the Tabernacle of the Congregation when he goeth to make atonement (verse 17).

Then he stops at the altar, which was in the Court of the Tabernacle, and takes a censer full of burning coals of fire from off the altar, and sweet incense, beaten small, and he puts the incense upon the fire, before the Lord, that the cloud of incense may cover the mercy seat, that he die not, for he has to go into the Holiest, where God himself dwells, into the immediate presence of God, and this cloud from the incense will rise, and break some of the glory of God's presence, that he may be able to bear it.

He now goes into the Holy Place, and there he strips himself of all his garments for glory and for beauty (a type of Christ, who was rich, yet for our sakes He became poor), and arrays himself in pure white linen. He then takes the blood from the bowl, and sprinkles his own garments. With the bowl of blood in one hand, and the censer, he now goes on to the Holiest, and draws aside the veil, and enters the very immediate presence of God, where he has to make an atonement for himself and his household. The first thing that he sees on entering is the Ark. The Ark was a wooden box, covered with gold, the wood and the gold typifying the divine and human nature of Christ. Inside the Ark was the table of the Law, which Law all the people had broken; but on the top of the Ark, and covering the Law altogether from sight, was a lid called the mercy-seat. The mercy-seat was composed of pure gold, typifying the divine nature of Christ.

Aaron makes the atonement by taking the blood of the bullock and sprinkling it upon the mercy seat seven times, for God had said, 'The life of the flesh is in the blood, and I have given it to you upon the altar to make an atonement for your souls, for it is *the blood that maketh an atonement for the soul*'. Two goats are then brought, one for the Lord and the other for the scapegoat, and Aaron shall bring the goat upon which the Lord's lot fell, and offer him for a sin offering, and his blood is brought within the veil. He does with that blood exactly as he did with the blood of the bullock, sprinkling it seven times upon the mercy-seat, to make an atonement for the people.

Aaron then comes forth and lays both hands upon the head of the live goat, and 'confesses over him all the iniquities of the children of Israel, all their transgressions in all their sins, putting them upon the head of the goat'; and by this act he transfers the sins from the people to the *scapegoat*. Now what is to be done with the scapegoat?

He is to be led away by the hand of a fit man into the wilderness, and the goat is to bear all their iniquities into a *land not inhabited*, or a *land of separation*; so the fit man goes, leading the goat away in the sight of all the people, to find this place not inhabited; on and on he goes out of the sight of the camp of Israel, past every bit of vegetation, on to the very heart of the desert. When he has reached this vast solitude, the fit man disappears quickly from the sight of the goat, and leaves him to die in that land of separation, having borne the sins of the people away where there is no one to bring them back again. For how long? Until the next Day of Atonement, when the same thing has to be repeated.

Aaron then goes into the Tabernacle of the Congregation, and puts off the linen garments, and washes his flesh with water in the Holy Place, and arrays himself once more in his garments for glory and for beauty. Now the people hear the tinkle of the golden bells as the blue robe is put on again, and they rejoice, for they know that soon the high priest will come forth to bless them. And have we nothing to correspond to the tinkle of the bells? Yes, indeed we have. Every time we get an answer to prayer, every time the Holy Spirit brings Christ's words to our remembrance, or the love of God is shed abroad anew in our hearts, it is a tinkle-tinkle from the golden bells on the robe of our High Priest, and we know that He is within the veil for us, and that soon, very soon, He will come forth to bless us. Have you heard the tinkle of the bells to-day?

And now will you let us look into the New Testament for a fulfilment of this type? Jesus Christ came down from Heaven to be the Scapegoat of His people, to bear their sins into a 'place of separation'—a 'place not inhabited'.

He goes to the Cross, not, as some would tell us to die a martyr's death, but to 'bear our sins on His own body on the tree', to die, 'the just for the unjust, that He might bring us to God'; and on the Cross Jehovah laid upon Him the iniquities of us all. For hours He hangs there, bearing our sins, taking upon Himself all the punishment due to us. What the wrath of God means Jesus knows, for He cries out, 'The pains of Hell gat hold on me. I sink in deep mire where there is no standing; lover and friend hast Thou put far from me, and mine acquaintance into darkness.' 'My God! My God! why hast Thou forsaken Me?' Has He found the 'land of separation' yet? No, He must go further down into the darkness—down, down, down into the solitude of death.[1]

The weary hours drag on, and, at last, there comes from the Cross a cry that has thrilled the universe, and made all hell stand back—a cry of a conqueror—'It is finished.' ... 'Father, into Thy hands I commend my spirit.' And the veil of the Temple was rent in twain from the top to the bottom; and our blessed Scapegoat has found in death the 'land of separation', the 'land not inhabited', 'and has borne His people's sins when there is no one to bring them back again'. 'He hath offered one sacrifice for sins for ever'; and to those who accept this atonement God says, 'Their sins and their iniquities will I remember no more'.[2]

But to those who commit the wilful sin of rejecting *this one sacrifice* there remaineth no more sacrifice for sins, but a *certain* fearful looking for judgement and *fiery* indignation; *that* sin is called by God, 'treading under foot the Son of God, and counting the blood of the covenant wherewith He was sacrificed an unholy thing'.[3] Oh! accept Christ and His atoning sacrifice; then you will never have the wrath of God abiding on you.

They take down the precious body and lay it in the tomb, and after three days He rises again. 'If Christ be not risen we are yet in our sins, our faith is vain; but now is Christ risen from the dead, and become the first fruits of them that sleep.'[4]

Very early on the first day of the week, Mary Magdalene goes to the grave, but finds it empty. Then Peter and John come—*they* go to their own homes, but *Mary* stands there weeping, and as she weeps, she looks into the sepulchre and sees two angels who speak to her, saying, 'Woman, why weepest thou?'[5]

'Because they have taken away my Lord, and I know not where they have laid Him'. She turns herself and sees Jesus standing, and knew not that it was Jesus.

Jesus said to her, 'Woman, why weepest thou? Whom seekest thou?'

She, thinking it was the gardener, said, 'Sir, if thou has borne Him hence, tell me where thou hast laid Him, and I will take Him away.'

How blessed for Jesus to see that He so filled her heart, that there was only one object there—*Himself*—and now He speaks one word—'Mary.'

That is enough. He calleth His own sheep by name. She falls at his feet with one word, 'Rabboni', which is to say, 'My own dear Master'.

Jesus says 'Touch Me not, for I am not yet ascended to My Father, but go to my brethren and say unto them, I ascend unto My Father and your Father, and to My God and your God'.

Why was she not to touch him? If you will turn to Leviticus, 16th chap. 17th verse, you will see—'There shall be no man in the Tabernacle of the Congregation when the high priest goeth in to make an atonement in the Holy Place *until he come out*. Under the Levitical Law it was defilement for the priest to come into contact with anyone on the *Day of Atonement until the atonement was complete*; and Jesus wished to fulfil the whole Law; until He had gone into heaven 'with His own blood' the atonement was not complete.[6]

No one saw that ascension; but we have His own word for it, when He said, 'I ascend.' We can imagine something of that scene, when the hosts of Heaven cry out. 'Lift up your heads, oh! ye gates, even lift up, ye everlasting doors, and the King of Glory shall come in.'[7] And the gates of Heaven are thrown open to welcome the Lord of Hosts, for He is the King of Glory. In He comes past the shining host of Angels, past the

Cherubim and Seraphim, on, on to the very Throne of God, and there, entering in by His own precious blood, presents Himself as the Lamb that was slain. And now that blood (His death on the Cross) has so atoned for sin, and made an end of it, that we His redeemed ones, can go right into the Holiest too.

For centuries Israel had a sanctuary on earth, and no one was to enter the Holiest except the high priest, and then only *once a year*, but now the veil is rent, the Holiest is open; God wants you to live in His presence.

The blood of Jesus! What does it mean to us? He has put away sin by sacrifice of Himself, and through His blood—and His blood alone—we can now draw nigh with boldness, and hear God's voice saying to us, 'Your sins and your iniquities will I remember no more forever.'

Glory be to the Father! Glory be to the Son! and Glory be to the Holy Ghost for such a salvation.

Mrs. E. L. Baeyertz

First published in *Six New Addresses* (Baeyertz E. L., 1904).

[1] 1 Peter 2:24 (paraphrased), 1 Peter 3:18. Psalm 116:3, 69:2, 88:18.

[2] John 19:30, Hebrews 10:12.

[3] Hebrews 10:29 (paraphrased).

[4] 1 Corinthians 15 (paraphrased).

[5] John 20.

[6] Hebrews 13:12.

[7] Psalm 24:9.

Notes on *This Is My Beloved*

These endnotes relate to the novel, *This Is My Beloved*, by Betty Baruch and Amanda Coverdale. There are no little numbers in the novel; instead, the notes are grouped here by chapter. Page numbers without other citation relate to this volume.

Preliminaries

1. The cover art of the novel and the Companion includes an illustration of Mrs. Baeyertz which was scanned for us by the Tasmanian Archive and Heritage Office. That illustration accompanied Emilia's testimony *From Darkness to Light* (see page 22) reproduced in the September 1886 edition of *The Pioneer*, which was published in Launceston, Tasmania and rediscovered by Elisabeth Wilson in the state archives during her research. *The Pioneer* was 'For the recording and Spreading of the Glad Tidings of Salvation. Published in connection with the Christian Mission Church.'
2. 'A Jewish Christian Lady Evangelist' is how Emilia billed herself (see page 93).
3. 'This is my beloved and this is my friend, O daughters of Jerusalem' is from Song of Solomon 5:16. This verse and the book title *This Is My Beloved* were selected by Betty.
4. See 'The Story behind the Story' in the novel for the dedication to David Perry.

Part 1

Chapter 1. Bangor, Wales, Thursday 29 March 1855

5. Emilia Louise was born on 29 March 1842, to John and Maria Aronson who headed a large Ashkenazi orthodox family of 'unblemished Jewish stocks' (Watson, 1894/1895, p. 2) from 'Russian Central Europe' (Dwyer,

2008, p. 3) who lived in Bangor, North Wales. In those days, Jewish families were emigrating out of necessity from Eastern Europe.

6   According to the 1841 Bangor Census, John was born in Prussia and was a jeweller. By 1851, his profession had become woollen draper on the Bangor High Street. At least five of his sons became jewellers, drapers or both.

7   The approximate birth years in the Chronology (see page 209) of the eleven Aronson children that we know of are based on the 1851 and 1861 UK Censuses and Births, Deaths and Marriages Victoria. There may have been others who died in infancy. We gleaned middle names as we found them in passing. Saul was also known as Samuel. Nuriel was also known as Norman. In 1851, Emilia was also known as Emma, and yes, she really did have a sister named Emily!

8   The name Emilia means 'industrious' (Dynes, 1984).

9   At the time, lilac on cotton was 'done by only one house in the United Kingdom and they get any price they wish for it' (Garfield, 2000, p. 38).

10 The story of the prescient visitor was told by Watson (1910, p. 3). If this story sounds familiar, perhaps you are remembering the meeting of Samuel and David in 1 Samuel 16:12.

11 For definitions of Hebrew terms in italics, such as *bar mitzvah*, see the Glossary in the novel.

12 Thomas Babington Macaulay (1800–1859) was a British poet, historian and politician who wrote several volumes of critical, historical and miscellaneous essays. In her interview by *The Nelson Evening Mail* (see page 62), Emilia states that she owed her elocutionary powers 'to the loving patient teaching' of her mother who was 'an exceedingly clever women, a wonderful linguist, and a beautiful reader … passionately fond of Shakespeare and Macaulay's essays'.

13 Rachel Aronson and Dora and Alexander Lazarus are fictional. The Aronson's had a family doctor whose name wasn't Dr Maurice Isaacs.

14 The Aronson family doctor did require Emilia to stay home from school. Her siblings all received Continental educations (Watson, 1910, p. 4).

Chapter 2. Bangor, 1855 to 1863

15 'Mrs. Baeyertz has often been heard to say that 1 Corinthians 1:27 is especially applicable to her—"God hath chosen the foolish things of the world to confound the wise; and God hath chosen the weak things of the world, to confound the things that are mighty" (Watson, 1910, p. 4).'

Chapter 3. Bangor, March 1863

16 Sydney Watson (1894/1895, p. 6) hints that the engagement fell in the year before her departure for Melbourne in 1864 and that the ball was 'nearly ten years' before 1871. Débutantes were usually a few years younger than twenty but Emilia had been sickly.

17 A landau is a kind of elegant carriage. The roof can be removed to display the passengers.

18 Watson (1894/1895, p. 13) talks of Emilia's 'married sister who had been [in Australia] for several years'. The registration (Births Deaths Marriages Victoria) of the birth of Eliza's daughter, Amy Berens, in October 1862 reveals that Eliza left Bangor for St Kilda after her marriage to Abraham in May 1861 and that Abraham was born in Posen, Prussia, now Poznań, Poland.

Chapter 4. Bangor, March 1863

19 We don't know the real name of Robert Newfield. Watson (1910, p. 9) refers to him discretely as 'Mr R——'

Chapter 5. Bangor, 1863

20 For *Second Seder*, see Glossary.

Chapter 6. Bangor, 16 Nisan 5623

21 16 Nisan in Anno Mundi 5623 began at sunset on 4 April in Anno Domini 1863.

22 For *matzot, charoseth, ma'ariv, yarmulke, haggadah* and *afikoman* see the Glossary. Emilia described this meal in her lecture 'The Jewish Passover' (see page 121).

23 Benjamin Disraeli (1804–1881) was a British author and Member of Parliament who would later become Prime Minister. The statements by

Disraeli in this chapter are fictional and based on the research of Christopher Hibbert (1978). Benjamin dropped the apostrophe from his father's surname, D'Israeli.

24 Disraeli, in his novel *Sybil* (1845, book 2, ch. 12), has Mr Lys ask, 'Was Moses then not a churchman? And Aaron, was he not a high priest? Ay! greater than any pope or prelate, whether he be at Rome or at Lambeth. In all these church discussions, we are apt to forget that the second Testament is avowedly only a supplement. Jehovah-Jesus came to complete the "law and the prophets". Christianity is completed Judaism, or it is nothing. Christianity is incomprehensible without Judaism, as Judaism is incomplete; without Christianity. What has Rome to do with its completion ... ? No; the order of our priesthood comes directly from Jehovah; ... The authenticity of the second Testament depends upon its congruity with the first ... '

Chapter 8. Bangor, 1863

25 The Sitting for Joy ceremony is referred to by Watson (1910, pp. 7–8).

26 *Chuppa*—see Glossary.

Chapters 9 & 10. Bangor, Wales and London, England, 1863

27 From Watson (1910, p. 7) we know that John Aronson required all his future sons-in-law to insure their lives. Just prior to the wedding, Emilia's fiancé was found to be in the last stages of tuberculosis. The wedding plans were cancelled. Emilia experienced a breakdown. Her fiancé left for the French Riviera where he died soon afterwards.

28 A hansom cab is a cabriolet designed by Joseph Hansom to be a vehicle for hire with a single horse, axle and driver and covered seating for two passengers.

Part 2

Chapter 11. At sea, February 1864

29 Emilia's dreams are entirely fictional and written by Betty. They are supposed to be from Emilia's memory; she could have encountered all those Scriptures previously within the Jewish community or in discussion with Robert.

30 'Behold, the Lord's hand is not shortened ... ' is from Isaiah 59:1–3.
31 The farewell blessing by John Aronson is described by Emilia in her short testimony (Baeyertz E. L., *From Darkness to Light*, 1875). The 'angel that redeemed (*goel*) us from all evil' is ultimately God (Genesis 48:15–16). For the Aaronic Blessing in its context, see Numbers 6.
32 Thornvalley is fictional as are the new characters in this chapter including Miss Nancy Wait. Nancy was created by Betty to give Emilia a correspondent and a way to meet Charlie Baeyertz.

Chapter 12. At sea, February 1864

33 Emilia Aronson, George Aronson, Louis Monash and Bertha Monash voyaged on *Empire of Peace*, a White Star Line clipper ship of 1,540 tons, which left Liverpool on 8 February 1864. Lewis and Bertha would later have a son who became famous as the civil engineer General Sir John Monash GCMG KCB VD (1865–1931) (Serle, 1982).
34 *Tanakh* is a name for the Hebrew Bible that is derived from the initials of its three parts, *Torah* (Teaching), *Nevi'im* (Prophets) and *Ketuvim* (Writings). These are the same three divisions that Jesus referred to in Luke 24:44, " ... all things must be fulfilled, which were written in the law of Moses, and in the prophets, and in the psalms, concerning me". In the Christian Bible, the books of the Tanakh have been merged, divided, renamed, sorted and supplemented.
35 Jeremiah 31:31–34 reads 'Behold, the days come, saith the Lord, that I will make a new covenant with the house of Israel, and with the house of Judah: Not according to the covenant that I made with their fathers in the day that I took them by the hand to bring them out of the land of Egypt; which my covenant they brake, although I was an husband unto them, saith the Lord: But this shall be the covenant that I will make with the house of Israel; After those days, saith the Lord, I will put my law in their inward parts, and write it in their hearts; and will be their God, and they shall be my people. And they shall teach no more every man his neighbour, and every man his brother, saying, Know the Lord: for they shall all know me, from the least of them unto the greatest of them, saith the Lord: for I will forgive their iniquity, and I will remember their sin no more.'

36 See also Psalm 103:2–4, Ruth and 1 Corinthians 6:11 & 20.
37 For *Pidyon haBen* and *goel*, see Glossary.
38 The Blackland family is fictional.

Chapter 13. At sea, February 1864

39 The *Lady Leonore* and the Misses Gantry are fictional.

Part 3

Chapters 15–17. Sandridge, St Kilda and Melbourne, Victoria, 5 and 6 June 1864

40 Sandridge was an early name for Port Melbourne.
41 *Empire of Peace* arrived at Sandridge on 5 June. A copy of the passenger list is in the Victorian Immigration Museum. *The Argus* records eleven first-class passengers, including the Aronsons and Monashes, 259 other passengers in the intermediate and steerage classes and none of the crew.
42 A waggonette is drawn by one or two horses and has seats for six passengers. They were readily available for hire.
43 Emilia's sister lived in St Kilda somewhere near the beach (Watson, 1910). The Aronson, Berens and Monash families are the only characters in these chapters that are not fictional.
44 The first railway line in Victoria opened in 1854 from Melbourne Terminus on Flinders Street to Sandridge; the second line, to St Kilda, opened in 1857. By 1864, from Prince's Bridge Station, on the eastern side of the bridge, you could catch a train to Swan Street (Richmond) and thence south through Elsternwick to (Brighton) Beach or east to Hawthorn (Watson & Johnson, 1994).

Chapter 18. Melbourne, late July 1864

45 *The Ugly Duckling* story by Hans Christian Andersen was first published in 1843. Sir James McCulloch and George Higinbotham were local politicians. The Vogel family is fictional.

Chapter 19. St Kilda, August 1864

46 Dr Ledler, his shop and Tarryever are fictional. Laudanum is a tincture of opium in alcohol that was then a popular treatment for pain. We don't

know what George did during his early years in Melbourne or when he returned Home to Bangor.

47   Abraham Berens had worked with David Rosenthal in Melbourne until 1859 (Dwyer, 2008, p. 2). For Rosenthal's business, see Chapter 57.

Chapter 22. Melbourne, August 1864

48   Prior to the *Married Women's Property Act 1870*, a married woman could not hold property in her own name. Single women like Nancy and Emilia could.

Chapter 23. St Kilda, January 1865

49   '[Charlie] was a true Christian, having been converted at his confirmation. He was a churchman, and he remained a churchman all his life, but was spared the folly of supposing that his baptism as an infant, and later still his confirmation, could in any sense alone entitle him to the glorious name and experience of a child of God' (Watson, 1910, p. 15). Charlie was known as Mr Bayertz, Mr Baeyertz, Charles, Chas. or Charles, jun., in formal documents and newspapers. Watson (1910, p. 46f) has Emilia call him Charlie so we went with that so you can tell him apart from all the others named Charles.

Chapter 25. St Kilda, February 1865

50   Charles Baeyertz, sen., was born around 1806. His father, Peter Baeyertz, gentleman, married his mother Elizabeth Tanner in London. Mary Anne, who married Charles, was born in Spain to Cornishman John Treleaven. Her mother's maiden name was Roscorlitz (Woods, 2008, p. 14).

51   Charles is the right age to be the Charles Baeyertz who was a witness for the notorious 4th Earl of Mornington in one of his many legal battles in England. This Charles lived with his married sister from the age of ten and became her husband's law clerk till Charles left the firm at the age of twenty-two (Wellesley, 1830).

52   After serving in the Royal Navy and as Private Secretary to a Governor in the West Indies, in 1852 Charles Baeyertz, sen., migrated to Melbourne during the height of the gold rush with his wife Mary Anne, daughter

Suzette and son Charlie (Watson, 1910; Woods, 2008). Their second son John was born after they arrived.

53   *The Argus* of 27 February 1862 carried this announcement: 'MARRIAGE. GIBBS—BAEYERTZ.—On the 26th inst., at Christ Church, St. Kilda, by the Rev. J. H. Gregory, Richard Berkett Gibbs, Ballarat, to Suzette Laura, daughter of Chas. Baeyertz, St. Kilda.' Christ Church is on Acland Street.

54   The Gibbs family appears to have lived in Ballarat where they had three children. Charlie and Suzette's thirteen-year-old brother John appears to be the Baeyertz who topped his class at Ballarat College (*The Ballarat Star*, 11 July 1868). Suzette's children were buried in the St Kilda Cemetery by 1867 to be joined by Richard in 1873 at the age of 44 (Batt). Woods (p. 25) suggests that Richard was wealthy and that Suzette later remarried.

55   The Baeyertz family lived in St Kilda as early as 1856 when Charlie was winning prizes at Mr C. A. Goslett's Collegiate School. The church, beach, pier and sea baths are nearby.

56   Charles Baeyertz, sen., was appointed Warehouse Keeper (reporting only to the Collector) at Customs House on 28 June 1850. By 1 February 1856, his annual salary had risen from £500 to £700. (Statistics Vic 1857, 1858–9, p. 54). Customs House is on the Birrarung (or Yarra Yarra River) close to the turning basin where Captain Lancey landed the schooner *Enterprize* in 1835 with John Pascoe Fawkner's settlers at John Batman's 'place for a future village'.

Chapters 29 & 30. St Kilda, November 1865

57   The National Bank of Australasia announced in *The Argus* on 18 October 1865 that their new branch at 231 Bridge Road in Richmond, Victoria had been opened under the management of Mr Charles Baeyertz. The building survived intact as a shop until 2013 when a block of flats was built in the garden.

58   Our extract from the marriage register on page 12 shows that the date of the wedding was 16 November 1865. *The Argus* carried this announcement under MARRIAGES on the following day: 'BAEYERTZ— ARONSON.—On the 16th inst, at Christ Church, Hawthorn, by the Rev.

W. Wood, B. A., Charles Baeyertz, jun., of Richmond, to Emilia, third daughter of John Aronson, Esq., Bangor, North Wales.'

59 'They were married by the Rev. [William] Wood, B. A., at Christ Church, Hawthorn, and having no friends of their own there, the clergyman's gardener and maidservant were called in to affix their signatures to the marriage certificate. Mr. Wood has said since that though he did not know it at the time, he did one of the best day's work of his life on that October morning' (Watson, 1910, p. 21). In those days, parish priests of the established Church of England, unlike other ministers, were pretty much obliged to conduct weddings when asked and the register records that Charlie was living in the Hawthorn parish.

60 Sydney Watson somehow reported the date of the wedding as 16 *October*, which later misled both Robert Evans and Joanna Woods.

61 The foundation stone of the church had recently been laid and bridges carrying the road and railway from Richmond now spanned the Yarra River. At that time, the Parish of Christ Church Hawthorn stretched from those bridges to far up the valley into the mountains.

62 Eliza's preference for putting Emilia on a homeward-bound ship is reported by Watson (1910, p. 16).

Chapter 31. Richmond, Victoria, November 1865

63 For *Sit shiva,* see Glossary.

Chapter 32. Bangor, February 1866

64 'Observant Jews could not hold to the 613 rules of dress, diet, hygiene and worship if they tried to live outside their own closed community; and intermarriage was strictly forbidden. Since Judaic law taught that Jewishness was biologically inherited in the maternal line, Jewish women were jealously protected. A girl who dared to marry out could expect to be disowned by her family and ritually pronounced dead' (Davies, 1997, p. 843).

65 'Emilia's mother, while she wept with sorrow at her child's awful sin (as she conceived it to be), yet let all the stirrings of her mother-love go out to the erring one, and forgave her freely. She wrote to Mrs. Baeyertz to this effect. When this letter reached her, and she recognised her

mother's well-known handwriting on the envelope, she handled it for some moments with fear and trembling. Turning it over to break the seal her heart gave great leap of joy as she saw inscribed in one corner, in the handwriting of her favourite brother—"George's love"' (Watson, 1894/1895, p. 25).

Part 4

Chapter 33. Colac, Victoria, 1867

66 The map of pertinent features of Colac was created by Garth Coverdale.
67 For Charlie's boats, see the note for Chapters 40–42.
68 Charles Nalder Baeyertz was born above the National Bank, Richmond on 15 December 1866 (Birth notices of *The Argus* on the 17th inst.).
69 Colac is about one hundred miles southwest of Melbourne and fifty miles west of the port of Geelong (Woods, 2008, p. 16). The nearest synagogue was in Geelong. There would be no railway for Colac until 1877 (*Colac: A Short History*, 1995, p. 10).
70 Charlie was the second manager of the only bank in Colac, the National Bank of Australasia (Hebb, 1888, p. 340).
71 Marion Cecilia Baeyertz was born at their home above the bank on 18 March 1869 (Birth notices of *The Argus*, 29th inst.). Marion was Eliza's middle name.
72 The Colac bank seems to have been established in 1864. Within a year, the branch moved into a purpose-built 'large two story brick building' at 26 Murray Street which 'at the time was considered quite an architectural adornment to the town' (Hebb, 1888) (see page 11). There the bank operated until 1885 when it was replaced by the 'present elegant and beautiful structure' on the same site. The current owners report that the name of the bank can just be seen above the doorway, there are two large ground floor rooms which were built for servants, the outside toilet block may belong to the original building and the original lot had a frontage of 66 feet and depth of 330 feet to the next street.
73 In time, a new National Bank branch was built on a street corner nearby and the old building was sold. Murray St is still the main street of Colac and is also known as the Princes Highway.

74 Joanna Woods (2008, p. 17) tells us that Charlie 'distinguished himself by burying the duplicate keys of the bank's main safe, because he did not want them in his house, then forgetting where they were interred' (*Colac Herald*, 23 June 1982).

75 Woods (p. 21) also tells us of George's wedding present of a white clock—appropriate for a family of jewellers.

76 Foxes were introduced for hunting in the preceding decades. Their rapid propagation followed that of the rabbit, introduced to Australia by Thomas Austin in October 1859 at Barwon Park near Winchelsea, twenty-four miles to the east of Colac.

Chapter 34. Colac, 1869

77 Emilia's account of Charlie praying for her is described by Watson (1910, p. 42).

78 The names 'Jesus' and 'Emmanuel', are described in Matthew 1:2–23.

79 Marion and Emilia would have been christened (Watson, 1910) in the Colac Temperance Hall where the Church of England had been meeting since April 1864. The first Vicar was Rev. Mr Thomas Sabine (Hebb, 1930).

Chapter 35. Colac, 1869

80 The silver tea and coffee service is described by Watson (1894/1895, p. 32).

81 'Speaking of this friend whom she asked to fill up the confirmation papers, Mrs. Baeyertz says: "After hearing nothing of her for over twenty years, she sent up her card to me on the platform of a meeting in London, only a few months ago, and on the card was written 'Mrs S——of the old Colac days'" (Watson, 1894/1895, p. 31)'.

82 The beginning of the Creed reported by Watson (1894/1895, p. 31) matches the current text of The Apostle's Creed in 'The Order for Morning Prayer'. The Creed in 'The Order for the Administration of the Lord's Supper or Holy Communion' is different (*Book of Common Prayer*, 1662/2015). Extracts from *The Book of Common Prayer*, the rights in which are vested in the Crown, are reproduced by permission of the Crown's patentee, Cambridge University Press.

Chapter 36. Colac, 25 February 1871

83 Tenders for the construction of a Church of England building in Colac were called in April 1869. The Church of St John the Evangelist opened on 8 May 1870. The name of St John the Baptist was added to their church in 1891, when they replaced the first building with the present one (Hebb, 1930).

84 The choir leader at the opening of St John's was the young Godfrey Blunden. The singing was 'above that of most country churches ... both effective and pleasing'. The first organist, until he retired in 1874, was R. C. Blunden (Hebb, 1930; Smith, 2010).

85 Sydney Watson refers to 'those old words' of *O Paradise* by Frederick W. Faber. They might have been old to him in 1894 but these events take place in 1871. That was only three years after the hymn set to Dr Dyke's popular tune was included in the Appendix to *Hymns Ancient and Modern*, only nine years after the hymns first publication (Julian, 1907) and seventeen years after it was written (*The Hymn Book*, 1909, p. 841).

86 Charles Baeyertz, sen., had retired from his post in Melbourne as Warehouse Keeper with a pension of £279/3/4 per year from 1 August 1867 (*Gippsland Times*, 16 July 1867). He and Mary Anne had come to live near Charlie and Emilia at a house on a farm called 'Nerennin', one and a half miles from the National Bank in Colac (Watson, 1894/1895, p. 36).

87 The name of the farm has been spelt 'Nerennin', 'Nerinnin', 'Nerinen' and 'Nerrenin'.

88 This advertisement appeared in *Colac Herald* of 25 December 1888 and 4 January 1889: 'TO LET FOR ONE YEAR. 58 ACRES SUPERIOR GRAZING LAND known as Nerinnin or Stodarts Point Paddock. Full particulars may be obtained from H. M. HEARN, Auctioneer, Colac.'

89 Stodarts Point overlooks Lake Colac. The point has been known as 'Ross Point' or 'Ross's Point' since 1892 when Alexander Ross replaced the original farmstead with his large house 'Balnagowan' (*Colac: A Short History*, 1995). The remainder of the farm has since been subdivided into house blocks.

90 The events on the lake are described by Sydney Watson (1894/1895, pp. 37–38).

NOTES ON *THIS IS MY BELOVED* 175

91 Prince Alfred (1844–1900), Duke of Edinburgh and a son of Queen Victoria, was the first member of the British royal family to visit Australia. His visit to Colac was cut short so he could extend his visit to Barwon Park, where, by December 1867, the rabbits were now so plentiful that the Duke could claim 416 of over 1000 shot in three hours. He returned in February for more. (*A Brief History of Colac*; National Trust). Charlie's 'dogs were so perfectly trained that they were specially selected for, and used by, Prince Alfred, when his Royal Highness visited the locality' (Watson, 1894/1895, p. 29).

92 Emilia wrote of her nervousness around horses (Reed, c. 1881, p. 239). We don't know the names of any of their horses or dogs, so we made up 'Banjo' for Charlie's favourite dog and 'Nimrod', from Genesis 10, for his favourite horse. By 1871, horse prices had tumbled. One could purchase a top four-year-old saddle horse for £6 or hire a hansom cab for 2/- (Carruthers, 2008, p. 30f).

Chapters 37 & 38. Colac, 4 March 1871

93 Thanks mostly to the *Australian Medical Pioneers Index* (Due), we know a little about Dr Rae and Dr Reid. They both migrated from England in 1859 and in 1871 were both about 38 years old.

94 In the year of Dr Thomas P. Rae's arrival, Dr H. E. Nankivell of 'Mooringarara' in Wallace Street, Colac, died and Dr Rae continued the practice (*Colac: A Short History*, 1995). By 1875, Dr Rae, and his new business partner, Dr John Blunden, father of Godfrey the musician, had moved into 'Nerinen' (Smith, 2010). In 1879, Dr Rae moved to Kerang, Victoria, and died at the age of 44.

95 Within a year of his arrival in Australia, Dr David Boswell Reid, jun., became one of the first players for Geelong, one of the oldest football clubs in the world (Walker, 1958, pp. 20, 51). During 1871, Dr Reid was Resident Surgeon at Geelong Infirmary and his villa, Belleville, was built. About 1891, Boswell returned to England where his father, Dr David Boswell Reid, sen., had famously promoted the ventilation of buildings.

Chapter 39. Colac, 5 to 9 March 1871

96 The death of Charlie Baeyertz was reported by *Geelong Advertiser* on Monday 6 March 1871, *Colac Herald* on 7 March (see page 13), and *Colac Observer* on 10 March.

97 The *Advertiser* mentions the chloroform. The *Herald* also reports the magisterial enquiry and that a buggy owned by Charles Baeyertz, sen., capsized near the brewery while being driven by a lad. Sydney Watson (1894/1895) transcribes the *Observer* article which describes the funeral. A local historian, Dawn Peel, has considered these accounts in a wider context (Death and Community in a Colonial Settlement, 2002)

98 There is no mention of Suzette or John at their brother's funeral. We assume that Ballarat and Melbourne were too far away for them to be notified and then to come by coach within two days.

99 In 2012, Amanda and Garth Coverdale visited Colac cemetery. We found Charles at plot C/E 518, which is enclosed by a unique iron chain and has the oldest memorial we saw. See the photo on page 108. Set into a concrete pedestal under a veiled urn is a white marble plaque which states 'SACRED TO THE MEMORY OF CHARLES BAYERTZ LATE MANAGER OF THE NATIONAL BANK OF AUSTRALASIA COLAC. DIED MARCH 6th 1871 AGED 28 YEARS. UNTIL THE DAY BREAK AND THE SHADOWS FLEE AWAY.' Attached to the foundation of the pedestal is another marble notice that reads: 'THIS MONUMENT IS ERECTED BY MANY FRIENDS TO MARK THEIR ESTEEM FOR HIS MEMORY.'

100 'Until the day break and the shadows flee away' is from Song of Solomon 2:17 and 4:6.

101 The spelling on the gravestone is 'Bayertz'. Isaac Hebb adopted the same spelling for his history of Colac in 1888. Charles Nalder Baeyertz would later sue a publisher for libel during the Great War, arguing that 'Bayertz' implies German ancestry whereas 'Baeyertz' implies Belgian (*The Advertiser*, 23 March 1915). After following the Baeyertz family trees and querying surname distribution at forebears.io/surnames, we think it's likely that everyone born today with the surname Bayertz has recent German ancestry and that those born a Baeyertz are descended from Charles Baeyertz, sen. His parents at least were English (Woods, 2008,

p. 14). Charles N. spoke fluent German and his maternal grandparents probably did too.

102 'One keen-eyed woman who watched the face of the poor tried tempted widow at this time, saw in it an expression that warned her of something of what was passing in her mind. This woman was so troubled by the expression she had seen in Mrs. Baeyertz's face that she could not rest, and later on followed the heart-stricken woman to her home, whither she had gone. Finding the door of her room unlocked, she went in, and found her lying upon the bed where he had died, with a bottle of laudanum in her hand. It was thus that God defeated Satan's plot, and gave the poor tempted one deliverance (Watson, 1910, p. 45).'

103 Emilia described her condoler in her address 'Tears' (Baeyertz E. L., *Six New Addresses*, 1904).

Chapters 40 to 42. Colac, Autumn and Winter 1871

104 Emilia would tell the story of these days of transformation again and again at her missions. Many times her tale was recorded, each time with different detail and emphasis that may reveal changes in her thinking and her memory as well as the different world views of the note-takers. The main sources for our synthesis in these chapters have been her testimony written in the year of her baptism at Aberdeen Street Baptist Church (Baeyertz E. L., 1875), reports of her return to Colac (Izaak, 1885), her version retold by Sydney Watson (1894/1895), her address to the next generation at Aberdeen Street (*Geelong Advertiser*, 11 April 1905), and our imagination where needed.

105 Emilia told Sydney Watson that Charlie's 'boats were the first that sailed upon the beautiful waters of Lake Colac' (Watson, 1894/1895, p. 29). Charlie could easily have built one or more boats after he arrived in 1867, before Mr Shattock placed his pleasure boats on Lake Colac in 1870. The Rowing Club formed in 1871. The Yacht Club formed in 1886 (*Colac: A Short History*, 1995). The Gulidjan Balug people, who had lived by the lake for countless generations, would have built their own water craft.

106 Now they could assemble a minyan (or quorum) of ten, the St Kilda Shule could hold its first meeting of members in September 1871, after two years of planning (www.stkildashule.org).

107 Page 3 of *The Argus* of 17 November 1871 includes a notice of application to the County Court for a rule granting administration of freehold land in the Estate of Charles Baeyertz the Younger to 'Emilie Louisa Baeyertz'.

108 The circumstantial evidence of an insurance policy on Charlie's life is compelling: Emilia lived without an obvious source of income for some years, her husband had been a banker, she had seen what had happened to Robert Newfield and her father was John Aronson!

109 '... had ye believed Moses, ye would have believed me: for he wrote of me.' John 5:46.

110 Robert Calvert owned Pirron Yallock Station eight miles west of Colac (*The Pastoral Review*, 16 April 1915 cited in oa.anu.edu.au/obituary/calvert-robert-188).

111 Charles, sen., and Mary Anne Baeyertz continued to participate in the life of the Colac district after Emilia and their grandchildren moved to Geelong. From the *Geelong Advertiser* of 22 October 1868, 8 July 1869 and 28 April 1874 we learn that Charles performed funny songs while fundraising for a library and a cricket club.

112 Suzie Zada maintains the enormous *Geelong & District and Bellarine Peninsula history web site*. A search in the databases for the names Baeyertz and Bayertz found matches in records of baptisms, burials, wills, rates, reports and books.

Chapters 43 to 46. Geelong, Victoria, 1871 to 1873

113 For background to life in Geelong at this time we refer to works by Catherine Bishop (2011), Geoffrey Blainey (2003), Davison, McCarty, & McLeary (1987) and Zada. Alison Bashford (1994) wrote about the roles of women in hospitals and Walter & Cox wrote about Geelong Infirmary. Stephen Due's *Australian Medical Pioneers Index* of doctors to 1875 was first digitized in Geelong.

114 These chapters draw from Watson and from Emilia's lectures 'The Great White Throne' and 'Holiness' (*Three Lectures*, 1890), 'The Clean Heart' (*Five Lectures*, 1891), 'The Baptism of the Holy Ghost' (*Twelve Addresses*, 1897), and 'Impossible to Renew' (*Six New Addresses*, 1904). The Bible

references are from Ezekiel 36, Mark 11, John 3, 11 and 16, 1 Thessalonians and Titus. Mrs Simpson, Bob and Violet are fictional.

115 According to the *North Melbourne Advertiser* of 29 February 1884, Pastor Wm. Christopher Bunning was called to the West Melbourne Baptist Church after 'more than eleven years' of ministry in Geelong. Chris Bunning was therefore at Aberdeen Street Baptist Church from about 1872. He experienced Emilia's early ministry in Geelong, became a good friend and baptised her by immersion in about 1875. Even so, Emilia always remained a member of the Church of England (Watson, 1910, p. 57). Whichever church she attended whilst in Geelong, it must have provided sound biblical teaching.

116 See page 113 for a paper that Emilia may have written for a conference at St Mary's Church of England in Caulfield in July 1874.

117 At this same conference, Henry Cooke (1874) spoke on the subject of 'Melbourne, as a field for Mission Work' wherein he called for 'a band of Christian ladies' to visit 'fallen and friendless' women. Within three weeks such a band of fifteen ladies was formed, in the first instance under the guidance of Cook and Dr John Singleton. This became an unsectarian and independent body called the Association of Female Workers for Melbourne and its Suburbs (AFWMS).

118 This Henry Cooke and the co-founder of *The Age* newspaper may be one and the same. Dr John Singleton established (with others) the Collingwood Free Medical Dispensary with bookshop, coffee shop and gymnasium, the Melbourne Children's Hospital, the Society for Promoting Morality, a Temporary Home for Fallen Women, the Prisoners' Aid Society, a Men's Model Lodging House, the Society for Prevention of Cruelty to Animals, and the Little Bourke Street Mission Hall in which Emilia would often speak in the following years (Watson, 1910, p. 63f; Prescott, 1994).

Chapter 47. Geelong, August 1876

119 The photo of young Charles Nalder Baeyertz taken at Turner's Rooms in Geelong on 16 February 1872, has been reproduced by Joanna Woods (2008, p. 48) along with photos of his mother, future wife Bella and

his grandfather Charles. We haven't discovered any images of Emilia's husband Charlie or daughter Marion.

120 The *Education Act of 1872* made school compulsory from the ages of six to fifteen for both boys and girls from January 1873. The new government-funded schools were free, secular and available for all children. Parents could still opt for private or denominational education.

121 Wesley College was established as a Methodist School in 1866 and operates on the same St Kilda Road campus to this day. Charles was a day boarder which means that he lived in private accommodation nearby. Suzette Gibbs may have been living in Ballarat and paying for his schooling or boarding (Woods, 2008, pp. 21, 25).

Chapter 48. Geelong, January 1877

122 Hussey Burgh Macartney, sen., sailed to Melbourne in 1847 with Charles Perry, the first Bishop of Melbourne in the Church of England. Hussey, sen., served God faithfully as the first Dean of Melbourne from 1852 to his death in 1894 (Robin, 1974).

123 Emilia was invited to Caulfield by one of the Dean's children, Rev. Mr Hussey Burgh Macartney, jun. As vicar of St. Mary's Church of England, from 1868 to 1898, Hussey, 'an ardent supporter of mission work', convened conferences in 1874 and 1875, and helped found the Church Missionary Association of Victoria (now CMS Vic) and the Evangelisation Society of Australasia (ESA), supported the Young Men's and Young Women's Christian Associations (YMCA & YWCA), Lighthouse Mission, Temperance Union and Bible Society and established new churches at East Malvern and Elsternwick (Cole, 1994). He published *The Missionary at Home and Abroad*, a monthly journal. Hussey, jun. died in 1908.

124 Some of Emilia's reflections in this chapter are from her lecture 'The Clean Heart' (Baeyertz E. L., *Three Lectures*, 1890).

Part 5

Chapter 49 to 51. Caulfield, Victoria, February to March 1877

125 The account of Marion's scarlet fever is from Watson (1894/1895, p. 59). Mrs Porter and Dr Bernard are fictional names.

126 Emily and Hussey Macartney had a daughter, Jane, and a son, Hussey (Lundy, p. 50261). The life of that son, Lieutenant Hussey Burgh George Macartney of the Royal Fusiliers, and his recovery from brain injury, deserves to be told—by a neurologist (*The Argus*).

127 St Kilda, Caulfield and their surrounding suburbs were then, and are now, home to many Jewish people. H. B. Macartney, jun., originally invited Emilia to Caulfield to minister to that community but she soon withdrew in the face of their strong opposition (Watson, 1910, p. 58).

Chapter 52. Melbourne, Early April 1877

128 Mrs Weinbeck is based on 'Mrs H——' as described by Watson (1910, p. 62).

129 *This Is My Beloved* is the story of a preacher who self-published at least twenty of her most popular addresses. so we have included some of her preaching in the novel, as well as in this *Companion*. This chapter draws from her address, 'Worry' (Baeyertz E. L., *Twelve Addresses*, 1904). Biblical passages referred to include Philippians 4:6, 1 Peter 5:7, Luke 12:7, 1 Corinthians 7:32, 1 John 1:9, Isaiah 66:13, 1 Peter 1:7, Genesis 21, 1 Kings 17, Matthew 14 and John 21.

130 The baize door in factories and large houses marked the boundary beyond which the staff ruled and the public and gentry were normally excluded. The rough woollen baize cloth helped muffle the sound of work behind the door.

131 Beath, Schiess and Co. was one of the clothing manufacturers on Little Flinders Street (now Flinders Lane), that commended Emilia's ministry (Evans, 2007, p. 220). In 1880, the Tailoresses Association of Melbourne (now the Textile, Clothing and Footwear Union of Australia) was formed and then, in December 1882, with the company's support, hundreds of their tailoresses led a widespread strike against pay cuts in the industry. This action soon led to the first major industrial action by women in the British Empire.

Chapter 53. Caulfield, April 1877

132 'We have heard it said that Mrs. Baeyertz, under God, was the first in that glorious city of Melbourne to get the factories opened for regular visitation' (Watson, 1894/1895, p. 62).

133 'The continuing basis of the work and witness of the Young Men's Christian Association is expressed in the *Paris Basis*, as adopted by the delegates of the First World Conference in Paris and reaffirmed by the 6th World Council of YMCAs in 1973: "The Young Men's Christian Associations seek to unite those young men who, regarding Jesus Christ as their God and Saviour, according to the Holy Scriptures, desire to be his disciples in their faith and in their life, and to associate their efforts for the extension of his Kingdom amongst young men. Any differences of opinion on other subjects, however important in themselves, shall not interfere with the harmonious relations of the constituent members and associates of the World Alliance." (Young Men's Christian Association, 1855/1973)'

134 The YWCAs adopted a similar basis to the *Paris Basis*. While the YWCAs and YMCAs had some paid staff such as General Secretaries, most of their work was carried out by their members, who were required to be believers and active members of their churches (Shedd, 1955).

135 The first Australian YWCA Chapter began in Geelong, and then closed in disorganisation, around the time Emilia was living there (Dunn, 1991).

136 Betty, drawing from Watson (1894/1895, p. 63), named 'Miss Thompson', active in 1877, as the first Secretary of the YWCA in Melbourne and Sarah (S. C.) Booth as the second. However, the official YWCA history (Dunn, 1991) has Sarah as the first Secretary, starting in 1883 after encouragement by H. B. Macartney, jun.

137 'Miss Thompson' was Mary Thomson. Sydney Watson got the spelling 'Thompson' from *The Nelson Evening Mail* (see page 62). Mary and Emilia appear to have been part of the AFWMS with Mary leading the association through the transition to join the YWCA, until she decided to marry and move to New Zealand (*150 Years*, 2008; Watson, 1894/1895). The Macartneys invited Sarah Booth to be the General Secretary at the incorporation of the Chapter in 1883 (Dunn, 1991).

138 The YWCA initially rented three rooms in the Protestant Hall in Stephen Street (renamed to Exhibition Street in 1898 and 1963). In 1885, when Mrs Emily Macartney was President and Sarah's sister Lila (E. W.) Booth was General Secretary, they moved to rooms at the Assembly Hall, where they started a library. Emilia conducted their first 'mission' (see page 56), in the YMCA Upper Hall (Dunn, 1991; Durie, 2007; Evans, 2007, pp. 179–183).

139 In 1890, 'Miss Thompson [was] now Mrs Downie Stewart of Otago' (*The Nelson Evening Mail* (see page 62) and *New Zealand Herald*, 2 September 1890). Mrs Stewart invited Mrs. Baeyertz to tour New Zealand beginning with a visit to the Dunedin YWCA. William Downie Stewart, sen., a lawyer, politician and Presbyterian elder of New Zealand (Dickson, 2011), married Mary Thomson at 'Kamesburgh, Brighton, Victoria, the residence of the bride's brother', on 24 February 1881. The celebrant was 'Rev. Mr. Clark, brother-in-law of the bride' (*Illustrated Australian News*, 12 March 1881, p. 62 and *Otago Daily Times*, 25 March 1881, p. 3). Both the Stewart and Thomson families were Scottish. Mary was 'of deep religious conviction and a stern Calvinist type' (Dickson, 2011). Kamesburgh mansion was the residence of William Kerr Thomson who had made his pile from the James McEwan & Co. hardware company and would lose it all in the crash of 1889 (Cannon, 1995, p. 112f).

Chapter 54. Tarryever, Victoria, April 1877

140 Tarryever, Dungower, Nancy, Martin and Tommy are all fictional.

Chapter 55. Melbourne, Early May 1877

141 Elsternwick Railway Station opened in 1859. Caulfield R. S. would not open until 1879 (Watson & Johnson, 1994).

Chapter 56. Melbourne, Early July 1877

142 For the events of this chapter, see Watson (1910, p. 63). The Assembly Hall of the Presbyterian Church of Victoria in Collins Street has since been replaced by a newer building, which we assume is on the same site.

Chapter 57. Melbourne, July 1877

143 William's Creek ran down the middle of Elizabeth Street through the City of Melbourne to the Yarra River. Wooden bridges crossed the creek (Twopenny, 1883/1973). Now the creek is barrelled and unseen until it floods.

144 Of the eleven Aronson children listed in the 1851 and 1861 Bangor censuses, at least five became jewellers, eight moved to Australia and two became religious leaders (Watson, 1910; Dwyer, 2008; Miskhel, 2011; Baruch, 1998; Abrams, 2007; *Australian Cemeteries*, 2010; *Index Search Historical*; SMCT, UK Census; *The Argus*).

145 John and Maria Aronson's eldest son, Lewis, stayed home to run the shop, which moved into 272 High St, Bangor, sometime between 1849 (Garfi, 2006) and 1883 (Abrams, 2007). That three-story building is now a branch of the HSBC Bank.

146 The story of the gold theft is from Dwyer (2008) and *The Argus* (1 & 2 February 1877).

147 Emilia and George followed Eliza to Melbourne. Then Emilia married Charlie and George returned Home to Wales. By 1874, Saul Aronson was in St Kilda, married to a sister of David Rosenthal, and partner in David Rosenthal and Co., a jewellery shop and manufactory at 15 Little Collins St West, Melbourne. Rosenthal sailed with his family to Europe leaving Saul in charge of Rosenthal, Aronson and Co. Their hallmark was the Southern Cross on a swallowtail flag. By 1877, George had returned to take over Rosenthal, Aronson and Co. in Melbourne from Saul who had left to set up a branch in London (Dwyer, 2008; Miskhel, 2011).

148 George married Philippa Solomon. Philippa died soon after their third child was born and is buried in the Hebrew section of St Kilda General Cemetery (Batt).

149 Charles Aronson married Emma Boseley (or Bosely or Bosley) in 1882 (Births Deaths Marriages Victoria). He then died at Prahran, Vic., in the following year and is also buried at St Kilda, in the Church of England section (Batt).

150 Frederick Aronson married Zara Baar in Sydney where she became famous as a writer and feminist (Rutledge, 1979). He established Lazarus and Aronson there—jewellers and importers like his brothers (Miskhel, 2011).

151 Lazarus was the maiden name of Maria Aronson (Woods, 2008). Aveline Lazzarus (sic) was a partner of Lewis in Bangor (Abrams, 2007). We assume, on no other evidence, that Frederick's partner, Maria and Aveline were all members of one Lazarus family. Amanda Coverdale created the characters Alexander and Dora Lazarus.

152 By 1892, the streets of Melbourne had been renumbered. The building previously known as 15 Little Collins Street West became 362 Little Collins Street, its present address. The upper storeys of the current façade may be original. Their postcard announced that Rosenthal, Aronson & Co were not only 'Wholesale and Manufacturing Jewellers' but now also stocked 'China, Glassware, Earthenware, Saddlery, Cutlery, Stationery, Fancy Goods, Watches, Clocks, Pianos, Concertinas, Plated Ware, Tobacconists' Goods, and Storekeepers Sundries of every description' (Miskhel, 2011). Today, 362 Little Collins Street hosts a Flight Centre travel agency.

153 Their brother Norman N. Aronson, also known as Nuriel, owned a similar shop in Launceston, Tasmania (Miskhel, 2011).

154 George and his second wife Charlotte (née Myers) had a son named John Joel Aronson. That family moved to Britain by 1895. John Aronson would later manage the shop in Brisbane.

155 The Bangor Hebrew Congregation (Ashkenazi Orthodox) was founded in 1894. The founders were Emilia's brother Lewis, as President, and father and son Morris and Isidore Wartski, as Treasurer and Secretary (Abrams, 2007). By 1897, the congregation had twenty families and sixteen singles paying for twelve seats. Sometime before 2007, they no longer had a minyan so the assets of the synagogue were stored at the Bangor Art Museum.

156 The Wartskis also founded a jewellery and drapery business that their descendants have made famous by trading in Fabergé eggs.

157 In 1900, George sold up his assets in Melbourne. Frederick came south from Sydney for a couple of years to float Rosenthal, Aronson & Co. for the partners into a public company with capital of £90,000.

158 Reed and Barnes was one of the oldest and most famous architectural partnerships in Melbourne. Before and after they designed the manufactory, they designed many of the grandest buildings in Melbourne including the Independent, Baptist and Scots' churches in Collins St, the Trades and Town Halls, the CBC, ANZ and NSW banks, and the Exhibition Buildings. Their successor today is Bates Smart.

159 Mrs Jones, Lizzie, Nancy and Dr Langmore are fictional characters. The shop, manufactory, picnic, gold theft, Rosenthals, Aronsons, Solomons, Brinkman, Coley and Smith all existed. Walter Walton was an employee of some kind. The picnic was held at Mordialloc (Dwyer, 2008) which in those days meant a journey by ferry across the bay. Rosenthal & Aronson fielded a cricket team for more than picnics; the *South Bourke and Mornington Journal* of 12 March 1890 records an away fixture against Ferntree Gully.

Chapter 58. Caulfield, Late July 1877

160 Charles and Mary Anne Baeyertz lived in their house in Black Street, Brighton, Victoria until their deaths. It was close to the Church Street shops and Middle Brighton Railway Station and they could walk to the church and the beach (Watson and Johnson, 1994). They both died in their house, Charles on 9 July 1879, then Mary Anne on 26 February 1891. Probate on 1 August 1879 was £1020 (Notices in *The Argus* and *Bendigo Advertiser*).

161 Sydney Watson (1910, p. 48) tells us that 'it was Mrs. Baeyertz who God eventually used for the conversion of her dear husband's mother.'

Chapter 59. Caulfield, Spring 1877

162 We don't have the name of the friend (Watson, 1910, p. 64) who sent Emilia a copy of *Our Coffee-Room* (Cotton, c. 1876/1884) so we called him Bob and conflated the man who invited Emilia to the week of prayer for enduement. Bob wasn't the only person who thought the book was

worth passing on. Florence Nightingale, the Nurse Educator, sent a copy to Henry Parkes, the Australian statesman (Dando-Collins, 2014).

163 Elizabeth Reid Cotton was a girls' Sunday School teacher in Dorking, Surrey. There she began teaching boys and then men which led to the establishment of an evangelistic temperance coffee-room (Cotton, 1876, p. 94).

164 The temperance movement called on people to give up the evils of drunkenness and to repent and submit to Christ. They often considered that to do one was to do the other (Howe, 1900; Evans, 2005; Evans, 2007; WCTU).

165 *Our Coffee-Room* had been newly published when Emilia read it in 1877 (see page 27). By 1884, over 15,000 copies had been printed. Cotton followed up with *More About Our Coffee-Room* (1878) and many other books.

166 We don't know the name or location of the Congregational Church in which Emilia first addressed an audience that included men.

Chapter 60. Hobart Town, Tasmania, January 1878

167 'The labourer is worthy of his reward' is from 1 Timothy 5:18.

168 *The Mercury* is still Hobart's daily paper. Most of the details of times and places are from accounts of the missions reproduced by Evans (2007).

169 The Edwards and Harris families are fictional members of the real Association of Christian Workers.

170 Charles Frederick Perrin was born to a Dublin merchant family in 1842. He married his cousin Sarah Deacon in Liverpool in 1866. Together they migrated to Melbourne in 1871 with a commission from the Open Brethren in Dublin, London and Liverpool to establish churches in the colonies of Australia. The Perrins ranged as far as the diggings near Sandhurst in Victoria and Table Cape, Launceston and Scottsdale in Northern Tasmania. Charles attended the 'first' 'conference' of 'believers' in the Australian colonies organised by the Open Brethren at Table Cape in 1873 and presented a paper at the Caulfield conference organised by H. B. Macartney in 1874. Charles Perrin died of consumption the

following year at Forth (at the time, Hamilton-on-Forth) in Tasmania, (Macartney H. B., 1874, July; Perrin, 1878; McDowell, 1994)

171 We assume that the tracts that were handed out here (Evans, 2007, p. 80) contained Emilia's testimony (see page 22) because they were distributed at other missions (*Colac Herald*, 3 April 1885).

Chapter 61. Hobart Town, February to April 1878

172 Thomas Spurgeon arrived in Geelong in August 1877 on doctor's orders to reside in a warm climate, with the intention of plying his trade as an engraver. His father, Charles Haddon Spurgeon, was preaching to crowds of five thousand at his Metropolitan Tabernacle in London. Thomas carried a letter to Pastor Bunning to which his father had added the postscript that Thomas 'could preach a bit'. Thomas spent a few quiet months early in 1878 recovering his health as guest of William and Mary Ann Gibson on their Native Point sheep station in Tasmania. William Gibson had built a Baptist Tabernacle at nearby Perth and Mary Ann would hand copies of C. H. Spurgeon's sermons to anyone interested.

There Thomas got to know Henry Varley and preached a bit. Thomas wrote from Native Point, 'When I see Mr. Varley preaching every day, I almost wish I could do the same, and thus devote my life'. As his health improved, Thomas was called to preach around Australia and New Zealand which he did. Upon the death of his father, in 1892, Thomas returned to London and, in time, assumed the care of his father's Tabernacle (Fullerton, 1919; Skinner, 1999; Rowston, 1994; Ray, n. d.).

173 'Henry Varley was probably the most significant evangelist to visit Australia at that time' (Paproth, 2004). The butcher from Lincolnshire first came to Australia to seek gold. He returned to England where he became an evangelist to pig feeders and was invited by C. H. Spurgeon to address his Tabernacle. After touring Canada, Varley came to Australia, this time to preach to large crowds at the Melbourne Cricket Ground (Evangelistic Services in Melbourne, 1877). He regarded Melbourne as home after 1888 (Lamb M. Y., 1994). His son Frank and at least two of his granddaughters became missionaries.

174 The morning after a prayer meeting in Dublin, Ireland, in 1872, Varley declared to a young American, 'Moody, the world has yet to see what

God will do with a man fully consecrated to him'. Dwight Lyman Moody decided he would be that man. Varley forgot the comment until D. L. Moody reminded him years later when Moody had become the best known evangelist of the age (Pollock, 1963; Gericke, 1978; Fackler, 1990; Paproth, 2004; Anon). Mrs. Baeyertz was compared with Mr Moody throughout her travels in North America and Britain.

175 The Sankey and Moody hymn-book was *Sacred Songs and Solos* compiled by Ira Sankey for use at D. L. Moody's missions. Sankey added more music with each edition. Mrs. Baeyertz included much less singing than was usual at missions.

Chapter 62. Launceston, Tasmania, April 1878

176 *The Examiner* is still Launceston's daily paper. Most of the details of times and places in Tasmania are from accounts of the missions reproduced by Robert Evans (2007). I have included one such account and some Letters to the Editor.

177 Henry Reed, a merchant's apprentice from Doncaster in Yorkshire, sailed to Tasmania in 1827 where he became both a rich merchant and an evangelist (Reed, c. 1881; Fysh, 1967; Fysh, 1973; Ely, 1994; Evans, 2007).

178 The earliest Christian sermons in the settlement that would be named Melbourne were preached in 1835, by Henry Reed 'in the spring' and John Pascoe Fawkner on 18 October (Reed, c. 1881, p. 26; Newnham, 1956; Renshaw, 2014). One person who appears to have attended them all was William Buckley, a Wathaurung man from Cheshire.

The first church service by an ordained minister was held by Rev. Joseph Orton, in April 1836 (Newnham and *The Age No 1 Vol 1* of 17 October 1854). Both Reed and Orton spoke on Batman's Hill. Reed was John Batman's best man, attorney and financier, loaning £3000 to establish the village and 'to devise some means of preserving the natives from destruction'.

During a previous attempt at European settlement, in 1803 at Sorrento near Port Phillip Heads, navy chaplain Rev. Robert Knopwood conducted a baptism, a wedding, church parades, divine services and, on 13 November, the first Christian sermon that we can find in Port

Phillip District. Present at Sorrento were Buckley, then a convict, and Fawkner, then a child (Nepean Historical Society, 1992).

179 After some years making money from land, shipping, sealing, whaling and trading in Tasmania and England, and spending money in England on buildings, gardens and worthy causes such as poor relief, mission and his seventeen children, Reed returned to Tasmania in 1873. In Launceston, he renovated Mount Pleasant into 'the finest house in Northern Tasmania'. That house has since been demolished. He also built Mountain Villa and a brick church on a large property he owned called Wesley Dale (not Wensleydale or Wesley Vale). Now you can go there for a holiday (oldwesleydaleheritage.com).

180 Of Henry Reed's many grandchildren, perhaps the best known are Hudson Fysh, jun., who co-founded QANTAS, John Reed of Heide, who published *Angry Penguins*, and Cynthia Nolan, who was an author, a sister of John Reed and a wife of artist Sidney Nolan.

181 Henry Reed bought an old hotel at 22 Wellington Street, Launceston, as a site for a church building. Emilia spoke in 'Mr Reed's Mission Room' (the hotel's skittle alley) in 1879 and then, in 1881, in the Mission Church building which would be completed by his widow, Margaret, in 1885.

Emilia 'supplied the pulpit' from June to August 1886 and then handed over a congregation of 1800, including 300 professed converts, to their new pastor George Soltau (Evans, 2007). In 1886, their church publication, *The Pioneer*, published several accounts of Emilia's visit, the complete text of her tract and the youthful portrait that graces the cover of this volume (Evans, 2007, pp. 190–193).

182 The church that meets at 22 Wellington Street has been known as the Christian Mission Church, Wellington St Temple, Henry Reed Memorial Church and Gateway Baptist Church.

183 Mrs Reed's memoir (Reed, c. 1881) includes an 'Appreciation of Henry Reed' written by Emilia (see page 43).

184 Emilia and Marion returned to stay with Mrs Reed at Mount Pleasant for more summer missions and holidays over the years, including on their way to New Zealand. Emilia visited again in 1905 on her brief return from Britain.

185 In June 1878, the Rev. Dr Alexander Somerville from Scotland arrived in Tasmania to find 'ground which had been well occupied by others' (*The Mercury*, 6 June 1878, p. 2). He persevered. He had, after all, left behind a barony and forty years of ministry in his Free Church parish to evangelize the English speaking world (Glasgow Story).

Chapter 63. Melbourne, Winter and Spring 1878

186 Throughout her ministry, Emilia almost always arranged to be by the sea during the heat of summer. In Australia, Tasmania was her usual summer seaside destination.

187 This chapter is based on letters published in *Willing Work* (Evans, 2007, pp. 92–93).

Chapter 64. Tasmania and Victoria, Summer to Winter 1879

188 Regattas have been popular in Tasmania since 1831. Regatta Day in Hobart is a public holiday.

189 Mechanics' Institutes provided technical education for working people and often included halls, libraries and schools.

190 The big mining town in Victoria that is now known as Bendigo was first called Bendigo Creek, then Castleton, then Sandhurst from 1853 to 1891. Bendigo Creek was named after Bendigo's Hut in which lived a shepherd and boxer, nicknamed Bendigo after Abednego Thompson, another boxer nicknamed Bendigo. Abednego Thompson was one of three triplets named after the brothers in the book of Daniel.

191 'During the [Sandhurst] mission some Jews sent to the committee, asking whether a box could be reserved for them if they paid the usual fee for the favour. The committee, of course, refused the money, and replied that they would reserve a box for them, on condition that they would *fill it with Jews*. This they did most effectually (Watson, 1910, p. 68; Evans, 2007, pp. 94–106).'

192 The passages Emilia used were from Luke 14–16, Isaiah 53:6, John 1:29 and 36, Matthew 11:28, Genesis 7:1 and Revelation 22:17. The scribes for *Willing Work* (Evans, 2007) paraphrased the Matthew passage.

193 Bendigo Baptist Church (2009) remembers this mission, citing an earlier history, *Until This Time* by Wesley C. Harry.

Chapter 65. Melbourne, Spring 1879

194 The events of this chapter are based on reports in *Willing Work* (Evans, 2007, pp. 107, 109).

Chapter 66. Tasmania and Victoria, Summer to Winter 1880

195 See *Willing Work* (23 July 1880, p. 502); Evans (2007, pp. 109–118); Watson (1894/1895, pp. 69–70).

196 The old Aberdeen St Baptist Church building was built in 1854; the new one, two doors down, was built in 1876. They are both in use today.

197 Ballarat (originally Balla-arat) is another big mining town in Victoria.

198 The Academy of Music is now known as Her Majesty's Theatre, 17 Lydiard Street South, Ballarat (hermaj.com).

Chapter 67. Adelaide, South Australia, Spring 1880

199 The picnic was described in *Truth and Progress* (1 October 1880, p. 120). See page 41 for the letter from the mission committee of the South Australian Baptist Association.

200 'It was while she was conducting meetings in the Adelaide Town Hall that Emilia first experienced a phenomenon that was to take place at least three times during her ministry. So great was the crowd waiting to enter the main hall that when the doors were firmly shut, there were as many outside as there were within. Those on the wrong side of the doors refused to leave. They waited until the meeting had concluded and those needing further help had been counselled, then as the hall emptied, they pushed their way in to take the place of those departing, and filled up the still-warm seats in the body of the hall. Emilia, who was in the counselling area, was informed of the situation, and she returned to the platform to repeat her message to the overflow audience, with the result that a harvest was gathered twice in one night' (Baruch, 1998). See also Watson (1910, p. 72) and Evans (2007, p. 119).

201 Belfast is now known as Port Fairy.

Chapter 69. Melbourne—Early March 1881

202 South Australia was the only Australian colony that was settled entirely by free settlers, who brought with them many different religious traditions. Adelaide soon became known as 'The City of Churches'.

203 Charles Nalder Baeyertz attended T. W. Boehm's school near Adelaide for a short while then settled into Prince Alfred College (also Methodist) for the rest of his formal schooling (Woods, 2008, pp. 24–27). PAC is named after the touring Prince Alfred.

204 C. N. Baeyertz had a 'prodigious memory' so could do his homework on the way to school, recite newspaper columns backwards and memorise dictionaries. Despite, or because of, these talents, Charles was near the bottom of the class at PAC (Woods, 2008).

Part 6

Chapter 71. South Australia, Winter 1881 to 1883

205 Emilia discusses her first men-only meetings in her interview with *The Nelson Evening Mail* (see page 62). One man stimulated to spiritual vitality through her meetings was John J. Virgo who became a leader of the YMCA (Evans, 2007, pp. 51, 115–214).

206 Sydney Watson tells us that Emilia read the news of her father's death in a newspaper. There was such a Death Notice, on the front page of *The Sydney Morning Herald* of 19 January 1882, which would have been placed by Frederick who lived in Sydney at that time.

207 Emilia's travels are chronicled by Sydney Watson (1910) and Evans (2007); the life of Charles Nalder Baeyertz is told by Joanna Woods (2008).

208 The Moonta Mines are described by Flinders Ranges Research (2015).

209 An October 1882 diary entry by James Bickford, a Wesleyan Methodist missionary, reads: 'Dr. Bollen and I called on Mrs. Baeyertz, a converted Jewess, and a successful evangelist, about the proposed services it is desired she should hold in the Semaphore Church. The interview was very pleasant, and I was impressed with her freedom from all foolish airs. She was natural, intelligent, self-possessed, and eminently religious in her whole bearing. We were much pleased with her. (Bickford, 1890)'

210 Mary Colton (1822–1898), the daughter of a boot-maker from London, married John, the son of a vigneron from Devon, in 1844. Together they demonstrated practical Methodist leadership. John went from saddler to chandler, from shopkeeper to manufacturer, from alderman to Premier of South Australia and from apprentice to Knight. He actively supported a hundred Wesleyan churches, the Bible Society, hospitals, Prince Alfred College, temperance and progressive taxes.

Once their ninth child was old enough, Mary was then free to support, start or prosper some twenty-two worthy causes for women such as the Nursing Sisters, Children's Hospital, YWCA and Women's Suffrage League (Parr, 1969; Jones, 2005). The Hundred of Colton on the Eyre Peninsula is named after John. The South Australian electoral district of Colton is named after Mary.

Chapter 72, Melbourne, 1884

211 The Melbourne International Exhibition of 1880 was the first World's Fair in the Southern Hemisphere. Smaller exhibitions were held in 1854 and 1888. The Exhibition Building, which hosts big events and exhibitions to this day, was designed by Joseph Reed of Reed and Barnes, the same firm that designed the Aronson's jewellery manufactory. The only World's Fair in Australia since has been World Expo 88 in Brisbane.

212 The exhibition was open from Monday to Saturday, from 10 a. m. until 6 p. m. Over 32,000 exhibits were displayed in national 'Courts' from Great Britain, France, Germany, India, Japan, China, the United States of America, and all Australian colonies. General admission cost 2/, 1/ or 6d (Museum Victoria).

213 St James' Cathedral was at the corner of Collins and William Streets.

214 The discussion of the music on offer in Melbourne is gleaned from *The Argus* (29 March 1884).

215 Emilia refers to 1 Corinthians 6 and 2 Corinthians 6.

216 Christians have always debated what behaviour and entertainment is and is not allowed. Emilia spelt out what she thought in her final address to the converts at Flinders St Baptist Church in 1881 (Evans, 2007, pp. 38–143f). In 1905, her interviewer for *Table Talk* recorded that

Mrs. Baeyertz 'believes in the religious value of beautiful music' (see page 101).

217 Emilia's statement that 'the great miracle of Christianity is its regenerating power today' was reported by *The Queensland Times* (19 September 1889, p. 2).

Chapter 73. Victoria, Winter 1884 to Summer 1885

218 The Victorian Bethel Union is now known as Mission to Seafarers Victoria.

219 For reports of the Echuca Gospel Temperance Union and the visit of Mrs. Baeyertz, refer to issues of *The Riverine Herald* in October 1884.

220 State Library of Victoria holds a copy of a similar pledge certificate completed in 1884 that is on display at Murray Breweries in Beechworth. On the obverse is the pledge 'I Promise in the Strength of God, Father, Son, and Holy Spirit, to abstain from all kinds of intoxicating liquor as a beverage, and to discourage as much as possible the drinking customs of society', quotes from Isaiah 61:1, John 15:5, Philippians 4:13 and Titus 2:11–12, the printers' name (Mason, Firth & M'Cutcheon) and the initials of a witness. The reverse states 'The work of the Victorian Gospel Total Abstinence Blue Ribbon Mission shall be to grapple with the evils of intemperance on distinctly Christian principles. The Officers and Members of Committee in the Central Organization, and in all the various Branches of the Blue Ribbon Mission, shall, in every instance, be avowedly Christian people. Blue Ribbon Literature Agency: Mr H. Cooke, 24 Swanston St., Melbourne. Single Cards, 3d. each. To Branches, &c., 5s. per 100.' (Blue Ribbon Literature Agency, 1884).

A similar pledge, 'I promise to abstain from all intoxicating drinks except used medically & by order of a medical man & to discountenance the cause & practice of intemperance', was signed by Father Theobald Mathew of Cork in Ireland in 1838 and had been promoted by him and thousands of others in Britain, America and Australia (Mathew, 1838/1885; Frost, 2012).

221 (Charles) Kerr Johnston and his wife Eliza migrated in 1853 from Greenock, Scotland, with six children, to Australia where they added another four (Phillips, 2005).

222 In 1872, Janet Johnston, Kerr and Eliza's youngest daughter, married Daniel Matthews from Cornwall, who had a business provisioning river steamers at the Port of Echuca on the Murray River. In 1874, Daniel and his brother William selected 800 acres at Moira, NSW, just south of Barmah and sixteen miles upriver from Echuca. They allocated twenty of those acres (now known as Maloga Park) for Daniel and Janet to establish the Maloga Mission School, a rare refuge for the dispossessed Yorta Yorta-speaking people of the area. Other Aboriginal people came from as far away as Queensland and Tasmania.

Daniel's advocacy helped form, in 1880, the New South Wales Aborigines Protection Association and, in 1883, Cummeragunja, a second community at a new Aboriginal reserve of 1800 acres abutting Maloga, three miles to the north. In time, to avoid the strict Methodist ways of the Matthews, which included early rising, daily prayer and temperance, the younger leaders took charge of the Association and moved their dwellings, school and kitchen from Maloga to Cummeragunja. Daniel and Janet then left to establish new Aboriginal missions, at first at Beulah House across the river in Victoria, and then downstream near Mannum in South Australia.

The NSW government later took full control of Cummeragunja. In 1939, Government policies led to many of the residents walking off in protest and crossing the river bridge into Victoria (Cato, 1974; Cato, 1976/1993; Coulson, 1979/2009; Fahey, 1988; Phillips, 2005; Franklin, 2014).

223 Charles N. Baeyertz would later write, in a long article for *Otago Witness*, 'My knowledge of [the Australian Aborigines] has been chiefly derived from a visit of some three months' duration paid to the Maloga mission station, ... from visits at various times to the Lake Tyers, Warangesda, and Corranderrk missions' stations, and also from contact with them in their untamed *aboriginality* in the northern areas ... the whole Yorta Yorta language consists of about 400 words.' (Baeyertz C. N., 1891). Of course, there were more words and stories that Charles was never made aware of. The people of Maloga, on the Murray River, Warangesda on the Murrumbidgee River, Lake Tyers in Gippsland and Corranderrk, east of Melbourne, spoke quite different languages.

224 On 21 December 1886, Charles Nalder Baeyertz married Janet's sister, Isabella Delgarno Johnston, at Kew Baptist Church in Victoria. Guests included Charles's aunt Suzette and her husband, Charles's uncle George Aronson and his wife and George's business partner, David Rosenthal (Baeyertz C. N., 1891; Woods, 2008, p. 32).

225 Prayer Unions were introduced from England in the 1880s. From 1884 to 1889, Emilia accepted invitations from strong prayer unions in Australia to conduct missions. When she arrived in England, she spoke at some missions sponsored by strong British prayer unions (Evans, 2005, p. 12; Evans, 2007, pp. 40, 175f).

226 Emilia's mission to Mornington in January 1885 is mentioned in *The Southern Cross* (Evans, 2007, p. 179). The current Mechanics' Institute building was opened at the end of that year.

227 Emilia promoted the cause of the Samaritan Brigade of the Salvation Army with which she volunteered. For example, they visited poor and distressed families, provided a dinner for over a thousand people and appealed for money and blankets in winter (*The Argus* 18, 21?, 23 and 24 and *Colac Herald* 24 June 1887).

Chapter 74. Melbourne, Summer 1889

228 Train and tram details are from maps by Stephen Watson and Ian Johnson (1993; 1994).

229 *I'll go where you want me to go* is a variation of a hymn usually attributed to Mary Brown and Charles Edwin Prior for the words and Carrie Rounsefell for the music.

230 Sydney Watson describes the prayer meeting where Emilia received the call to New Zealand and America and Emilia's mention of her picture of the women of the 'Great Temperance Crusade' (Watson, 1894/1895, pp. 79, 99).

Chapter 75. Victoria and Queensland, Autumn to Spring 1889

231 Sources for this chapter include Watson (1894/1895), Evans (2007), *Alexandra and Yea Standard* (28 October 1892), *The Queensland Times* (19 and 28 September and 1 October 1889) and *The Brisbane Courier* (12, 16, 24 September 1889 and 24 November 1889).

232 One night while Emilia spoke at the Brisbane Opera House, the Courier Hall had its usual Sunday evangelistic meeting. Unfortunately for those at the Hall, their choir was away singing for Emilia so the attendance was down and the collection amounted to only £2/12/1. A gentleman kindly offered to make up any deficiency.

233 Marion did write the words 'home to England' (Watson, 1894/1895, p. 81) even though neither she nor mother had ever lived in that country. The word 'England' was commonly used to refer to England and Wales together and sometimes with other parts of Britain.

234 Jessie Ackermann had been appointed by the World's Woman's Christian Temperance Union (WCTU) as a 'round the world missionary'. In 1891, Miss Ackermann became the inaugural President of the Woman's Christian Temperance Union of Australasia, which was later renamed National Women's Christian Temperance Union of Australia. 'The Pledge' is still the basis of WCTU membership.

Chapter 76. Sydney, New South Wales, October 1889

235 The encounter in Sydney is mostly derived from Sydney Watson (1894/1895, pp. 80–81), *The Illustrated Sydney News* (7 February 1889) and *The Sydney Morning Herald* (19 October 1899 and 21 January 1915).

Chapter 77. Kew, Victoria, November 1889

236 For the account of Emilia praying while prone, see Watson (1894/1895, p. 82). For the family of Charles Nalder Baeyertz, refer to his biography (Woods, 2008).

Chapter 78. Melbourne, December 1889

237 Charles and Bella lived at 3 College Parade, Kew till 1888 when they moved up to 44 College Parade to have their first child. Charles Kerr Johnston Baeyertz, known as Carl, was named Charles Kerr Johnson after his maternal grandfather and Charles after his father, grandfather and great grandfather on the other side (Woods, 2008, pp. 13,32).

238 On 15 December 1889, Charles and Bella had a girl, Maida Estelle Isabel Baeyertz, at Burke St, Hawthorn. They then moved to 'the small house in which Emilia had lived at 9 Studley Park Road, Kew'. Charles was then a tea merchant (Woods, 2008). The Birth Register (Births Deaths

Marriages Victoria) for Maida describes her father as a 'Commercial Traveller'.

239 Miss Lydia Von Finkelstein was born in Jerusalem. With her family, she migrated to New York. As a child, she heard preachers explain the Bible quite wrongly through misunderstanding her culture so, as an adult, she created her 'relentlessly operatic' travelling show, leading a large cast of costumed assistants to illustrate life in Bible times (*The Mercury*, 24 November 1888, *The Argus*, 17 December 1889). Her book is *Jesus Christ in his Homeland* (Mountford, 1911).

240 Matthew Burnett 'told of the wonders of this meeting' and commended Mrs. Baeyertz to New Zealand in *The Southern Cross* (*The Press*, 24 April 1890; Watson, 1910; McHarg, 2005). There is also an unattributed account in Emilia's scrapbook (Evans, 2007, p. 218f). Robert Evans has also written his biography, *Matthew Burnett, The Yorkshire Evangelist* (2010).

241 Beath, Schiess and Co. might have owned the factory mentioned in Chapter 52.

242 The *Circular Letter* signed by the fifteen ministers (Paton, et al., 1899) was reproduced by Watson (1910, pp. 83–84). See page 59.

Epilogue

Tasmania, January 1890

243 An account of the visit to the Sailors' Home in Hobart is in *The Mercury* of 4 February 1890.

New Zealand, Autumn to Spring 1890

244 In 1890, Henry Brett of Auckland printed *Three Lectures Delivered by Mrs Baeyertz*. See pages 121 and 135 for two of these lectures, where 'she wanted no "ranting", shouting, clapping, screaming, and thumping at her meetings, and would have none of it. But instead quiet, order, reverence.' Brett also published the weekly *New Zealand Graphic* which Watson (1910, p. 89) tells us included 'an excellent portrait' of Emilia and allotted 'considerable space to accounts of her work'. As of 2015, NZG had yet to be digitised into PapersPast.

245 Watson (1910), *New Zealand Methodist* and many local papers describe her tour. Evans (2007, pp. 216–238) quotes a few from the C. N. Baeyertz Collection. Other papers are reproduced by PapersPast.

246 A writer in Auckland recorded this of Emilia: 'Her power of describing the unseen world from her own imagination (based, of course, upon Scripture hints), have, perhaps, never been equalled, except by Mrs. Oliphant, in *The Land of Darkness*. Her language is simple, but very expressive, and without being lurid, she infuses plenty of colour into her descriptions. Without unduly pressing on the horrors of hell, she still strongly maintained that there was such a place, and quoted Scripture to prove her point. She closed with a fervid, passionate appeal to the vast audience to see that their names were written in the Book of Life.' (Watson, 1910, pp. 87–88).

247 In the words of Rev. Dr Frost (c. 1890), 'Mrs. Baeyertz, though a sincere Christian, is nevertheless a Jewess and faithful to her people. She believes in the near advent of our Lord and the return of the twelve tribes to the promised land, the conversion of all Israel, and their mission to the Gentiles, and the reign of universal righteousness in the millennial age' (Evans, 2007, p. 240).

In Auckland and California, Emilia often spoke on this theme (Evans, 2007, pp. 226, 230 & 240) which explains why 'at the close of one of her meetings the Jewish Rabbi stepped up to the carriage, and, with his head uncovered, thanked her on behalf of the Jews, whom he represented, for her noble tribute to the nation, and the glorious future awaiting them, and thanking her on their behalf for her visit to Auckland (Watson, 1894/1895, p. 90)'. In 'The Coming of the Lord' (Baeyertz E. L., *Twelve Addresses*, 1904), Emilia refers to the First Zionist Congress held in Basel in 1897.

248 The account of the conclusion of the Auckland mission is from *The New Zealand Herald* of 6 October, p.10. 'She arrived just at a moment when the spirits of men and women were depressed with strikes, turmoil, and conflicts ... there were often 1,000 to 1,500 at the afternoon Bible readings; and ... great were the crowds at night.' (Watson, 1910, p. 88)

249 John MacNeil's note in *The Southern Cross* is reported by Evans (2007, pp. 56, 216). John MacNeil was a local Presbyterian evangelist. He is not

to be confused with another Presbyterian evangelist, John McNeill, who visited Australia from Scotland at around this time.

250 Watson (1894/1895, p. 92f) records that Marion counted seven sea voyages from leaving Victoria to leaving New Zealand and that Emilia exclaimed 'Goodbye dear Australia!' on leaving New Zealand for Hawaii.

In the 1890s, the antipodean colonies were still deliberating how best to federate. The last act of the New Zealand delegation before withdrawing from the constitutional convention was to move that the name of the federation be Australia (meaning South Land) rather than Australasia (meaning South of East Land). The constitution of the Commonwealth of Australia since 1901 contains a standing invitation for New Zealand to join. The National Bank of Australasia did not operate in New Zealand, where there was a separate National Bank of New Zealand.

North America, Fall 1890 to Spring 1892

251 In New Zealand, C. N. Baeyertz put his prodigious talents to work as writer, teacher of elocution, public speaker and commentator, through his magazine *The Triad*, on all manner of public art and entertainment. He described the singer Nellie Melba as both 'brilliant and moving' and 'liquid as a crystal snow-fed brook—and as cold'. He was better than most at football, snooker, chess, whist, organ, piano, writing, reciting, storytelling, shooting and directing concerts. He was a master of English, French, German and Italian languages and could converse in seventeen, including Yorta Yorta and Maori. He also wrote a *Guide to New Zealand* (1908) for tourists. Joanna Woods has written his biography (*Facing the Music: Charles Baeyertz and The Triad*, 2008).

252 The contents of the Brighton house were sold into a housing market that had recently crashed at the end of the land boom. Suzette and Bella appear to have been the closest relatives Mary Anne had in Melbourne when she died on 26 February 1891. Note the name of the house in the following advertisement that appeared in *The Argus* on 22nd and 26th August 1891: 'Sales by Auction. FRIDAY, AUGUST 28 On the Premises At Eleven O'Clock. Nereim, Black-street, MIDDLE BRIGHTON. HOUSEHOLD FURNITURE and EFFECTS. In the Estate of the Late Mrs.

Baeyertz Under Instructions From the Executors. UNRESERVED SALE by AUCTION OF HOUSEHOLD FURNITURE, Comprised In Sitting and Dining Rooms, Bedrooms, Kitchen, and Yard. F. L. FLINT has received Instructions to SELL by AUCTION, on the premises as above, The whole of the household furniture and personal effects Without reserve. Terms—cash F. L. Flint auctioneer, Camberwell and Collins-st.'

253 For the story of Emilia and Marion in San Francisco, see Watson (1894/1895, pp. 95–96). Henry J. McCoy was the first General Secretary of the San Francisco YMCA, from 1881–1915 (McCoy Chapter, AYR). Watson (1894/1895, p. 96) unambiguously tells us that the commending letter from another YMCA arrived in the mail from Mr Walker in Sydney, yet Emilia was recorded later saying that the letter may have come from New Zealand (Celia, 1905).

254 John Thornton Francis Baeyertz, the much younger brother of Charles and Suzette, was born in Victoria in 1855. By 1886, he had migrated to California. In 1892, he married Olivia Sarah Phelps in Santa Maria and was Chief Clerk at the Santa Fe Freight Depot in Los Angeles. In 1895, John became a naturalized citizen of the USA (Woods, p. 32 and *Los Angeles Herald*). They would name their home in the suburb of Whittier "Nerrenin" (San Francisco Blue Book, 1931).

255 Henry Wadsworth Longfellow (1807–1882) was famous for poems such as *The Arrow and the Song, The Song of Hiawatha, The Wreck of the Hesperus, Paul Revere's Ride* and *The Village Blacksmith*, which opens with 'Under a spreading chestnut-tree'. Emilia would have been shown the chair made from that tree at Craigie House, Longfellow's home in Cambridge, Massachusetts. Craigie House was General George Washington's headquarters during the Siege of Boston in the American Revolutionary War of 1776.

256 The sojourn of Emilia and Marion in Boston and Canada was described by Watson (1894/1895).

Britain, Spring 1892 to 1904

257 This story of T. C. Hammond comes from his biography by Warren Nelson (1994, p. 37).

258 Robert Evans (2007, pp. 58–60) devotes a chapter to Emilia's ministry in Britain. He concludes, 'there are a number of reasons for claiming that the British period of her work represents the climax of her ministry, and in some ways, her most fruitful years'.

259 *The Argus* of 5 December 1895 noted: 'MARRIAGES. KIRKLAND-BAEYERTZ.—On the 29th October, at St Thomas's Church, Edinburgh, by Rev. Howard Coclough, Dr James Kirkland, eldest son of Rev. James Kirkland, to Marion, only daughter of Mrs Charles Baeyertz, late of Kew, Melbourne.'

260 Betty says that Marion met Dr Kirkland in Edinburgh at one of her mother's meetings. Dr Kirkland came from New Zealand, possibly from the family of Kirklands who were in the church at Dunedin when Marion visited. Both of Emilia's children married 'preacher's kids'.

261 James and Marion Kirkland had a daughter and two sons, Gerald, a doctor, and Derek, an engineer. When the family sailed to Perth, Western Australia, in 1904, Emilia joined them before resuming her missions in Australia and later in Britain.

Australia, 1904 to 1906

262 Gerald Kirkland later wrote about his time in Perth in an autobiography, under his pseudonym Frederick Kaigh (1946). He later married the actress Jose Collins (Darwin, 2012).

Britain, Summer 1906 to Spring 1926

263 James and Marion settled for a time by the beach at St Leonards, East Sussex. Emilia died at Marion's house (Baruch, 1998).

264 The summary of probate (Government Digital Service) states: 'BAEYERTZ Emelia Louisa of 42 Leigham Court-road Streatham Surrey widow died 29 April 1926 at 84 Gleneldon-road Streatham. Probate London 29 January to Marion Cecily Kirkland (wife of James Kirkland). Effects £94/15/11.' Streatham is two miles south of the City of London. Their terrace houses are about a mile apart.

The Immediate Family of Emilia Baeyertz

265 The family tree was created by Garth Coverdale.

Glossary

266 The Glossary of Hebrew and Yiddish terms was especially written for this book by Betty's friend Merle Roseman in 2006 and revised in 2014 (Bridger & Wolk, 1962; Jessup, 1976; Kac, 1986; Wilson M. R., 1989).

Authors' Notes

267 Betty refers to Sydney Watson (1904/1905). Amanda refers to Betty Baruch (*Gifted Evangelist*, 1998) and Robert Evans (2007).

The Story Behind the Story

268 The words of The Preacher are from Ecclesiastes 1:9 and 12:12–14.

About the Authors

269 The inscription on Betty's memorial plaque concludes with M. H. D. S. R. I. P, a common Jewish epitaph derived from 1 Samuel 25: 29.

270 The photo of Betty was taken by Gwen McKelvie. The photo of Amanda was taken by Garth Coverdale.

Places Where Mrs Baeyertz Preached and Chronology

271 In compiling the list of Emilia's missions (just the places we know of) and the Chronology, I am especially indebted to Robert Evans (2007) for permission to mine his List of Missions. Other sources Amanda and I mined included UK Census (1841, 1851 & 1861), Sydney Watson (1910), Ruth Dwyer (2008), Joanna Woods (2008), Maurice Miskhel (2011) and newspapers.

Bibliography

272 Our Bibliography includes some references we quoted from, some we used for context and some we hope to read one day.

Back Cover

273 The sources I used for the quotes on the back cover are Paton, et al., (1899), Baruch, (1998, p. 11), Evans, (2007, pp. 8, 259) and the Foreword that we asked Lawrence Hirsch to write but decided not to use.

274 Reading all the footnotes is fun, isn't it? (Adams & Meretzky, 1984).

Places where Mrs Baeyertz Preached

California
Los Angeles
Monterey
Pacific Grove
Sacramento
San Francisco

England
Anerley
Bath
Battersea
Bayswater
Bedford
Berkhamsted
Birmingham
Brighton
Bristol
Blackburn
Blackheath
Blackpool
Blofield
Boscombe
Brantham
Brenchley
Bridlington
Bristol
Brixton
Brynn, now Bryn
Carlisle
Chester
Clitheroe
Crowborough
Croydon
Doncaster
Dudley
Felixstowe
Gloucester
Godalming
Great Wakering
Hadleigh
Harlesden
Harrogate
Heaton
Hebburn
Hastings
Huddersfield
Hull
Ipswich
Jarrow
Kendal
Kilburn Gate
Kings Cross
Leicester
Lewes
Liverpool
London
Loose
Lowestoft
Macclesfield
Maidstone
Manchester
Margate
Nayland
Newbury
Newcastle upon Tyne
Newington Butts
Norbury
North Shields
Norwood
Norwich
Notting Hill
Nottingham
Oswaldthistle

Otley
Portsmouth
Reading
St Leonards-on-Sea
St John's Wood
Sevenoaks
Shrewsbury
Southborough
Southport
Stansfield
Stockport
Sunderland
Taunton
Thornton Heath
Tilehurst
Tunbridge Wells
Uckfield
Upper Sydenham
Wandsworth
Wattisfield
Whyteleafe
Wimbledon
Winchester
Woodbridge
Worcester
Worle

Ireland
Belfast
Cork
Dublin
Queenstown, now Cobh

Isle of Man
Douglas

Massachusetts
Boston

New South Wales
Albury
Maloga
Sydney

New Zealand
Ashburton
Auckland
Christchurch
Dunedin
Nelson
Oamaru
Wanganui, now Whanganui
Wellington

Ontario
Brockville
Hamilton
Kingston
London
Ottawa
Peterborough
Smiths Falls
Toronto

Quebec
Montreal
Quebec City

Queensland
Brisbane
Ipswich

Scotland
Aberdeen
Ancrum
Annan
Anstruther
Arbroath
Ayr
Broughty Ferry
Campbelltown
Coatbridge
Dumfries
Dundee
Edinburgh
Elgin
Forfar
Glasgow
Hamilton
Hawick
Helensburgh

PLACES WHERE MRS BAEYERTZ PREACHED

Inverness
Kilmarnock
Kirkaldy
Langholm
Leith
Limehouse
Motherwell
Newbattle
Paisley
Pollokshields
Rutherglen
Saltcoats
Stirling
Uddingston
Wishaw

South Australia
Adelaide
Alberton
Angaston
Burra
Clare
Gawler
Gladstone
Glenelg
Jamestown
Kanmantoo
Kapunda
Laura

Magill
Mitcham
Moonta
Mount Barker
Nairne
North Rhine, now Somme Creek
Norwood
Parkside
Port Adelaide
Port Pirie
Semaphore
Terowie
Woodside

Tasmania
Deloraine
Hobart Town, now Hobart
Launceston
Longford
New Norfolk
New Town
O'Brien's Bridge, now Glenorchy
Port Esperance
Richmond
Sandy Bay
South Bruny Island

Victoria
Alexandra
Ballarat
Belfast, now Port Fairy
Birregurra
Box Hill
Brunswick
Camperdown
Caulfield
Chilwell
Clifton Hill
Cobden
Colac
Eaglehawk
Echuca
Emerald Hill, now South Melbourne
Fitzroy
Footscray
Geelong
Gisborne
Kew
Koroit
Mansfield
Maryborough
Melbourne
Mornington
Newstead
Pomborneit

Preston
Queenscliff
St Kilda
Sandhurst, now Bendigo
Stawell
Strangways
Warrnambool
West Melbourne
Williamstown
Winchelsea
Yarraville

Yea

Wales
Aberavon
Abergavenny
Barry Dock
Brecon
Cardiff
Dowlais
Maesteg
Merthyr Tydfil
Morriston

Newport
Newstead
Port Talbot
Rhayader
Swansea
Wrexham

Western Australia
Fremantle
Geraldton
Kalgoorlie
Perth

Chronology

THIS CHRONOLOGY IS AN INCOMPLETE LIST OF HISTORICAL EVENTS IN the life and times of Emilia Baeyertz, including every mission that I know of that she led. All dates and sequences are approximate unless the exact date is given.

Date	Location	Venue	Event
1806	England?		Charles Baeyertz, sen., is born
1807	Prussia?		John Aronson is born
1813	England	London?	Maria Lazarus is born
1822	Spain		Mary Anne Treleaven is born
1826	England		Charles Baeyertz, sen., leaves employment as a law clerk
	England		Charles Baeyertz, sen., joins the Royal Navy
	West Indies		Charles Baeyertz, sen., serves as Private Secretary to a Governor
1834	Posen, Prussia		Abraham Berens is born
30 Aug 1835	Port Phillip, New South Wales	Schooner *Enterprize*	Captain John Lancey begins permanent European settlement
1837	Port Phillip, NSW	Melbourne	The settlement is named after the Prime Minister
	Bangor, Wales?		Maria Lazarus marries John Aronson
1838	Bangor, Wales	High St	John & Maria's first child Julia Aronson is born
1838?			Mary Anne Treleaven marries Charles Baeyertz
1838?			Charles & Mary Anne's child Suzette Laura Baeyertz is born

Date	Location	Venue	Event
1840	Bangor, Wales	High St	Eliza Marion Aronson is born
1841	Bangor, Wales	High St	John Aronson is a jeweller
1841	Bangor, Wales	High St	Lewis Henry Aronson is born
29 Mar 1842	Bangor, Wales	High St	Emilia Louise Aronson is born
Oct 1842	Wandsworth, Eng		Charlie Baeyertz, son of Charles & Mary Anne, is born
1845	Bangor, Wales	High St	Saul Philip Aronson is born
1846	Bangor, Wales	High St	Charles Henry Aronson is born
1847	Bangor, Wales	High St	George Alfred Aronson is born
25 June 1847	Melbourne, NSW		Melbourne Town becomes the City of Melbourne
11 Nov 1850	Melbourne, NSW	Separation Tree	Governor La Trobe announces that the Port Phillip District is to be separated from NSW
1 July 1851	Sydney, NSW	Legislative Council	The separation of the Colony of Victoria from NSW takes effect
5 July 1851	Victoria		Discoveries of gold are announced
1851	Victoria	Clunes, Warrandyte, Mt Alexander, Ballarat & Bendigo Creek	Gold rushes
1852	Bangor, Wales		Emilia Aronson has a visitor
1852	Melbourne, Vic		Charles Baeyertz, sen., migrates with family, including his wife Mary Anne, son Charlie, & daughter Suzette
1852	Melbourne, Vic	Customs House	Charles Baeyertz, sen. is appointed Warehouse Keeper
Nov 1852	Melbourne, Vic	*SS Sydney*	David Rosenthal, jeweller, arrives from London
1853	Bangor, Wales?		Frederick Aronson is born

CHRONOLOGY   211

Date	Location	Venue	Event
Sep 1854	Melbourne & Sandridge, Vic	Melbourne Terminus on Flinders St & Station Pier	Melbourne & Hobson's Bay Railway is opened
1855	Bangor, Wales		Emilia Aronson turns 13 & starts home-schooling
1855	Bangor, Wales		Emily Aronson, Emilia's sister, is born
24 Feb 1855	St Kilda, Vic?		John Thornton Francis Baeyertz, son of Charles & Mary Anne, is born
June 1856	St Kilda, Vic	Goslett's Collegiate School	Charlie Baeyertz wins prizes at exams
1857	Bangor, Wales?		Arthur Aronson is born
13 May 1857	St Kilda, Vic	Railway station	The second of many Victorian railways is opened
1859	Bangor, Wales?		Nuriel Aronson is born
1859	Melbourne, Vic	33 Little Collins St West	Abraham Berens leaves work with David Rosenthal for Bangor
1860	Melbourne, Vic	Governor's Prize for rifle shooting	Charlie Baeyertz qualifies for the final round
1 May 1861	Bangor, Wales		Eliza Aronson marries Abraham Berens
27 Feb 1862	St Kilda, Vic	Christ Church	Suzette Baeyertz marries Richard Berkett Gibbs
31 Oct 1862	St Kilda, Vic		Amy Berens, daughter of Abraham & Eliza, is born
1863	Bangor, Wales		Emilia debuts, engages & disengages
8 Feb 1864	Liverpool, Eng	*Clipper Empire of Peace*	Emilia & her brother George Aronson leave for Melbourne
11 Apr 1864	Colac, Vic	Temperance Hall	Anglicans begin to meet
6 June 1864	Sandridge, Vic	*Clipper Empire of Peace*	Abraham & Eliza Berens welcome Emilia & George

Date	Location	Venue	Event
17 Oct 1865	Richmond, Vic	National Bank, 231 Bridge Rd	Charlie Baeyertz opens his new branch as Manager
16 Nov 1865	Hawthorn, Vic	Christ Church (Church of England)	Charlie Baeyertz & Emilia Aronson marry
1866	Bangor, Wales		John Aronson removes Emilia's name from the Aronson family register
1866	Bangor, Wales		Maria Aronson & son George write to Emilia
15 Dec 1866	Richmond, Vic	231 Bridge Rd	Charles Nalder Baeyertz is born to Charlie & Emilia
1867	Colac, Vic	National Bank, 26 Murray St	Charlie Baeyertz is appointed Manager
1867	Richmond to Colac, Vic		Charlie, Emilia & Charles N. Baeyertz move
1867	Colac, Vic	'Nerennin' farm	Charles Baeyertz, sen., & Mary Anne retire
21 Oct 1868	Colac, Vic	Temperance Hall	Charles, sen., is elected to the library committee
18 Mar 1869	Colac, Vic	26 Murray St	Marion Cecilia Baeyertz is born
1869	Colac, Vic		Emilia & Marion Baeyertz are christened on the same day
1869	Victoria	Church of England	Emilia Baeyertz is confirmed
2 July 1869	Colac, Vic	New schoolroom	Charles Baeyertz, sen., sings *The Comic History of England*
8 May 1870	Colac, Vic	Church of St John the Evangelist in Hesse St	Church of England dedicates their building
4 Mar 1871	Colac, Vic	Racecourse paddock	Charlie Baeyertz suffers an accidental gunshot wound
6 Mar 1871	Colac, Vic	26 Murray St	Charlie Baeyertz dies
9 Mar 1871	Colac, Vic	Cemetery plot C/E 518	Charlie Baeyertz is buried

CHRONOLOGY 213

Date	Location	Venue	Event
1871	Colac, Vic	From the bank to a cottage	Emilia, Charles N. & Marion Baeyertz move
1871	Pirron Yallock, Vic	Mr Calvert's farm	Emilia declares 'Christ is God & He died for me'
3 Sep 1871	St Kilda, Vic	Hebrew Congregation	First meeting of members
1871	From Colac to Geelong, Vic		Emilia, Charles N. & Marion Baeyertz move
1871	Geelong, Vic	Church of England	Emilia teaches lads at Sunday school
1871	Geelong, Vic	Homes, hospital & prison	Emilia regularly visits women & men
1871	Geelong, Vic	Presbyterian manse	Emilia offers her first prayer in public
1872	Geelong, Vic		The first Young Women's Christian Association in Australia is founded
1872	South Australia	Overland telegraph	Eastern Australia is connected to the world
Nov 1872	Melbourne, Vic	Rear of 15 Little Collins St West	David Rosenthal opens his jewellery manufactory
1 Jan 1873	Victoria	Education Act	Schooling becomes compulsory for boys & girls from ages 6 to 15
Jan 1873	Table Cape, Tas	Tollymore	Open Brethren hold a conference
1873	Geelong, Vic		Emilia 'consecrates' herself to God
1874	Melbourne, Vic	15 Little Collins St West	David Rosenthal & Saul Aronson have a jewellery business
Apr 1874	Birregurra, Vic	State schoolroom	Charles Baeyertz, sen., sings at a fundraiser for cricket
July 1874	Caulfield, Vic	St Mary's Church of England	Conference of ministers & laymen
Aug 1874	Melbourne & suburbs, Vic		Association of Female Workers sets to work
Jan 1875	Melbourne, Vic		David Rosenthal sails for Europe

Date	Location	Venue	Event
1875	Melbourne, Vic		Emilia writes her testimony
1875	Geelong, Vic	Aberdeen St Baptist Church	Emilia is baptised by immersion
8 Sep 1876	Melbourne, Vic	Wesley College, 577 St Kilda Rd	Charles N. starts school as a day boarder
Jan 1877	Melbourne, Vic	15 Little Collins St West	George Aronson helps catch a gold thief
Jan 1877	Mordialloc, Vic	Rosenthal, Aronson & Co annual picnic	Saul Aronson is farewelled to establish a shop in London
Feb 1877	Caulfield, Vic	St Mary's Church of England	Emilia joins the parish as an evangelist
6 Mar 1877	Caulfield, Vic		Marion survives scarlet fever
1877	Melbourne, Vic		Emilia starts speaking to factory girls in their lunchtimes
1877	Melbourne, Vic		Emilia begins a Bible Class for six young women
1877	Melbourne, Vic	Collins St Assembly Hall	Emilia's Bible Class for women is now weekly
1877	Melbourne, Vic	Dr Singleton's Mission Hall in Little Bourke St	Emilia speaks to 'crowded congregations' of women
1877	St Kilda, Vic	Blanche St Gospel Hall	Emilia addresses women & girls
1877	Emerald Hill, Vic	Clarendon St Presbyterian Church	Emilia addresses women & girls
1877	Melbourne, Vic	Albert St & Collins St Baptist Sunday Schools	Emilia addresses children
Oct 1877	East Melbourne, Vic	Melbourne Cricket Ground	Henry Varley preaches to large crowds
1877			Emilia declines many invitations to speak at churches
1877	Victoria		Emilia reads *Our Coffee Room*
1877	Victoria	A Congregational Sunday School	Emilia addresses women, men & children

CHRONOLOGY

Date	Location	Venue	Event
Dec 1877	Hobart Town, Tas	Bathurst St Peoples' Hall & Brisbane St Independent Memorial Church Schoolroom	Emilia begins leading her first Mission
Jan 1878	Hobart Town, Tas	Peoples' Hall & Ebenezer United Methodist Chapel in Murray St	Mission
1878	New Town, Tas	Congregational Church	Mission
1878	O'Brien's Bridge, Tas	Chapel	Mission
1878	Richmond, Tas		Mission
1878	South Bruny Island, Tas		Mission
1878	Port Esperance, Tas		Mission
1878	New Town, Tas	Independent Church	Mission
1878	New Norfolk, Tas		Mission
1878	Launceston, Tas	Pavilion, Mechanics' Institute & Tamar St Congregational Church	Mission
1878	Deloraine, Tas	Town Hall	Mission
1878	Wesley Dale, Tas	Mountain Villa	Emilia & children 'rest awhile'
3 May 1878	From Launceston, Tas to Melbourne, Vic	*SS Mangana*	Henry Varley and Baeyertz family travel
1878	Melbourne, Vic	15 Little Collins St West	George Aronson is a partner in Rosenthal, Aronson & Co
1878	London, Eng	Camomile St	Saul Aronson expands Rosenthal, Aronson & Co
1878	Victoria		George Aronson marries Philippa Solomon
Aug 1878	St Kilda, Vic	Town Hall	Mission

Date	Location	Venue	Event
1878	Melbourne, Vic	Assembly Hall	Regular Bible Classes for women
22 Nov 1878	Birmingham, Eng	Edgbaston	Maria Aronson dies
Jan 1879	Hobart Town, Tas	Peoples' Hall	Mission
Feb to Mar 1879	Launceston, Tas	Mechanics Institute, Mr Reed's Mission Room & Tamar St Congregational Church	Mission
9 July 1879	Brighton, Vic	Black St	Charles Baeyertz, sen., dies
July 1879	Sandhurst, Vic	Wesleyan & Eaglehawk Presbyterian Churches, Princess Theatre, Palmerston Hall in Quarry Hill & Masonic Hall	Emilia's first 'big' mission
31 Aug 1879	Sandhurst, Vic	Princess Theatre	Two evangelistic services
Aug to Oct 1879	Melbourne, Vic	Assembly Hall	Meetings for women on alternate Wednesdays
Oct to Nov 1879	Melbourne, Vic	YMCA Hall	Meetings for women on three Wednesdays
24 Nov 1879	Sandhurst, Vic		Evangelistic meeting with Thomas Spurgeon
Nov to Dec 1879	Melbourne, Vic	Stephen St (now Exhibition St) Protestant Hall	Meetings for women on alternate Wednesdays
1880	Hobart Town, Tas	People's Hall	Mission
1880	Sandy Bay, Tas		Mission
1880	Deloraine, Tas		Mission
1880	Longford, Tas		Mission
28 June 1880	Glenrowan, Vic	Anne Jones' Inn	Ned Kelly is captured

CHRONOLOGY

Date	Location	Venue	Event
1880	Melbourne, Vic	Assembly Hall	Wednesday evening meetings for women
July 1880	Geelong, Vic	Aberdeen St Baptist Church, YMCA rooms & Mechanics Hall	Mission
1880	Queenscliff, Vic		Mission
Aug 1880	Ballarat, Vic	Dawson St Baptist Church & Academy of Music	Mission
Sep 1880	Mt Lofty, South Australia	Mr Fowler's	Baptist Association decides to invite Mrs Baeyertz
10 Oct 1880	Launceston, Tas	Mount Pleasant	Henry Reed dies
1 Oct 1880 to 30 Apr 1881	Carlton, Vic	Exhibition Buildings, Exhibition St	International Exhibition (a World's Fair) is held
Dec 1880	Adelaide, SA	Town Hall & Flinders St & North Adelaide Baptist Churches	Mission
1 Jan 1881	Hobart, Tas		Hobart Town becomes the City of Hobart
Feb 1881	Launceston, Tas	Wellington St Christian Mission Church	Mission
21 Feb 1881	Launceston, Tas to Melbourne, Vic	*SS Flinders*	Emilia & Marion travel
1881	Victoria		Emilia & children begin to travel west
Apr 1881	Birmingham, Eng	Edgbaston	Abraham & Eliza Berens are on the census
Apr 1881	Warrnambool, Vic		Mission
Apr 1881	Koroit, Vic	Temperance Hall	Mission
May 1881	Belfast, Vic	Wesleyan Church	Mission

Date	Location	Venue	Event
June 1881	Stawell, Vic	Town Hall & Scallan St Welsh Baptist Church	Mission
1881	South Australia		Baeyertz family arrive
1881	Hahndorf, SA	T. W. Boehm's school	Charles N. Baeyertz briefly boards
Aug 1881	Adelaide, SA	Prince Alfred College	Charles N. B. begins day boarding
Aug 1881	Norwood, SA	Baptist Church	Mission
1881	Parkside, SA	Baptist Church	Mission
Sep to Dec 1881	Adelaide, SA	Flinders St Baptist Church	Emilia's mission includes meetings for men only for the first time
6 Dec 1881	Birmingham, Eng	Edgbaston	John Aronson dies
1882	Mitcham, SA		Mission
1882	Mount Barker, SA	Institute Hall	Mission
1882	Clare, SA		Mission
1882	Kapunda, SA	Baptist & Wesleyan Churches	Mission
1882	Gawler, SA	Baptist, Wesleyan & Congregational Churches	Mission
1882	Moonta, SA		Mission
1882	Moonta Mines, SA		Mission
1882	North Rhine, SA		Mission
1882	Angaston, SA	Union Church	Mission
1882	Port Adelaide, SA		Mission
1882	Alberton, SA	Baptist Church	Mission
25 Oct 1882	Sydney, NSW	Great Synagogue	Frederick Aronson marries Zara Baar
Nov 1882	Semaphore, SA	Methodist Church	Mission

CHRONOLOGY

Date	Location	Venue	Event
Nov 1882	Melbourne, Vic	A public meeting for ladies only	A YWCA Chapter is founded
1882	Kapunda, SA	Congregational Church	Mission
Dec 1882	Glenelg, SA	1859 & 1879 buildings at the Congregational Church in Jetty Rd	15-year-old Charles N. Baeyertz presides at the organ during a mission
1883	Bangor, Wales	272 High St	Lewis Aronson is a jeweller & goldsmith
14 May 1883	Prahran, Vic		Charles Aronson (brother of Emilia) dies
1883	Nairne, SA		Mission
1883	Mount Barker, SA		Mission
1883	Kanmantoo, SA		Mission
1883	Woodside, SA	Institute Hall	Mission
1883	Burra, SA	Kooringa	Mission
June & July 1883	Norwood, SA		Charles N. Baeyertz suffers from typhoid fever
1883	Magill, SA		Mission
1883	Terowie, SA		Mission
1883	Jamestown, SA		Mission
1883	Laura, SA		Mission
1883	Port Pirie, SA		Mission
1883	Gladstone, SA	Institute Hall	Mission
Jan to June 1884	Melbourne, Vic	Theatre Royal, Bourke St	Emilia preaches each Sunday night
July 1884	Stawell, Vic	Primitive Methodist, Wesleyan & Welsh Baptist Churches	Mission
Aug 1884	West Melbourne, Vic	Baptist Church	Mission

Date	Location	Venue	Event
Sep 1884	Sandhurst, Vic	Masonic Hall & Hargreaves St Baptist Church	Mission
Oct 1884	Echuca, Vic	Temperance Hall & Baptist & Wesleyan Churches	YMCA and Temperance Union Mission
Nov 1884	Maloga, NSW	Mission School	Baeyertz family assists
Dec	Brunswick, Vic	Baptist Church	Emilia speaks at a mission
1884	Sydney, NSW	2 Wynyard St ?	Frederick Aronson opens a Lazarus & Aronson shop
Aug 1884	Launceston, Tas	57 George St	Norman Aronson opens a Rosenthal, Aronson & Co shop
Jan 1885	Mornington, Vic	Mechanics' Institute	Mission
Apr 1885	Colac, Vic	Oddfellows' Hall	Mission
July 1885	Melbourne, Vic	YMCA Upper Hall	Emilia speaks at YWCA Mission
Aug 1885	Fitzroy, Vic	Gore St Bible Christian Church	Mission
Oct 1885	Echuca, Vic		Mission
Dec 1885	Williamstown, Vic	Wesleyan Church	Mission
1886	Mansfield, Vic	Shire Hall & Presbyterian Church	Mission
1886	Colac, Vic	Wesleyan Church	Mission
1886	Birregurra, Vic		Mission
June 1886	Geelong, Vic	Aberdeen St Baptist Church	Mission
June to Aug 1886	Launceston, Tas	Wellington St Temple	Mission
1886	Kew, Vic	'in & around'	Great spiritual blessing attends the labours of Mrs Baeyertz
21 Dec 1886	Kew, Vic	Baptist Church	Charles Nalder Baeyertz marries Isabella Delgarno Johnston

CHRONOLOGY

Date	Location	Venue	Event
1886	Williamstown, Vic	United Free Methodist Church	Mission
1886	Yarraville, Vic	United Free Methodist Church	Mission
7 Jan 1887	Melbourne, Vic	Assembly Hall Collins St	Emilia speaks at a 'Service of Song' for Aborigines of Maloga Mission
Jan 1887	Yea, Vic	Presbyterian Church & Temperance Hall	Mission
Mar 1887	Gisborne, Vic		Mission
Apr 1887	Camperdown, Vic		Mission
May 1887	Pomborneit, Vic		Mission
May 1887	Cobden, Vic	Temperance Hall & Presbyterian, Bible Christian & Wesleyan Churches	Mission
1887	Winchelsea, Vic		Mission
1887	Sandhurst, Vic	Temperance & Masonic Halls	Women's Prayer Union mission
1887	Ballarat, Vic	Ebenezer Presbyterian Church	Mission
1887	Newstead, Vic		Mission
1887	Strangways, Vic		Mission
19 Dec 1887	Kew, Vic	60 Denmark St	Railway terminus opens
1887	Yea, Vic	Presbyterian Church	Mission
Dec 1887	Chilwell, Vic	Wesleyan Church	Mission
12 Feb 1888	Kew, Vic	44 College Parade	Carl is born to Charles & Bella Baeyertz
Apr 1888	Alexandra, Vic	Presbyterian Church	Missions
31 May 1888	Melbourne, Vic	Athenæum Hall	Charles N. Baeyertz sings for, & Emilia addresses, the YWCA annual coffee supper

Date	Location	Venue	Event
June 1888	Maryborough, Vic	Primitive Methodist Church	Mission
July 1888	Melbourne, Vic	Theatre Royal, Collins St Baptist Church & Assembly Hall	YWCA Mission
July to Aug 1888	Melbourne, Vic	Theatre Royal, Bourke St	Emilia speaks each Sunday night
Dec 1888	Chilwell, Vic		Mission
1889	Victoria	Everywhere	Land boom ends, land prices fall & economic depression starts
Apr 1889	Alexandra, Vic	Presbyterian Church	Mission
July 1889	South Preston, Vic	Wesleyan Church	Mission
Aug 1889	Eaglehawk, Vic	Presbyterian Church & Skating Rink	Mission
Sep 1889	Brisbane, Queensland	YMCA, Princess St Wesleyan & Wharf St Baptist Churches, Courier Hall & Opera House	Mission
Sep 1889	Ipswich, Qld	Church of England Schoolroom, Congregational Church & School of Arts Hall	Mission
10 Oct 1889	Wallangarra, Qld	Railway Station	Emilia 'breaks gauge'
20 Oct 1889	Sydney, NSW	YMCA	Emilia speaks to only men
Nov 1889	Albury, NSW	Temperance Hall	Mission
15 Dec 1889	Hawthorn, Vic	Burke Rd	Maida Baeyertz is born to Charles & Bella Baeyertz
17 Dec 1889	Melbourne, Vic	Athenæum Theatre	Lydia von Finkelstein completes her tour
19 Dec 1889	Melbourne, Vic	Collins St Baptist Church	Emilia farewells her supporters

CHRONOLOGY

Date	Location	Venue	Event
27 Dec 1889	Melbourne, Vic		Emilia's friends farewell her
31 Dec 1889	Sandridge, Vic	SS *Pateena*	Emilia & Marion farewell Charles, Bella, Carl & Maida
Jan 1890	Launceston, Tas	Mount Pleasant	Emilia & Marion begin a family holiday
Jan 1890	Hobart, Tas		Emilia & Marion continue their holiday
2 Feb 1890	Hobart, Tas	Town Hall	Emilia gives an address
3 Feb 1890	Hobart, Tas	Sailors' Home	Emilia gives an address
11 Feb 1890	Dunedin, NZ		Emilia & Marion arrive from Hobart
Feb to Mar 1890	Dunedin, NZ	YWCA, Trinity Wesleyan Church & Garrison Hall	Mission
1890	Kew, Vic	9 Studley Park Rd	Charles & Bella move into what had been Emilia's rented house
April	Oamaru, NZ	Congregational, Presbyterian & Methodist Churches	Mission
May 1890	Christchurch, NZ	Oddfellows' Hall	Mission
June 1890	Ashburton, NZ	Hall & Wesleyan Church	Mission
June 1890	Nelson, NZ		Mission
July to Aug 1890	Wellington, NZ	Opera House, Central Hall & Salvation Army Barracks	Mission
Aug 1890	Wanganui, NZ	Oddfellows' Hall	Mission
1890	Auckland, NZ		Henry Brett prints *Three Addresses*
Sep to Oct 1890	Auckland, NZ	City Hall & Baptist Tabernacle	Mission
6 Oct 1890	Wellington, NZ	SS *Zealandia*	Emilia & Marion set sail for USA

Date	Location	Venue	Event
19 Oct 1890	Honolulu, Hawaii	Home of Dr & Mrs Whitney	Emilia & Marion visit in passing
27 Oct 1890	San Francisco, California	SS Zealandia	Emilia & Marion arrive
Nov 1890	San Francisco, Cal	YMCA & First Baptist Eddy St & First Presbyterian Churches	Mission
Nov 1890	Sacramento, Cal	First Baptist Church	Mission
Dec 1890	Monterey, Cal		Mission
Dec 1890	Pacific Grove, Cal		Mission
24 Feb 1891	Melbourne, Vic	SS Hauroto	Charles N. Baeyertz sails for Dunedin, NZ
26 Feb 1891	Brighton, Vic	At home, Black St	Mary Anne Baeyertz dies
Mar 1891	Los Angeles, Cal	YMCA & First Presbyterian Church & Simpson Tabernacle	Mission
May 1891	Melbourne, Vic		Bella, Carl & Maida sail for Dunedin, NZ
1891	Southern California		Marion suffers from malaria
1891	Chicago, Illinois		Emilia & Marion visit
1891	Hamilton, Ont		Mission
July 1891	Toronto, Ont	Association Hall	Mission
1891	Boston, Mass	J. A. Gordon's Church	Mission
1891	Massachusetts	'a lovely seaside resort'	Rest during 'the intense heat of the hot season'
1891	Cambridge, Mass	H. W. Longfellow's house	Emilia is a tourist
28 Aug 1891	Brighton, Vic	'Nereim', Black-street	Furniture & personal effects are auctioned without reserve
Sep 1891	Quebec City, Que	YMCA	Mission

Date	Location	Venue	Event
1891	Ottawa, Ont	Dominion & Knox Churches	Mission
1891	Toronto, Ont	Temperance St	Hill & Weir prints *Five Lectures*
Dec 1891	London, Ont	St Andrew's Church	Mission & sleigh-ride in the snow
Dec 1891	Toronto, Ont	Home of Mr & Mrs Henry O'Brien & family	Christmas
	Peterborough, Ont		Mission
Jan 1892	Kingston, Ont	Congregational Church	Mission
Feb 1892	Brockville, Ont		Mission
1892	Smiths Falls, Ont		Mission
1892	Montreal, Que	St James' Methodist Church	Mission
13 Apr 1892	New York, NY	*SS Teutonic*	Emilia & Marion depart for Britain
May 1892	Queenstown (now Cobh), Ire	Parochial School House & Methodist Church	Mission
1892	Cork, Ire	Assembly Rooms & Patrick St Methodist Church	Mission
1892	Glengarriff, Ire		Emilia & Marion rest
1892	Killarney, Ire		Emilia & Marion rest
1892	Belfast, Ire		Mission
June 1892	Dublin, Ire	YWCA at Christian Union	Mission
July 1892	London, Eng	YMCA Aldersgate St & West London Tabernacle	Mission
1892	Notting Hill, Eng		Mission

Date	Location	Venue	Event
17 Aug 1892	Santa Maria, Cal		John T. F. Baeyertz marries Olivia Sarah Phelps
1892	Notting Hill, Eng	Westbourne Grove Baptist Chapel	Mission
1892	Dundee, Scot	Free St Andrew's Church & YMCA Hall	Mission
1892	Limehouse, Scot	Dr Barnardo's Edinburgh Castle Mission Church	Mission
1893	Cardiff, Wales	Park Hall & Wood St Chapel	Mission
1893	Winchester, Eng	Hyde St Soldiers' Home	Mission
1893	Birmingham, Eng	Longmore St Baptist Church	Mission
Apr 1893	New Zealand		Charles N. Baeyertz begins publishing *The Triad*
1893	Edinburgh, Scot	YMCA, Free Assembly Hall & Carrubbers Close Mission Hall	Mission
1893	Broughty Ferry, Scot		Mission
1893	Dundee, Scot	YMCA Hall	Mission
1893	Glasgow, Scot	Christian Institute & Cowcaddens Free Church	Mission
1893	Notting Hill, Eng	Westbourne Grove Baptist Chapel	Mission
1893	Bayswater, Eng	YMCA	Mission
1893	Winchester, Eng	Hyde St Soldiers' Home	Mission
1894	Cork, Ire	70 Patrick St	Guy & Co. begins printing *Ten Addresses* & *From Darkness to Light*

CHRONOLOGY

Date	Location	Venue	Event
1894	Abergavenny, Wales	Town Hall, Wesleyan & Presbyterian Churches & Frogmore St Chapel	Mission
1894	Cardiff, Wales	YWCA, East Moors Mission, Tredegarville & Bethany Baptist Churches	Mission
1894	Birmingham, Eng	Mt Zion Baptist Church & YMCA	Mission
1894	Shrewsbury, Eng		Mission
1894	Carlisle, Eng		Mission
1894	Glasgow, Scot	Cowcaddens & Trinity Free Churches	Mission
1894	Ayr, Scot	Town Hall & Newton Free Church	Mission
May 1894	Bangor, Wales	Hebrew Congregation (Ashkenazi Orthodox)	Lewis Aronson and Morris Wartski found the congregation
1895	Glasgow, Scot	Langside Free Church	Mission
1895	Kilmarnock, Scot	Grange Free Church	Mission
1895	Saltcoats, Scot	Christian Institute & Town Hall	Mission
1895	Paisley, Scot	Free High Church	Mission
1895	Kirkaldy, Scot	St Brycedale's Free Church	Mission
1895	Motherwell, Scot		Mission
1895	Rutherglen, Scot	Free & Parish Churches & Town Hall	Mission
1895	Inverness, Scot	Market Hall & Free High, Free East & Union St United Presbyterian Churches	Mission
29 Oct 1895	Edinburgh, Scot	St Thomas's Church	Marion Baeyertz marries Dr James Kirkland

Date	Location	Venue	Event
1895	Edinburgh, Scot	Dalry Free Church	Mission
1896	Hull, Eng	Prospect St & Newington Presbyterian Churches	Mission
1896	St Leonards-on-Sea, Eng		Mission
1896	Kings Cross, Eng	Vernon Baptist Church	Mission
1896	Liverpool, Eng	Kirkdale Tabernacke	Mission
1896	Kilburn Gate, Eng	Kilburn Hall	Mission
1897	Cork, Ire	70 Patrick St	Guy & Co. prints *Twelve Addresses*
1897	Hull, Eng	Holderness Rd Presbyterian Church	Mission
1897	Wandsworth, Eng	Down Hall Lodge	Mission
Apr 1897	Notting Hill, Eng	Westbourne Grove Baptist Chapel	Mission
Jun 1897	Cardiff, Wales	Grangetown Hall	Mission
July 1897	Newbattle, Scot		Mission
Sep 1897	Hull, Eng	Newington Presbyterian Church	Mission
Oct 1897	Blackheath, Eng	Rink Hall	Mission
Dec 1897	Liverpool, Eng	Edge Hill Congregational Church	Mission
1897	Gloucester, Eng	Presbyterian Church	Mission
Jan 1898	Huddersfield, Eng	Ramsden St Church	Mission
Feb 1898	Liverpool, Eng		Mission
1898	Blackburn, Eng	St George's Presbyterian Church	Mission
May 1898	Aberdeen, Scot	Music Hall, YMCA Union St & West & St Clement's Free Churches	Mission

CHRONOLOGY

Date	Location	Venue	Event
June 1898	Clitheroe, Eng	St James' Church	Mission
July 1898	Limehouse, Scot	Dr Barnardo's Edinburgh Castle Mission Church	Mission
Sep 1898	Glasgow, Scot	Shamrock St United Presbyterian Church	Mission
Oct 1898	Liverpool, Eng	Byrom Hall	Mission
Dec 1898	Chester, Eng	Queen St Congregational Church	Mission
Jan 1899	Reading, Eng	Women's United Prayer Union	Mission
Feb 1899	Dumfries, Scot	St George's Free Church	YMCA & YWCA Mission
Mar 1899	Southport, Eng	Temperance Institute & Hoghton St Baptist Church	Mission
Apr 1899	Sunderland, Eng	Bethesda Free Church	Mission
May 1899	Newcastle-upon-Tyne, Eng	Blackett St Presbyterian Church & Trinity	Mission
June 1899	Annan, Scot	Free & Congregational Churches	Mission
July 1899	Jarrow, Eng		Mission
Sep 1899	Pollokshields, Scot	Kinning Park Free Church	Mission
1899	London, Eng	7 Ladbroke Square, Nottinghill	Emilia's postal address
Oct 1899	North Shields, Eng	Howard Hall, YMCA, Methodist New Connexion and Baptist Churches	Mission
Dec 1899	Bedford, Eng	YMCA	Mission
Jan 1900	Bristol, Eng		Mission

Date	Location	Venue	Event
Feb 1900	Kendal, Eng	Free Churches, YMCA Rooms & Friends' Meeting House	Mission
Mar 1900	Helensburgh, Scot	United Presbyterian, Congregational & Park Free Churches	Mission
June 1900	Hebburn-on-Tyne, Eng	St Andrew's Presbyterian Church	Mission
July 1900	Heaton & Heaton Moor, Eng	Chapel & Public Hall	Mission
Sep 1900	Langholm, Scot	North United Presbyterian Church	Mission
Oct 1900	Hawick, Scot	Public Hall	Mission
1900	Ancrum, Scot		Mission
1900	Glasgow, Scot	Wellpark United Free Church	Mission
3 Dec 1900	Windsor, Vic	'Linden', The Avenue	George Aronson sells up & leaves for Europe
1901	Melbourne, Vic	297 Little Collins St	Frederick Aronson floats Rosenthal, Aronson & Co for £90,000
Jan 1901	Wimbledon, Eng		Simultaneous mission
Feb 1901	Leith, Scot	Ebenezer, North Leith & Junction Rd United Free Churches	Christian Fellowship Union Mission
Mar 1901	Dudley, Eng		Mission
May 1901	Bristol, Eng	Methodist Free Church	Mission
June 1901	Great Wakering, Eng	Congregational Church	Mission
July 1901	Brynn (now Bryn), Eng	Baptist Church	Mission
Sep 1901	Arbroath, Scot		Christian Endeavour Mission

CHRONOLOGY 231

Date	Location	Venue	Event
Oct 1901	Paisley, Scot	Good Templar Hall & Free High, Primitive Methodist & Victoria Hall Baptist Churches	Christian Endeavour Mission
1901	Nottingham, Eng	Noel St Presbyterian Church & Belgrave Square	Mission
Dec 1901	Portsmouth, Eng	Soldiers' Home	Mission
Jan 1902	London, Eng	Church St Baptist Chapel, Edgeware Rd	Mission
Feb 1902	Sevenoaks, Eng	Baptist Church	Mission
1902	Coatbridge, Scot		Mission
1902	Newport, Wales	Malpas Hall	Mission
1902	London, Eng	Eccleston St Conference Hall	Mission
1902	Cardiff, Wales		Mission
1902	Felixstowe, Eng		Mission
1902	Battersea Park, Eng	Tabernacle	Mission
1902	Anstruther, Scot	Cellardyke Parish & Chalmers' Uniting Free Churches & Town Hall	Mission
Dec 1902	Wrexham, Wales		Mission
Jan 1903	Wandsworth, Eng	Earlsfield Congregational Church	Mission
1903	Bath, Eng	King St Wesleyan, Manvers St Baptist, Countess of Huntingdon's & Argyle St Chapels	YMCA Mission
1903	Tunbridge Wells, Eng	Crabb Memorial Institute	Mission
1903	St John's Wood, Eng	YWCA Institute	Mission

Date	Location	Venue	Event
1903	Norwich, Eng	Agricultural Hall	Mission
1903	Blofield, Eng		Mission
1903	Newport, Wales		Mission
1903	Cardiff, Wales	Mount Stuart Square Church	Mission
1903	Taunton, Eng	Temple Chapel	Mission
Nov 1903	Maidstone, Eng	Corn Exchange	Mission
Dec 1903	Crowborough, Eng		Mission
1904	Bristol, Eng		Mission
1904	Edinburgh, Scot	Kirk Memorial Congregational Church	Mission
1904	Bayswater, Eng	Paddington Baths Hall, Queens Rd	Mission
1904	Tunbridge Wells, Eng	Victoria Hall, Southborough	Mission
1904	England		The Kirkland family with Emilia sail to Western Australia
1904	Melbourne, Vic	326–328 Flinders Lane	Varley Brothers prints *Twelve Addresses*
1904	Perth, WA	221 Murray St	City Printing Co. prints *Six New Addresses*
1904	Perth, WA	Queen's Hall	Mission
1904	Fremantle, WA		Mission
1904	Kalgoorlie, WA		Mission
1904	Geraldton, WA		Mission
30 Mar 1905	Melbourne, Vic		Emilia arrives without Marion
Apr 1905	Geelong, Vic	Aberdeen St Baptist Church	Mission

CHRONOLOGY

Date	Location	Venue	Event
May 1905	Melbourne, Vic	Collins St Baptist, Central Baptist & Independent Churches	Mission
June 1905	Ballarat, Vic	Dawson St Baptist & Lydiard St Methodist Churches	Mission
July 1905	Footscray, Vic	Baptist Church & Federal Hall	Mission
1905	Box Hill, Vic	Baptist Church	Mission
1905	Clifton Hill, Vic	Baptist Church	Mission
Oct 1905	West Melbourne, Vic	Baptist Church	Mission
Nov 1905	Launceston, Tas	Henry Reed Memorial Church	Mission
Nov 1905	Hobart, Tas	Baptist Tabernacle	Mission
Feb 1906	Hobart, Tas		Charles N. Baeyertz visits his mother
1906	Perth, WA		Emilia returns via Melbourne
June 1906	England		Emilia arrives from Australia
1906	Taunton, Eng	Gloucester Hall	Mission
1906	Norbury, Eng	King Edward's Hall	Mission
1906	Bath, Eng	Hay Hill Baptist Church	Mission
1906	Barry Dock, Wales	Presbyterian Forward Movement	Mission
1906	London, Eng	Charlton	Mission
1907	Swansea, Wales	Central Hall	Mission
1907	Wrexham, Wales	Victoria Hall	Mission
1907	Sevenoaks, Eng	Baptist Church	Mission
1907	Morriston, Wales		Mission
1907	Worle, Eng		Mission
1907	Harlesden, Eng	Christ Church	Mission

Date	Location	Venue	Event
1907	Brecon, Wales	Bethel Hall & Plough Congregational Chapel	Mission
1908	Hastings, Eng	Railway Mission Hall	Mission
1908	Newport, Wales	YMCA	Mission
1908	Thornton Heath, Eng	Thornton Heath Mission	Mission
1908	Berkhamsted, Eng	Town Hall	Mission
1908	Newport, Wales	Maindee United Methodist Church	Mission
1908	Lowestoft, Eng	YMCA Hall	Mission
1908	Manchester, Eng	Chapman St Hall, Hulme	Mission
1908	Nayland, Eng		Mission
1908	Hadleigh, Eng	Town Hall	Mission
1908	Dowlais, Wales		Mission
1908	Abergavenny, Wales		Mission
1908	Rhayader, Wales		Mission
1909	Merthyr Tydfil, Wales	Central Mission	Mission
1909	Felixstowe, Eng	Oddfellows' Hall & Hamilton Hall	Mission
1909	Coatbridge, Scot	Christian Union & Lesser Hall	Mission
1909	Glasgow, Scot	Highland & Open Air Mission Oswald St	Mission
1909	Aberdeen, Scot	YMCA & St Clement's & West United Free Churches	Mission
1909	Campbelltown, Scot	Albert Hall	Mission

CHRONOLOGY

Date	Location	Venue	Event
1909	Wishaw, Scot	Pavilion & Parish, Baptist & Christian Union Churches	Mission
1909	Glasgow, Scot	Mt Florida Church	Mission
1909	Forfar, Scot		Mission
1909	Hamilton, Scot	Baptist Church & Town Hall	Mission
1910	Brantham, Eng		Mission
1910	England		George Aronson dies
1910	Swansea, Wales	Central Hall	Mission
1910	Uddingston, Scot		Mission
1910	Stansfield, Eng	Congregational Church	Mission
1910	Port Talbot, Wales		Mission
1910	Aberavon, Wales		Mission
1910	Oswaldthistle, Eng		Mission
1910	Cork, Ire	70 Patrick St	Guy & Co. prints the final edition of *From Darkness to Light*
1910	Godalming, Eng	Baptist Church & Town Hall	Mission
1910	Edinburgh, Scot	Dalry United Free Church	Mission
1910	Woodbridge, Eng		Mission
1910	Wattisfield, Eng		Mission
1911	Blackpool, Eng	Queenstown Mission Hall	Mission
1911	Stirling, Scot	British Women's Temperance Association	Mission
1911	Douglas, Man	YWCA	Mission

Date	Location	Venue	Event
1911	Ipswich, Eng	St Nicholas Congregational Church	Mission
1911	Loose, Eng		Mission
1911	Brenchley, Eng	Walnut Tree Hall	Mission
1912	Macclesfield, Eng		Mission
1912	Whyteleafe, Eng	Tabernacle	Mission
1912	West Norwood, Eng	Bethel Chapel & Lansdowne Hall	Mission
1912	Croydon, Eng	Temperance Hall	Mission
1912	South Norwood, Eng		Mission
1912	Taunton, Eng		Mission
1912	Bridlington, Eng		Mission
1913	Blackpool, Eng	YWCA & Queenstown Hall	Mission
1913	Winchester, Eng	Hyde St Soldiers' Home	Mission
1913	Lewes, Eng		Mission
1913	Maidstone, Eng	YWCA & St Faith's Church	Mission
1913	Uckfield, Eng		Mission
1913	South Norwood, Eng		Mission
1913	Boscombe, Eng		Mission
1913	England		Emilia & two 'loved ones' undergo medical operations
1913	Doncaster, Eng	Presbyterian Church	Mission
1913	Harrogate, Eng	Town Mission Hall	Mission
Jan 1914	London, Eng	186 Aldersgate St	Daily noon prayer meetings
1914	Maesteg, Wales	Trinity Presbyterian Church	Mission

CHRONOLOGY

Date	Location	Venue	Event
1914	Upper Sydenham, Eng	Well Rd	Mission
26 June 1914	Wellington, NZ	*SS Ulimaroa*	Charles N. Baeyertz migrates to Sydney, NSW
1914	Elgin, Scot	Baptist Church	Mission
1914	Worcester, Eng	Red Hill Baptist Church	Mission
1915	Hawick, Scot		Mission
1915	Paisley, Scot		Mission
Mar 1915	Glasgow, Scot	Tent Hall	Mission
May 1915	Glasgow, Scot	Grove St Institute	Mission
1915	Otley, Eng		Mission
1915	Southborough, Eng	St Matthew High Brooms Church	Mission
1915	Leicester, Eng	Carley St Baptist Church	Mission
1916	Brixton, Eng	YWCA Institute	Mission
10 Jan 1917	Newington Butts, Eng	Metropolitan Tabernacle of C. H. Spurgeon	Emilia speaks at a special gospel meeting
1917	Margate, Eng	Congregational Church	Mission
1917	Tilehurst, Eng	Village Hall	Mission
1918	Anerley, Eng	Parish Hall	Mission
1918	Newbury, Eng		Mission
1918	London, Eng	42 Leigham Court Rd, Streatham Hill, Surrey	Emilia retires from public speaking
29 Apr 1926	London, Eng	84 Gleneldon Rd, Streatham, Surrey	Emilia dies at Marion's house

Bibliography

Books and Articles

150 Years "Naming the Wells". (2008). Caulfield, Vic: St Mary's Anglican Church. Retrieved from oaktreeanglican.org.au

A Brief History of Colac. (2012). Colac ... A Community Website. Retrieved from otway.biz/history.html

A Post Card Photograph of Mrs. Baeyertz. (n.d.). London: Mrs. Baeyertz.

Abrams, N. (2007, April 27). Historian Goes Big on Small Communities. In *Roots Directory*. Jewish Telegraph. Retrieved from jewishtelegraph.com

Adams, D., & Meretzky, S. (1984). *The Hitchhiker's Guide to the Galaxy*. Cambridge, Mass.: Infocom.

Alexander Somerville. (n.d.). Retrieved from theglasgowstory.com

Anon. (n.d.). Dwight Lyman (D. L.) Moody. In *Faith Hall of Fame*. European–American Evangelistic Crusades. Retrieved from eaec.org/faithhallfame/dlmoody.htm

Applebee, P. (2010). *Australian Cemeteries*. Retrieved from australiancemeteries.com

Badger, I. (1976). Horse-drawn Vehicles in South Australia. *Journal of the Historical Society of South Australia*(2), 18–29.

Baeyertz, C. N. (1891, December 22 & 31). The Australian Aborigines. *Otago Witness*, p. 8f & 38f.

Baeyertz, C. N. (1892). *Voice Culture*. Dunedin: Dresden Piano Co.

Baeyertz, C. N. (Ed.). (1893–1927). *The Triad*. Dunedin, Wellington and Sydney.

Baeyertz, C. N. (1908). *Guide to New Zealand*. Dunedin: Mills Dick & Co.

Baeyertz, C. N. (c. 1920). *Self-training Method of Instruction in Correct English, Public Speaking, Elocution, Voice Production*. Sydney: C. N. Baeyertz Institute.

Baeyertz, E. L. (n.d.). *My Authority as a Woman for Preaching the Gospel*. London: Mrs Baeyertz.

Baeyertz, E. L. (n.d.). *Can God's Children expect Answers to Prayer?* London: Mrs. Baeyertz.

Baeyertz, E. L. (n.d.). *Rest—Deliverance from Worry*. London: Mrs. Baeyertz.

Baeyertz, E. L. (1875). *From Darkness to Light*. Melbourne: Mrs. Baeyertz.

Baeyertz, E. L. (1890). *Three Lectures Delivered by Mrs. Baeyertz, the Converted Jewess with the Story of her Conversion from Judaism to Christianity*. Auckland: H. Brett.

Baeyertz, E. L. (1891). *Five Lectures Delivered by Mrs. Baeyertz, the Converted Jewess with the Story of her Conversion from Judaism to Christianity* (2 ed.). Toronto, Ontario: Mrs. Baeyertz. Retrieved from eco.canadiana.ca

Baeyertz, E. L. (1894 c.). *Ten Addresses delivered by Mrs. Baeyertz*. London: Mrs. Baeyertz.

Baeyertz, E. L. (1897). *A Sixteen Days' Mission in the Rink Hall, Blackheath*. London: Mrs. Baeyertz. Retrieved from lcje.net

Baeyertz, E. L. (1897). *Twelve Addresses delivered by Mrs. Baeyertz with the Story of her Conversion from Judaism to Christianity* (Enlarged ed.). Cork: Mrs. Baeyertz.

Baeyertz, E. L. (1904). *Six New Addresses Delivered by Mrs. Baeyertz (Jewish Evangelist)*. Perth, WA: Mrs. Baeyertz. Retrieved from nla.gov.au/nla.aus-vn4933889

Baeyertz, E. L. (1904). *Twelve Addresses Delivered by Mrs. Baeyertz* (New ed.). Melbourne: Varley Bros. Retrieved from catalogue.statelibrary.tas.gov.au/item/?id=2611

Baruch, B. (1994, January 14). Emilia Baeyertz of Melbourne, Jewish Evangelist. In *New Life*. Melbourne.

Baruch, B. (1997, April). The Jewish Lady Evangelist from Melbourne. In *On Being Magazine*. Hawthorn, Vic: 36 Media.

Baruch, B. (1998). *Emilia Baeyertz: Gifted Evangelist 1842–1926*. Chadstone: Unpublished manuscript.

Baruch, B. (1998). *This Is My Beloved*. Chadstone: Unpublished manuscript.

Baruch, B. & Coverdale, A. (2017). *This Is My Beloved: The Story of Emilia Baeyertz, Jewish Christian Lady Evangelist*. Melbourne: Emilia Baeyertz Society.

Bashford, A. (1994). Respectability, Morality, Cleanliness: The Feminisation of Hospitals in Colonial Australia. *Working Papers in Australian Studies*(92). Retrieved from kcl.ac.uk/artshums/ahri/centres/menzies/research/Publications/Workingpapers/WP92Bashford.pdf

Batt, G. (n.d.). St. Kilda General Cemetery. In *Australian Cemeteries*. Retrieved from australiancemeteries.com/vic/ptphillip/stkilda.htm

Baughen, G. A. (2012). Baeyertz, Charles Nalder. In *Dictionary of New Zealand Biography Te-Ara – the Encyclopedia of New Zealand*. NZ: Ministry of Culture and Heritage. Retrieved from TeAra.govt.nz/en/biographies/2b1/baeyertz-charles-nalder

Bendigo Baptist Church. (2009). *Until This Time*. Bendigo Baptist Church.

Bickford, J. (1890). *James Bickford: An Autobiography of Christian Labour in the West Indies, Demerara, Victoria, New South Wales and South Australia 1838–1888*. London: Charles H Kelly. Retrieved from archive.org/details/jamesbickfordauto0bick

Births Deaths Marriages Victoria. (n.d.). Search your Family History. BDMV. Retrieved from bdm.vic.gov.au

Bishop, C. (2011). Women of Pitt Street. In *The Dictionary of Sydney*. Retrieved from dictionaryofsydney.org

Blainey, G. (2003). *Black Kettle and Full Moon: Daily Life in a Vanished Australia*. Penguin.

Blue Ribbon Literature Agency. (1884). *Victorian Gospel Total Abstinence Blue Ribbon Mission Pledge Certificate*. Melbourne, Vic: BRLA. Retrieved from handle.slv.vic.gov.au/10381/243734

Book of Common Prayer. (1662/2015). Retrieved from The Church of England: churchofengland.org/prayer-worship/worship/book-of-common-prayer.aspx

Bridger, D., & Wolk, S. (Eds.). (1962). *The New Jewish Encyclopedia*. New York: Behrman House.

Cannon, M. (1995). *The Land Boomers: The Complete Illustrated History*. Melbourne University Press.

Carroll, B. (1980). *Getting Around Town—A History of Urban Transport in Australia*. Cassell Australia.

Carruthers, F. (2008). *The Horse in Australia*. Sydney: Knopf.

Cato, N. (1974). Matthews, Daniel (1837–1902). In *Australian Dictionary of Biography* (Vol. 5). Melbourne University Press. Retrieved from adb.anu.edu.au

Cato, N. (1976/1993). *Mister Maloga*. St Lucia: University of Queensland Press.

Celia. (1905, April 20). An Interview with Mrs. Baeyertz. In *Table Talk*. Melbourne.

Charlwood, D. (1981). *The Long Farewell*. Penguin.

Colac Heritage Walk. (c. 2012). Apollo Bay, Vic: Otway Tourism.

Colac—A Short History from 1837. (1995). Colac, Vic: Colac and District Historical Society.

Cole, K. (1994). Macartney, Hussey Burgh (?–1908). In *Australian Dictionary of Evangelical Biography*. Sydney: Evangelical History Association. Retrieved from webjournals.ac.edu.au

Cooke, H. (1874, July). Melbourne, as a Field for Mission Work. In H. B. Macartney (Ed.), *Caulfield Addresses*, (pp. 80–86).

Cotton, E. R. (1878). *More About Our Coffee-Room*. London: James Nisbet & Co.

Cotton, E. R. (c. 1876/1884). *Our Coffee-Room*. London: James Nisbet & Co.

Coulson, H. (1979/2009). *Echuca–Moama River Neighbours*. Killawarra, Vic: McCabe Prints.

Dando-Collins, S. (2014). *Sir Henry Parkes: The Australian Colossus*. Random House Australia.

Darwin, L. (2012, December 4). The Actress and the Impecunious Doctor. In *Little Darwin*. Blogspot. Retrieved from littledarwin.blogspot.com.au

David, J. (1969). *Hilltop House*. London: Victory Press.

David, T. (n.d.). *Bernie Cohen*. Sh'ma Israel Distributors.

David, T. (n.d.). *Ruth*.

David, T. (n.d.). *The Havilah*.

Davies, N. (1997). *Europe—a History*. London: Pimlico.

Davison, G., McCarty, J., & McLeary, A. (1987). *Australians 1888*. Sydney: Fairfax, Syme & Weldon.

Dickson, A. R. (2011). Lieutenant-Colonel George Hepburn Stewart. In *Families and Farming from West Otago*. Rootsweb. Retrieved from rootsweb.ancestry.com/~nzlwo/stewartgh.html

Disraeli, B. (1845). *Sybil, or The Two Nations*. London: Henry Colburn. Retrieved from gutenberg.org/ebooks/3760

Due, S. (Ed.). (n.d.). *Australian Medical Pioneers Index*. Retrieved from medicalpioneers.com

Dunn, M. (1991). *The Dauntless Bunch. The Story of the YWCA in Australia*. Clifton Hill, Vic: Young Women's Christian Association of Australia.

Durie, M. (2007, April 27). God's Smile. In *Oaktree Anglican Vicar's Blog*. Oaktree Anglican. Retrieved from oaktreevicar.blogspot.com.au/search?q=god's+smile

Dwyer, R. (2008). A Jewellery Manufactory in Melbourne. *The Journal of Public Record Office Victoria*(7).

Dynes, C. (1984). *The Complete Australian and New Zealand Book of Names*. North Ryde, NSW: Angus & Robertson.

Echuca Heritage Walk. (n.d.). Echuca, Vic: Shire of Campaspe.

Ely, R. (1994). Reed, Henry (1806–1880). In *Australian Dictionary of Evangelical Biography*. Sydney: Evangelical History Association. Retrieved from webjournals.ac.edu.au

Evangelistic Services in Melbourne—Mr. Varley in Richmond Park. (1877, October 3). *The Illustrated Australian News*. Retrieved from handle.slv.vic.gov.au/10381/250806

Evans, R. (2005). *Evangelism and Revivals in Australia 1880 to 1914* (Vol. 1). Hazelbrook, NSW: Research in Evangelical Revivals.

Evans, R. (2007). *Early Evangelical Revivals in Australia* (2 ed.). Hazelbrook, NSW: Research in Evangelical Revivals.

Evans, R. (2007). *Emilia Baeyertz—Evangelist: Her Career in Australia and Great Britain*. Hazelbrook, NSW: Research in Evangelical Revivals.

Evans, R. (2010). Evangelicalism in Victoria—1910. *Charles Perry Lecture*. Parkville: Ridley College.

Evans, R. (2010). *Matthew Burnett, The Yorkshire Evangelist*. Hazelbrook, NSW: Research in Evangelical Revivals.

Fackler, M. (1990). The World has Yet to See .... In *Christian History*. Christianity Today. Retrieved from christianitytoday.com/ch/1990/issue25/2510.html

Fahey, C. (1988). *Barmah Forest—A History*. Vic: Historic Places Section, Department of Conservation Forests & Lands.

Flinders Rangers Research. (n.d.). The Moonta Mine. In *South Australia and the Northern Territory*. Flinders Rangers Research. Retrieved from southaustralianhistory.com.au/moonta.htm

Franklin, L. (2014). *Bass Straitsmen and their Wives—Their Journey c.1800–1940*. Barmah Forest Heritage Education and Visitor Information Centre, Nathalia.

Freeman, J. (1888). *Lights and Shadows of Melbourne Life*. London: Sampson Low Marston Searle & Rivington.

Freier, P. (2010, July). Spirit's Call to Affirm Women's Ministry. *The Melbourne Anglican*(483), p. 2.

Frost, S. (2012, December 14). Purifying the Nation: Father Theobald Mathew. In *Prezi*. Retrieved from prezi.com/wd4b94hqfxpi/purifying-the-nation-father-theobald-mathew

Fullerton, W. Y. (1919). *Thomas Spurgeon, A Biography*. London: Hodder and Stoughton. Retrieved from archive.org/details/thomasspurgeonbi00fullrich

Fysh, H. J. (1967). Reed, Henry (1806–1880). In *Australian Dictionary of Biography* (Vol. 8). Melbourne University Press. Retrieved from adb.anu.edu.au/biography/reed-henry-2582

Fysh, H. J. (1973). *Henry Reed: Van Diemen's Land Pioneer*. Hobart: Cat and Fiddle Press.

Garfi, S. (2006, October 6). HSBC Bank, 274 High Street, Bangor. In *Coflein*. Royal Commission on the Ancient and Historical Monuments of Wales. Retrieved from coflein.gov.uk/en/site/26627/details

Garfield, S. (2000). *Mauve*. London: Faber and Faber.

Gericke, P. (1978). *Crucial Experiences in the Life of D. L. Moody*. New Orleans: Insight Press.

Government Digital Service. (n.d.). Wills and Probate 1859–1996. In *Find a Will*. GOV.UK. Retrieved from probatesearch.service.gov.uk/#wills

Griffin, G. (1829/n.d.). *The Collegians or The Colleen Bawn*. Coles Victoria Library.

Hauser, I. (2006). *Printers of the Streets and Lanes of Melbourne 1837–1975*. Melbourne: Nondescript Press.

Hebb, I. (1888/1970). *The History of Colac and District*. Melbourne: The Hawthorn Press.

Hebb, I. (1930). *Sixty Years' Historical Sketch of S. S. John's Parish, Colac 1870–1930*. Colac, Vic: S. S. John's Church of England. Retrieved from slv.vic.gov.au/10381/119080

Hibbert, C. (1978). *Disraeli and his World*. London: Thames & Hudson.

Hickman, J. (2003). Betty Baruch and her Mother Shoshana Rosa Baruch, age 94. In J. Hickman, *Messiah's Shalom in Jewish Lives*. Auckland: Messiah House Ministries Trust.

Hilliard, D. (1982). Popular Revivalism in South Australia. *Gordon Rowe Memorial Lecture*. Uniting Church Historical Society.

Howe, H. (Ed.). (1900). *Historical Collections of Ohio* (Centenial ed., Vol. 1). The State of Ohio. Retrieved from digital.case.edu/concern/texts/ksl:howhis00

(1881). Hymns for Mrs. Baeyertz's Evangelistic Services. In *Australian Hymnody Database*. Adelaide: R. K. Thomas. Retrieved from pandora.nla.gov.au/pan/54223/20060208-0000/dlibrary.acu.edu.au/msm/acm/browse9b45.html?l=h

Izaak. (1885, April 10). Mrs. Baeyertz in Colac. *Colac Herald*. Retrieved from trove.nla.gov.au

Jessup, G. (1976). *No Strange God*. London: Olive Press.

Jones, H. (2005). Colton, Mary (1822–1898). In *Australian Dictionary of Biography* (Vol. Suppl.). Melbourne University Press. Retrieved from adb.anu.edu.au

Julian, J. (1907). *Dictionary of Hymnology*. London: John Murray.

Kac, A. W. (1986). *The Messiahship of Jesus*. Grand Rapids: Baker Book House.

Kaigh, F. (1946). *Ninety Nine and All That*. London: Richard Lesley.

Kjær-Hansen, K. (Ed.). (1994, August). Discovering Emilia. *Lausanne Consultation on Jewish Evangelism Bulletin*(37).

Kjær-Hansen, K. (Ed.). (1994, August). The Memory of them is not Forgotten. *Lausanne Consultation on Jewish Evangelism Bulletin*(37).

Kjær-Hansen, K. (Ed.). (2007, February). The Jewish Lady Evangelist from Melbourne. *Lausanne Consultation on Jewish Evangelism Bulletin*(187).

Lady, A. (1874, July). Consecration. In H. B. Macartney (Ed.), *Caulfield Addresses*, (pp. 121–128).

Lady, A. (1874, July). The Right of Holiness Purchased by the Cross, Co-equally with the Right of Salvation. In H. B. Macartney (Ed.), *Caulfield Addresses*, (pp. 29–34).

Lamb, C., & Lamb, M. (1807/1910). *Tales from Shakespeare*. London/New York: Ernest Nister/EP Dutton.

Lamb, M. Y. (1994). Varley, Henry (1835–1912). In *Australian Dictionary of Evangelical Biography*. Sydney: Evangelical History Association. Retrieved from webjournals.ac.edu.au

Lundy, D. (n.d.). *The Peerage*. Retrieved from ThePeerage.com

Macartney, H. B. (Ed.). (1873–1898). *The Missonary at Home and Abroad (Monthly Journal)*. Caulfield.

Macartney, H. B. (Ed.). (1874, July). *Conference Addresses Delivered at St. Mary's, Caulfield, by Ministers and Laymen of Different Denominations*. Melbourne: Mason, Firth & M'Cutcheon. Retrieved from handle.slv.vic.gov.au/10381/172988

Mathew, T. (1838/1885). Medal—Roman Catholic Total Abstinence Pledge. In *Collections*. Museum Victoria. Retrieved from museumvictoria.com.au/collections/items/280540/medal-roman-catholic-total-abstinence-pledge-australia-circa-1885

McCoy Chapter, Association of YMCA Retirees. (n.d.). McCoy Chapter, AYR. Retrieved from facebook.com

McDowell, I. (1994). Perrin, Charles Frederick (1842–1875). In *Australian Dictionary of Evangelical Biography*. Sydney: Evangelical History Association. Retrieved from webjournals.ac.edu.au

McHarg, T. (2005, October 29). List of References to Emilia in The Southern Cross. *Letter to Robert Evans*. Boronia, Vic.

Messianic Passover Haggadah. (2013). Caulfield South, Vic: Celebrate Messiah.

Miller, J. G. (1994). Paton, John Gibson (1824–1907). In *Australian Dictionary of Evangelical Biography*. Sydney: Evangelical History Association. Retrieved from webjournals.ac.edu.au

Miskhel, M. (2011). Rosenthal, Aronson & Co., Wholesale & Manufacturing Jewellers & General Merchants. In *Australian Postal History and Social Philately*. APHSP. Retrieved from auspostalhistory.com

Mountford, L. M. (1911). *Jesus Christ in his Homeland.* Cincinnati: Press of Jennings and Graham. Retrieved from openlibrary.org/books/OL7161689M/ Jesus_Christ_in_his_homeland

Museum Victoria. (n.d.). The Courts. In *Royal Exhibition Building.* Museum Victoria. Retrieved from museumvictoria.com.au/reb/history/visions-of-colonial-grandeur/the-courts

National Bank of Australasia, Colac [Picture]. State Library of Victoria. Retrieved from handle.slv.vic.gov.au/10381/276349

National Trust. (n.d.). Barwon Park. In *National Trust.* Retrieved from nationaltrust.org.au/places/barwon-park

Nelson, W. (1994). *T. C. Hammond: Irish Christian: his Life and Legacy in Ireland and Australia.* Edinburgh: Banner of Truth Trust.

Nepean Historical Society. (1992). First Settlement 1803. In *The Peninsula Story.* Sorrento, Vic: NHS. Retrieved from nepeanhistoricalsociety.asn.au/history/first-settlement-1803

Newnham, W. H. (1956). *Melbourne.* Melbourne: Cheshire.

Ng, S. (1988, January 21). New Life at 93! In *New Life.* Melbourne: New Life.

Ng, S. (1988, January 21). On Special Assignment. In *New Life.* Melbourne: New Life.

Oliphant, M. (1888). *The Land of Darkness.* London: Macmillan.

Paproth, D. (2004, June). Henry Varley and the Melbourne Evangelicals. *The Journal of Religious History, 25,* 173.

Parr, S. R. (1969). Colton, Sir John (1823–1902). In *Australian Dictionary of Biography* (Vol. 3). Melbourne: Melbourne University Press. Retrieved from adb.anu.edu.au

Paton, J. G., Macartney, H. B., Langley, H. A., Campbell, A. J., Chapman, S., Watsford, J., Mead, S. (1899). Circular Letter. In Watson, *From Darkness to Light* (1910 ed., pp. 83–84).

Peel, D. (2002, December 1). Death and Community in a Colonial Settlement. *Journal of the Royal Australian Historical Society.* Retrieved from thefreelibrary.com/Death+and+community+in+a+colonial+settlement.-a095913546

Perrin, S. (1878). *One Thing I do; or Memorials of Charles F. Perrin by his Widow.* Melbourne: Bible & Tract Repository. Retrieved from handle.slv.vic.gov.au/10381/173070

Phillips, W. (2005). Johnson, Kerr (1812–1887). In *Australian Dictionary of Biography* (Vol. Suppl.). Melbourne University Press. Retrieved from adb.anu.edu.au

Piggin, S. (2004). *Spirit of a Nation: The Story of Australia's Christian Heritage.* Sydney: Strand.

Pollins, H. (2013, Feb 18). Press Reports relating to the Bangor Jewish Community 1843–1959. In *Jewish Communities and Records UK.* JewishGen. Retrieved from jewishgen.org/jcr-uk/community/bangor/Press_Reports_Bangor.htm

Pollock, J. C. (1963). *Moody without Sankey.* London: Hodder and Stoughton.

Post, E. (1922). *Etiquette in Society, in Business, in Politics and at Home* (2 ed.). New York: Funk & Wagnalls Co. Retrieved from gutenberg.org

Prescott, A. W. (1994). Singleton, John (1808–1892). In *Australian Dictionary of Evangelical Biography*. Sydney: Evangelical History Association. Retrieved from webjournals.ac.edu.au

Railway Map—Victorian Lines showing Passenger Mileages. (1968). Melbourne: Victorian Railways.

Ray, T. (n. d.). Thomas Spurgeon The Forgotten Spurgeon. In *Baptist Bible Tribune*. BBT. Retrieved from tribune.org/?p=1916

Raymond, B. (1983). The Melbourne Tailoresses' Strike 1882–1883: An Assessment. In *Labour History* (Vol. 44). Sydney: Australian Society for the Study of Labour History.

Reed, M. S. (c. 1881). *Henry Reed An Eventful Life devoted to God and Man by his Widow*. London: Morgan and Scott.

Renshaw, W. (2014). *Marvellous Melbourne and Spiritual Power*. Moreland, Vic: Acorn Press.

Robin, A. D. (1974). Macartney, Hussey Burgh (1799–1894). In *Australian Dictionary of Biography* (Vol. 5). Australian National University. Retrieved from adb.anu.edu.au

Rowston, L. F. (1994). Gibson, William (1820–1892). In *Australian Dictionary of Evangelical Biography*. Sydney: Evangelical History Association. Retrieved from webjournals.ac.edu.au

Rubinstein, H. L. (1986). *The Jews in Victoria 1835–1985*. Sydney: George Allen and Unwin.

Rutledge, M. (1979). Aronson, Zara (1864–1944). In *Australian Dictionary of Biography* (Vol. 7). Melbourne University Press. Retrieved from adb.anu.edu.au

San Francisco Blue Book and Club Directory. (1931). San Francisco: Jed J. Boag. Retrieved from archive.org/details/sanfanciscoblue31sanf

Sankey, I. D. (n.d.). *Sacred Songs and Solos*.

Serle, G. (1982). *John Monash*. Melbourne University Press.

Shedd, C. P. (1955). *History of the World Alliance of YMCAs*. London: SPCK.

Skinner, C. F. (1999). *Spurgeon & Son*. Grand Rapids: Kregel Publications.

Smith, J. W. (2010). Blundens in Australia. In *Smith Family*. JWS and Co. Retrieved from family.jwsmith.com.au/family_history_jws/jws_blundens/jws_blundens_in_australia.htm

Southern Metropolitan Cemeteries Trust. (n.d.). Deceased Search. In *SMCT*. Melbourne: SMCT. Retrieved from smct.org.au

Statistics of the Colony of Victoria for the Year 1857. (1858–9). Melbourne: Parliament of Victoria. Retrieved from parliament.vic.gov.au/papers/govpub/VPARL1858-59No46P1-64.pdf

Swain, S. (2002, February 1). In these Days of Female Evangelists and Hallelujah Lasses: Women Preachers and the Redefinition of Gender Roles in late Nineteenth-Century Australia. *The Journal of Religious History* (26), 65–77.

The Book of Common Praise being The Hymn Book of The Church of England in Canada. (1909). Toronto: Henry Frowde.

The Church of England. (1662/2015). *Book of Common Prayer.* Retrieved from The Church of England: churchofengland.org/prayer-worship/worship/book-of-common-prayer.aspx

The Holy Bible containing the Old and New Testaments. (1611/1890). London: The British and Foreign Bible Society.

Torrey, R. A. (1923). *Why God Used D. L. Moody.* The Bible Institute Colportage Association. Retrieved from eaec.org/faithhallfame/dlmoody.htm#Torrey

Twopenny, R. (1883/1973). *Town Life in Australia.* Penguin Colonial Facsimiles.

Walker, C. S. (1958). *The Earlier Days of Newtown & Chilwell.* Newtown: City of Newtown & Chilwell. Retrieved from handle.slv.vic.gov.au/10381/109965

Walter, F., & Cox, H. (n.d.). *Index to the Admission Books of the Geelong Infirmary and Benevolent Asylum.* FW Walter. Retrieved from fredwalter.com/infirmary

Watson, S. (1894/1895). *From Darkness to Light—The Life and Work of Mrs. Baeyertz.* London: Mrs. Baeyertz. Retrieved from lcje.net

Watson, S. (1904/1905). *From Darkness to Light—The Life and Work of Mrs. Baeyertz* (2 ed.). Perth, WA: Mrs. Baeyertz.

Watson, S. (1910). *From Darkness to Light—The Life and Work of Mrs. Baeyertz* (New, revised and enlarged ed.). London: Mrs. Baeyertz.

Watson, S. (1993). *The Melbourne Tramways—a Pictorial History* (1 ed.). Moonee Ponds, Vic: Stephen Watson.

Watson, S., & Johnson, I. (1994). *Melbourne's Metropolitan Railway System 1854–1994* (1 ed.). Moonee Ponds, Vic: Stephen Watson & Ian Johnson.

WCTU. (n.d.). Crusades. In *Women's Christian Temperance Union.* WCTU. Retrieved from wctu.com/crusades.html

WCTUA. (n.d.). WCTU—Our History. In *WCTU Australia.* WCTU Australia. Retrieved from wctu.com.au/pages/history.html

Wellesley, W. L. (1830). *Illustrations of Chancery Practice.* Picadilly: James Ridgeway. Retrieved from books.google.com.au

Wilson, E. K. (2002, September). "Totally Devoid of Sensationalism": Mrs. Baeyertz the Jewish Lady Evangelist from Melbourne. *Tasmanian Historical Research Association Papers and Proceedings* (49), 153–166. Retrieved from eprints.utas.edu.au/8969

Wilson, E. K. (2011). *Wandering Stars—The Impact of British Evangelists in Australia 1870s–1900.* Hobart, Tas: University of Tasmania. Retrieved from eprints.utas.edu.au/12522/2/Revised_thesis.pdf

Wilson, M. R. (1989). *Our Father Abraham: Jewish Roots of the Christian Faith*. Grand Rapids: Eerdmans.

Woods, J. (2008). *Facing the Music: Charles Baeyertz and The Triad*. Dunedin: Otago University Press.

Young Men's Christian Association. (1855/1973). Paris Basis—1855. In *World YMCA*. World Alliance of YMCAs. Retrieved from www.ymca.int/who-we-are/mission/paris-basis-1855

Zada, S. (2015). Search the Geelong and District Database. In *Geelong and District*. Geelong & District and Bellarine Peninsula History Site. Retrieved from zades.com.au

Collections

Alexander Turnbull Library Archive. National Library of New Zealand. natlib.govt.nz

A. N. S. Coombe Archive. Melbourne School of Theology Library. Australia. mst.edu.au.

Baeyertz Family Scrapbook. Baeyertz family.

Baillieu Library Special Collections. The University of Melbourne. Australia. lib.unimelb.edu.au/collections/special

California Digital Newspaper Collection. USA. cdnc.ucr.edu.

C. N. Baeyertz Collection. Hocken Collections. University of Otago Library. New Zealand. otago.ac.nz/library/hocken.

Early Canadiana Online. Canada. eco.canadiana.ca

Elizabeth Wilson Collection of Sarah Perrin papers. Australia.

Gertrude Snyers Collection of Betty Baruch papers. Australia.

PapersPast. National Library of New Zealand. paperspast.natlib.govt.nz

Robert Evans Collection of Emilia Baeyertz Sources. Australia. revivals.arkangles.com.

Trove. National Library of Australia. trove.nla.gov.au.

Webjournals. Australian Pentecostal Studies. webjournals.ac.edu.au.

Journals and Newspapers

Advertiser, The. South Australia

Alexandra and Yea Standard. Victoria

Areas' Express and Farmers' Journal, The. South Australia

Argus, The. Victoria

Ashburton Guardian. New Zealand

Australasian, The. Victoria

Australian Town and Country Journal. New South Wales

Ballarat Star, The. Victoria

Bendigo Advertiser. Victoria

Brisbane Courier, The. Queensland

Christian, The. England

BIBLIOGRAPHY 249

Christian Weekly and Methodist Journal, The. South Australia
Christianity Today. USA
Colac Herald. Victoria
Colac Observer. Victoria
Daily Alta California. USA
Dunedin Press. New Zealand
Examiner, The. Tasmania
Goulburn Herald, The. New South Wales
Geelong Advertiser. Victoria
Illustrated Australian News, The. Victoria
Illustrated Sydney News, The. New South Wales
Irish Times, The. Ireland
Jewish Chronicle. England
Jewish Telegraph. England
Journal of Religious History, The. New South Wales
Journal of the Historical Society of South Australia. South Australia
Journal of the Royal Australian Historical Society. New South Wales
Lausanne Consultation on Jewish Evangelism Bulletin. Denmark
Los Angeles Churchman. USA
Los Angeles Herald. USA
Mercury, The. Tasmania
Missionary at Home and Abroad, The. Victoria
Nelson Evening Mail, The. New Zealand
New Life. Victoria
New Zealand Graphic. New Zealand
New Zealand Herald, The. New Zealand
New Zealand Methodist. New Zealand
North Melbourne Advertiser. Victoria
On Being. Victoria
Otago Daily Times. New Zealand
Otago Witness. New Zealand
Pastoral Review, The. Victoria
Pioneer, The. Tasmania
Press, The. New Zealand
Quebec Morning Chronicle. Canada
Queensland Times, The. Queensland

Queenslander, The. Queensland
Riverine Herald, The. Victoria & New South Wales
Sacramento Daily Union. USA
San Francisco Call. USA
Spectator and Methodist Chronicle, The. Victoria
South Australian Weekly Chronicle. South Australia
South Bourke and Mornington Journal. Victoria
Southern Cross, The. Victoria
Star. New Zealand
Sydney Morning Herald, The. New South Wales
Table Talk. Victoria
Tasmanian Historical Research Association Papers and Proceedings. Tasmania
Triad, The. New South Wales and New Zealand
Tribune. Tasmania
Truth and Progress. South Australia
Willing Work. Victoria
Wodonga and Towong Sentinel. Victoria

About the Editor

Garth Coverdale (GradAIEAust) was born in England and grew up in Australia. When he is not advising civil engineers and surveyors on their software, Garth likes to walk, read, edit and stare out of the window while thinking. He has a Diploma in Bible and Mission from Ridley College, Melbourne, and is the husband of one wife named Amanda, without whom Betty's manuscript might never have seen the light of day.

Photographer: Heather Aeschlimann

CATTAC PRESS
cattac.com.au

www.ingramcontent.com/pod-product-compliance
Lightning Source LLC
Chambersburg PA
CBHW020610300426
44113CB00007B/592